B

&

The African Origin of Islam

Black Arabia
&
The African Origin of Islam

By

Wesley Muhammad, PhD

A-Team Publishing

Atlanta

Black Arabia

Second Printing; Second Edition
December 2009

A-Team Publishing
PO Box 551036
Atlanta GA, 30355

To order additional copies or to reach Dr. Muhammad for speaking engagements, please contact the Publisher.

Contents

Abbreviations

ABD	*Anchor Bible Dictionary*
AcOr	*Acta Orientalia*
ANE	Ancient Near East(ern)
BCE	Before the Common Era
BP	Before the Present (Day)
BSOAS	*Bulletin for the School of Oriental and African Studies*
CAD	*The Assyrian Dictionary of the Oriental Institute of the University of Chicago*
CE	Common Era
DDD	*Dictionary of Deities and Demons in the Bible*
EI[1]	*Encyclopedia of Islam. First Edition* Leiden 1913-38
EI[2]	*Encyclopedia of Islam. New Edition* Leiden 1954-
EQ	*Encyclopedia of the Qur'ān*
ER	*Encyclopedia of Religion*
ERE	*Encyclopedia of Religion and ethics*
HAR	*Hebrew Annual Review*
HB	*Hebrew Bible*
HTR	*Harvard Theological Review*
IJMES	*International Journal of Middle East Studies*
IOS	*Israel Oriental Studies*

JANES	*Journal of the Ancient Near Eastern Society*
JANESCU	*Journal of the Ancient Near Eastern Society of Columbia University*
JAOS	*Journal of the American Oriental Society*
JBL	*Journal of Biblical Literature*
JJS	*Journal of Jewish Studies*
JNES	*Journal of Near Eastern Studies*
JNSL	*Journal of Northwest Semitic Languages*
JQR	*Jewish Quarterly Review*
JRAS	*Journal of the Royal Asiatic Society*
JRelS	*Journal of Religious Studies*
JSAI	*Jerusalem Studies in Arabic and Islam*
JSS	*Journal of Semitic Studies*
ky	Thousand years
kya	Thousands of years ago
LXX	Septuagint
MT	Masoretic Text
MW	*The Muslim World*
NOAB	*New Oxford Annotated Bible*
REI	*Revue des Etudes Islamiques*
Rel. Stud.	*Religious Studies*
TDOT	*Theological Dictionary of the Old Testament*
UF	*Ugaritische Forschungen*

ya	Years Ago
ZA	*Zeitschrift für Assyriologie und Verwandte Gebiete*
ZAW	*Zeitschrift für alttestamentliche Wissenschaft*

Chapter One

Afrabia and its People

I. *The Peoples of Arabia*

In his ground-breaking book, ***The Destruction of Black Civilization***, Chancellor Williams suggests that "Blacks are in Arabia for precisely the same reasons Blacks are in the United States, South America, and the Caribbean Islands-through capture and enslavement."[1] Archaeology, anthropology and ethno-historical studies have now demonstrated the error of this postulate. A more accurate assessment is certainly that of Runoko Rashidi who documents that:

> The Arabian Peninsula...was, like much of Asia, first populated by Black people...Some of the surviving Black populations, known as the Veddoids, are major portions of the Mahra population found still in the extremities of Arabia.[2]

This suggestion of a 'Black Arabia' might seem counter-intuitive – the Arab with which most are familiar is the very fair-skinned, hawk-faced Semite (Figure 1). It is the case however that the latter shares the peninsula today with a much different type of Arab. As Major-General Maitland, Political Resident in Aden for Britain, noted in 1932:

---

[1] Chancellor Williams, ***The Destruction of Black Civilization: Great Issues of a Race From 4500 B.C. to 2000 A.D.*** (Chicago: Third World Press, 1987) 23. For an important, though relatively unknown, African American Muslim critical review of Williams and ***The Destruction*** see Ameen Yasir Mohammed, ***Afrocentricity, Minus al-Islam, Cheats...Exposing the conspiracy to rob African Americans of their most precious heritage*** (Los Angeles: Dawahvision, 1994).

[2] Runoko Rashidi, "Africans in Early Asian Civilizations: A Historical Overview," in Runoko Rashidi and Ivan Van Sertima (ed.), ***African Presence in Early Asia*** (New Brunswick: Transaction Publishers, 1999) 28f.

> The people of Arabia...belong to two distinct and apparently quite different races.[3] The common idea of the Arab type...(is) tall, bearded men with clean-cut hawk-like face. The Arabs of South Arabia are smaller, darker, coarser featured and nearly beardless[4]...All authorities agree that the southern Arabs are nearly related by origin to the Abyssinians.[5]

This black-skinned southern Arab is best represented today by the Mahra, Qara, and Shahra tribes of Oman and Hadramawt (Figures 2-4).[6]

---

[3] Sir Arthur Keith noted as well: "all observers agree in recognizing a profound difference between the Arab of the north and the Arab of the south." Sir Arthur Keith and Dr. Wilton Marion Krogman, "The Racial Characters of the Southern Arabs," in Bertram Thomas, ***Arabia Felix, Across the 'Empty Quarter' of Arabia*** (New York: Charles Scribner's Sons, 1932) 305. Henry Field suggested that Arabia's current ethnography is the result of the mixing of two distinct basal stocks: The dolichocephalic (long-headed), dark-skinned Mediteranean/Eur-African and the brachycephalic (round-headed) fair-skinned Armenoid. "Ancient and Modern Inhabitants of Arabia," ***The Open Court*** 46 (1932): 854 [art.=847-869]. See also Bertram Thomas, "Racial Origin of the Arabs," in idem, ***The Arabs: The life-story of a People who have left their deep impress on the world*** (London: Thorton Butterworth Ltd., 1937) 353-359; C.G. Seligman, "The Physical Characters of the Arabs," ***Journal of the Royal Anthropological Institute of Great Britain and Ireland*** 47 (1917): 214-237.

[4] See also Baron von Maltzan's description of the Southern Arab ("Geography of Southern Arabia," ***Proceedings of the Royal Geographical Society of London*** 16 [1872]: 121 [art.=115-123]: "Their complexion is almost as black as that of the Abyssinians; their bodies are very finely formed, and with slender, yet strong limbs; their faces are Semitic, noses generally aquiline, eyes full of fire, lips small, and mouths of very diminutive proportions. They are generally thin, and never fat; they have little or no beard, their hair is long, but curly, not woolly."

[5] Major-General Maitland, Preface to Wyman Bury's ***The Land of Uz*** (London: Macmillan & Co., Ltd., 1911), xiiif.

[6] On these tribes see J. E. Peterson, "Oman's diverse society: Southern Oman," ***The Middle East Journal*** 58 (Spring 2004): 254ff; ***Encyclopedia of Islam*** [Second Edition; hereafter ***EI²***] 6:81-84 s.v. Mahra by W.W. Müller; Bertram Thomas, "Among Some Unknown Tribes of South Arabia," ***Journal of the Royal Anthropological Institute*** 59 (1929): 97-111; For photos of these black-skinned South Arabians see further D. Van der Meulen, "Into Burning Hadhramaut" ***The National Geographic Magazine*** 62 (1932): 393-421; Richard F. Nyrop (ed.), ***The Yemens Country Studies*** (Washington D.C.: The American University, 1985): 5-7; Sir Arthur Keith and Dr. Wilton Marion Krogan, "The Racial Characteristic of the Southern Arabs," in Thomas, ***Arabia Felix***, 327 facing, 330 facing 333.

Figure 1
Traditional (White) Arab

Figure 2
Mahra Arab of South Arabia

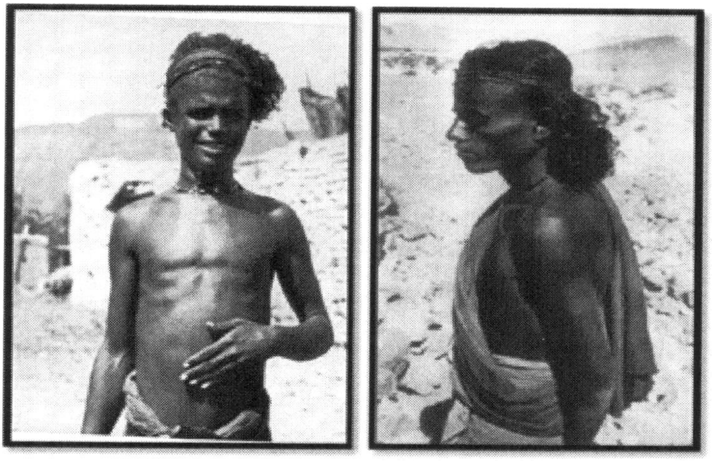

Figures 3-4
Black Arabs from Hadramawt (South Arabia)

Undoubtedly a modified version of Arabia's original inhabitants,[7] these groups show an affinity to both the so-called 'Hamites' of East Africa (Somalis, Abyssinans) and the South Indian Dravidians,[8] and they possibly represent a 'genetic link' between these two populations.[9] These Black Arabians should be

---

[7] The dark South Arabian today is short and "extremely round-headed (brachycephalic)" (Henry Field, "Racial Types From South Arabia," ***The Open Court*** 50 [1936]: 33-39) but was no doubt originally much taller and dolichocephalic. In the 13th century CE the Muslim traveler Ibn al-Mujāwir described the Mahra as "*tall*, handsome folk" (*Tārīkh al-mustabṣir*, 271.1.17; trans. G. Rex Smith in ***A Traveller in Thirteenth-Century Arabia: Ibn al-Mujāwir's*** Tārīkh al-mustabṣir [London: Ashgate, 2008] 268-69) and early pre-Christian skulls found in Hadramawt were markedly dolichocephalic (G.M. Morant, "A Description of Human Remains Excavated by Miss G. Gaton Thompson at Hureidha" in G. Caton Thompson, ***The Tombs and Moon Temple of Hureidha (Hadhramaut)*** [Reports of the Research Committee of the Society of Antiquaries of London # 8; Oxford: University Press, 1944] 107-112; Scott, ***High Yemen***, 200f). It has been suggested that the 'definite change' in the racial constitution of the people of Hadramawt resulted from the invasion and inbreeding of brachycephalic whites (Armenoids or Persians; see ibid; Jivanji Jamshedji Modi, "The Physical Character of the Arabs: Their Relations with Ancient Persians" ***Anthropological Society of Bombay*** 7 [1919]: 724-68; Keith and Krogan, "Racial Characteristic,"301-333). Major R.E. Cheesman already in 1925 suggested that the Mahra were remnants of Arabia's earliest civilization: "The Deserts of Jafura and Jabrin," ***Geographical Journal*** 65 (1925): 125.

[8] ***West Arabia and the Red Sea*** (Official Report: Naval Intelligence Division, June 1946) 365-66; Hugh Scott, ***In the High Yemen*** (London: John Murray, 1942) 202-203; Keith and Krogan, "Racial Characteristic," 327; Thomas, "Racial Origin," 359; Bertram Thomas, "Anthropological Observations in South Arabia," ***Journal of the Royal Anthropological Institute of Great Britain and Ireland*** 62 (1932): 83-103; Henry Field, "The Arabs of Iraq," ***American Journal of Physical Anthropology*** 21 (1936): 49-56 (53); Carleton Stevens Coon, ***The Races of Europe*** (New York: The Macmillian Company, 1939) 402-03, 411, 429. ***The Encyclopedia Britanica*** [9th Edition; 1:245-46 s.v. Arabia] lists ten literary, linguistic, cultural, and ethnological evidences indicating a relation between South Arabians and Africa. On the other hand, Sir Arthur Keith is convinced that "Often the features of the more Negroid Arabs are derivatives of Dravidian India rather than inheritances of Hamitic Africa." Sir Arthur Keith, "Arabs in Central Iraq: Introduction," in the Field Museum of Natural History's ***Arabs of Central Iraq: Their History, Ethnology, and Physical Characters*** by Henry Field (Chicago, 1935), 14. Henry Field even suggested that "Dravidian and Arab have in them an inheritance from a common stock – an inheritance which has been retained more completely by the natives of India than by the people of Arabia." Field, ***Arabs of Central Iraq***, 27.

[9] There has been in certain anthropological circles a search for the 'bridge' connecting the western and eastern branches of the 'black belt,' i.e. for a transitional stage between the Dravidian race in India and the Ethiopian in Africa. The long noted similarity between the two suggests the existence of a continuous genetic gradient. It has been suggested that this bridge has been located in the mountain dwellers on the island of Socotra off the coast of southern Arabia. Socotra's ancient inhabitants, who had South Arabian roots, are akin to the Veddo-Dravidoid racial type of India, according to Vitaly V. Naumkin (***Island of the Phoenix, an Ethnological Study of the People of***

understood in the context of what 19th – 20th century European adventurers and anthropologists dubbed 'the Black Belt of mankind.' Sir Arthur Keith, renowned anthropologist from the Field Museum of Natural History, observed:

> The enigma of modern anthropology is the Black Belt of mankind. It commences in Africa and peters out amongst the natives of the Melanesian Islands of the Pacific. At each extremity of the belt, in Africa as in Melanesia we find peoples with black skins, woolly hair, more or less beardless, prognathous and long-headed. We cannot suppose these negro peoples, although now widely separated, have been evolved independently of each other. We therefore suppose that at one time a proto-negroid belt crossed the ancient world, occupying all intermediate lands, Arabia, Baluchistan, India, Further India, the Philippines and Malay Archipelago.[10]

This enigmatic "Black Belt" of mankind is the more peculiar because it apparently consists of two different parent stocks, both with Black skins but differing in almost every other ethnologic feature. The "intermediate lands" of this proto-negroid belt – the regions of West Asia, North Africa and southern India – seem to be home to a markedly different black face than the one we generally associate with 'Black/African' peoples. West African scholar Cheik Anta Diop explained:

> There are two well-defined Black races: one has a black skin and wooly hair; the other also has black skin, often exceptionally black, with straight hair, aquiline nose, thin lips, and acute cheekbone angle. We find a prototype of this race

Socotra, trans. by Valery A. Epstein [Ithaca Press Reading, 1993]) who notes that: "Socotra, and possibly all of Southern Arabia, may after all be the missing intermediate link in the race-genetic 'west-east' gradient for which anthropologists search in order to fill the gap between the African Negroids and the Australo-Veddo-Melanesian types in the equatorial area." (67).

[10] Keith and Krogan, "Racial Characteristics," 320f. Sees also Henry Field, "Racial Types from South Arabia," ***The Open Court*** 50 (1936): 33-39; Sir Harry H. Johnston, ***The Negro in the New World*** (1910; rp. 1969: New York, Johnson Reprint Corporation), 25f; Percy Sykes who wrote in ***History of Persia*** (London: Routledge and Kegan Paul, 1969) 51.

> in India: the Dravidian. It is also known that certain Nubians likewise belong to the same Negro type, as this sentence by the Arab author, Edrissi, indicates: "The Nubians are the most handsome of Blacks; their women have thin lips and straight hair." [11]

While the (stereo) typical "negroid" stock (the *Broad type*; Figure 5) characterized by dark skin, a broad nose (platyrhine), full lips, prognathism (protruding upper jaw/lower face), high facial index (short broad face) and wooly (ulotricous) hair seems to have its origin in sub-Saharan Africa, the second parent stock (the *Elongated type*; Figure 6), characterized by exceptionally dark skin, narrow head, aquiline nose, thin lips, high cheek bones and straight or wavy hair is normally located further east. It is in India where we find the typical representative of this type in the Dravidian (Figure 7). However, North Africa is also home to such a population (the so-called Hamites).[12] The *Elongated type*, called variously (erroneously) Hamitic, Mediterranean, or the Brown Race, had (also erroneously) been understood to be a brunet type of the Caucasian race and therefore ethnically distinct from the chromatically similar yet phenotypically distinct African *Broad type*.[13] However, as Keith W. Crawford, M.D. has well pointed out, scientific studies calculating the degree of relatedness between world populations based on genetic similarities for certain proteins reveal that present day African populations with differing morphologies cluster together as a group distinct from other world populations.[14] Thus sub-Saharan Senegalese (*Broad type*) and Ethiopians from the Horn of Africa

---

[11] ***The African Origin of Civilization*** (Westport: Lawrence Hill & Company, 1967) 164.

[12] See Oric Bates, ***The Eastern Libyans*** (1914; Frank Cass & Co. Ltd., 1970), 39: "The original pure Hamitic type seems to be that found among the Saharan Berbers-a type tall, spare, long-limbed, and dark (*brun*); hair black or dark brown, straight or wavy; head dolichocephalic (long), orthognathous (no protruding upper jaw/lower face); nose slightly aquiline or straight; eyes dark and piercing, set rather wide apart; mouth well defined; facial capillary system slightly developed; movements generally slow and dignified."

[13] See especially Dana Reynolds-Marniche, "The Myth of the Mediterranean Race," in Ivan Van Sertima (ed.), ***Egypt: Child of Africa*** (New Brunswick and London: Transaction Publishers, 1994) 109-125; Wyatt MacGaffrey, "Concepts of Race in the Historiography of Northeast Africa," ***Journal of African History*** 7 (1966) 1-17.

[14] Keith W. Crawford, "The Racial Identity of Ancient Egyptian Populations Based on the Analysis of Physical Remains," in van Sertima, ***Egypt,*** 55-56 [art.=55-73].

(*Elongated type*) show a genetic kinship that distinguishes them from European, Asian, and indigenous American populations. Other studies suggest that the *Elongated type* itself is "a product of a long evolution in African ecosystems".[15] That is to say, the *Broad type* and the *Elongated type* do not actually represent two distinct parent stocks, but two morphological variations of a single, black stock. It is this African *Elongated type* to which the Black Arabian shows an affinity.[16] Not only the original Arabian, but the original Near Easterner in general appears to have his prototype in the Dravidian that is now inhabiting India but who seems to himself have originated in Arabia.[17]

Figure 5

Broad type (Nuba chief from Kenya). From Ivan van Sertima, ***Egypt: Child of Africa*** (1994)

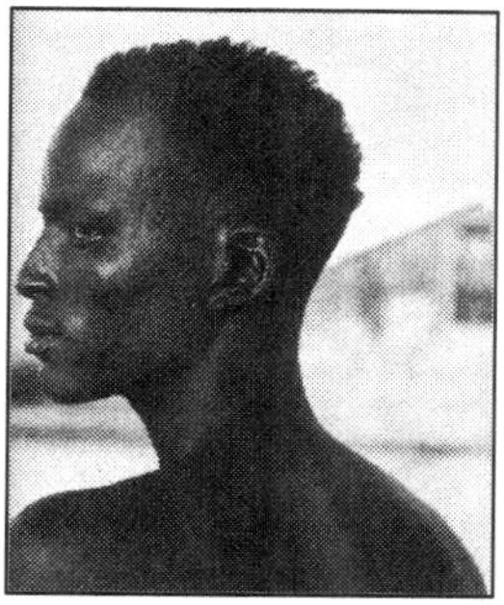

Figure 6

Elongated type (Somali). From Carleton S. Coon and Edward E. Hunt Jr., ***The Living Races of Man*** (1965)

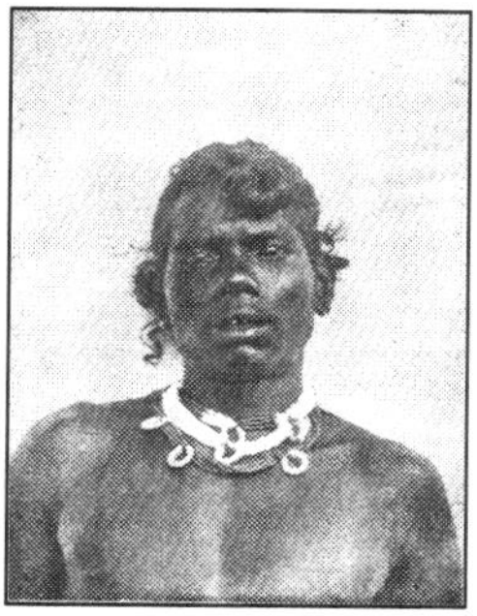

Figure 7

Vēdan (Dravidian) of India. From Edgar Thurston, ***Casts and Tribes of Southern India*** (1909)

[15] Reynolds-Marniche, "Myth," 110; On the *Broad* as well as *Elongated* types as indigenous to Africa see also S.O.Y. Keita, "Studies in Ancient Crania from Northern Africa," ***American Journal of Physical Anthropology*** 83 (1990): 35-48; idem, "Further Studies of Crania from Ancient Northern Africa: An Analysis of Crania From First Dynasty Egyptian Tombs, Using Multiple Discriminant Functions," ***American Journal of Physical Anthropology*** 87 (1992): 245-254; J. Hiernaux, ***The People of Africa*** (New York: Charles Scribner's Sons, 1975).

[16] Craniofacial measurements in nearly 2000 recent and prehistoric crania from major geographical areas of the Old World indicated that ancient West Asians and Africans resembled each other. See Tsunehiko Hanihara, "Comparison of Craniofacial Features of Major Human Groups," ***American Journal of Physical Anthropology*** 99 (1996): 389-412.

[17] P. Molesworth Sykes et all suggested that "one Dravidian race stretch(ed) from India to the Shatt-el-Arab": "Anthropological Notes on Southern Persia," ***Journal of the Anthropological Institute of Great Britain and Ireland*** 32 (1902): 343. Genetic evidence now indicates that the Dravidians of India originated in West Asia: Partha P Majumder, "Ethnic Populations of India as seen from an evolutionary perspective." ***Journal of Bioscience*** 26 (2001): 541.

II. *Afrabia*

This ethnological kinship with *Elongated type* East Africans comes as no surprise: Arabia itself, we are assured, is but "the geological extension of Africa."[18] As Maurizio Tosi has pointed out in his discussion, "The Emerging Picture of Prehistoric Arabia": "Physically the (Arabian) peninsula is a part of Africa, landscaped by the same geological and climate processes as the eastern Sahara and the Ethiopian highlands."[19] The ***Encyclopedia Britanica*** explains:

> Western Arabia formed part of the African landmass before a rift occurred in the Earth's crust, as a result of which the Red Sea was formed and Africa and the Arabian Peninsula finally became separated some five to six million years ago. Thus, the southern half of the peninsula has a greater affinity with the regions of Somalia and Ethiopia in Africa than with northern Arabia or the rest of Asia.[20]

Plate tectonics separated Africa and Arabia sometime during the Precambrian (c. 5, 000 million – 590 million BP), the Miocene (c. 25-12 million BP) or maybe as late as the Pliocene (c. 5.3 – 1.8 million BP) period when the Arabian plate broke off from the African shield, creating the Red Sea. Nevertheless Arabia remains the geological and ecological continuation of Africa.

> In general, Arabia is the continuation of the African system across the Red Sea, spanning the Saharo-Arabian

---

[18] Words of Maurizio Tosi, "The Emerging Picture of Prehistoric Arabia," ***Annual Review of Anthropology*** 15 (1986): 462 [art.=461-490. See also J.A. Rodgers, ***Sex and Race: Negro-Caucasian Mixing in All Ages and All Lands, Vol. I: The Old World*** (St. Petersburg, Fl: Helga M. Rogers, 1967) I:95: "Arabia is but an extension of Africa"; William H. Worrell, ***A Study of Races in the Ancient Near East*** (Cambridge: W. Hiffer & Sons Ltd., 1927) 6: "Geologically Africa includes that part of Asia which we now call Mesopotamia, Palestine and Syria…Arabia and the Syrian Desert are merely the extension of the great deserts of Northern Africa".

[19] Tosi, "Emerging Picture," 462. See also D.T. Potts, ***The Arabian Gulf in Antiquity, Vol. I: From Prehistoric to the Fall of the Achaemenid Empire*** (Oxford: Oxford University Press, 1990) 9: "During the Precambrian time…Arabia was part of Africa".

[20] ***Encyclopedia Britanica*** s.v. Arabian Desert. ***Britanica Online*** at http://www.britannica.com/EBchecked/topic/31610/Arabian-Desert. Accessed February 12, 2009.

phytogeogrphical region comprising its northern and central parts and the Sudanese one for its tropical southern and eastern coastlands.[21]

Put simply, the Arabian Peninsula is actually just the north-eastern extremity of the African continent, a fact which the 'tyranny of the Red Sea' obscures. As Ali Mazrui notes:

> a European decision to make Africa end at the Red Sea has decisively de-Africanized the Arabian peninsula…the tyranny of the sea is in part a tyranny of European geographical prejudices. Just as European map-makers could decree that on the map Europe was above Africa instead of below (an arbitrary decision in relation to the cosmos) those map-makers could also dictate that Africa ended at the Red Sea instead of the Persian Gulf. Is it not time that this dual tyranny of the sea and Eurocentric geography was forced to sink to the bottom?[22]

The terminology *Afrabia* is proposed, and used here, as a pointer to this ancient cultural, geographical and historical relationship between Africa and Arabia and as a means of transcending the tyranny of the Red Sea.[23] *Afrabia* as used here is not the same as the area popularly called 'Arabia,' i.e. Saudi Arabia. The latter is defined by European and Wahhabi political boundaries and excludes areas such as Yemen in the South and the Levant in the north (Israel, Lebanon, Syria, Palestinian territories, Jordan). *Afrabia* includes the whole area between the Mediterranean Sea in the north and the Arabian Sea to the south, i.e the whole of the Arabian Peninsula.

II.1. *Afrabia: Doorway to the World*

Afrabia is also an *ethnological* extension of Africa. As Michael D. Petraglia remarks, the Arabian peninsula was "a key geographic region that, without doubt, played a critical role in Out of Africa

---

[21] Tosi, "Emerging Picture," 476.
[22] Ali A. Mazrui, ***Euro-Jews and Afro-Arabs: The Great Semitic Divergence in World History*** (Lanham: University Press of America, 2008) 140.
[23] Mazrui, ***Euro-Jews and Afro-Arabs***, Chapter Seven.

dispersals."[24] In fact, Arabia is likely the first territory that hominids encountered as they expanded outside of the African mainland.[25] They entered the peninsula by the south over the Bab el-Mandeb and by the north through the Levantine corridor (Figure 8). We are therefore not taken aback by the discovery that Lower Miocene (c. 17-14 million BP) hominid remains similar to those found in East Africa have been found in Arabia.[26] Africa and Arabia would have still been connected during this time according to some theories. The faunal remains imply a tropical or subtropical climate during this time. The environment of central and eastern Arabia during the Miocene and Pliocene "has been called 'lush' and compared to that of a tropical Savanah."[27] At that time, as Michael Rice suggests, "Arabia probably would have looked much like East Africa now".[28] Geomorphological evidence suggests great rainfall during the Pliocene (5.3 million – 1.8 million BP). Thus, prehistoric Arabia was a home-away-from-home for the early African colonists. Archaeogenetics indicates that the progenitor African group of today's human population migrated out of Africa into Arabia about 70,000 years ago.[29] It was from Arabia, after adapting there for approximately 5000 years,[30] that these

---

24 "The Lower Paleolithic of the Arabian Peninsula: Occupations, Adaptations, and Dispersals," ***Journal of World History*** 17 (June 2003): 173 [art.=144-179].

25 Norman M. Whalen and David E. Peace, "Early Mankind in Arabia," ***ARAMCO World*** 43:4 (1992): 20, 23 and below. On the colonization of Western Asia from Africa see Ofer Bar-Yosef, "Early colonizations and cultural continuities in the Lower Palaeolithic of western Asia," in Michael D. Petraglia and Ravi Korisettar (edd.), ***Early Human Behaviour in Global Context: The Rise and Diversity of the Lower Palaeolithic Record*** (London: Routledge, 1998): 221-279.

26 P. Andrews, W.R. Hamilton and P.J. Whybrow, "Dryopithecines from the Miocene of Saudi Arabia," ***Nature*** 274 (1978): 249-51; Pott, ***Arabian Gulf in Antiquity***, 11.

27 Pott, ***Arabian Gulf in Antiquity***, 16.

28 Michael Rice, ***The Archaeology of the Arabian Gulf*** (London and New York: Routledge, 1994) 69.

29 Richard Gray, "African tribe populated rest of the world," http://www.telegraph.co.uk/science/science-news/5299351/African-tribe-populated-rest-of-the-world.html. Accessed July 25, 2009.

30 On the development of modern man in the Near East see Erik Trinkaus, "Western Asia," in Fred H. Smith (ed.), ***The Origin of Modern Humans: A World survey of the Fossil Evidence*** (New York: Alan R. Liss, 1984) 251-293 (287).

Afrabians went on to populate the rest of the world.[31] As Norman M. Whalen and David E. Peace point out:

> whether migration proceeded by way of the north or the south, it was necessary to cross Arabia first before continuing further. For that reason, the oldest cites in the world, next to those in Africa, should be found in Arabia, which occupied a pivotal position astride the path of early intercontinental migration in Lower Pleistocene times...Arabia (is) humankind's doorway to the world.[32]

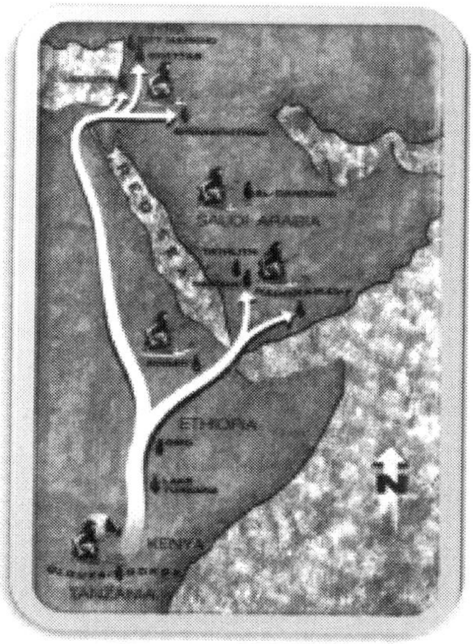

Figure 8
Initial Out-of-Africa dispersal routs.
From ***ARAMCO World*** 43:4 (1992)

[31] P.A. Underhill et al have done genetic research with the non-recombining portion of the Y-chromosome (NRY) polymorphisms suggesting that human diversity today can be traced back to a migration out of Africa *ca* 50-45 kya to the Middle East. From there, after adapting for *ca* 5-10 ky, these groups expanded North to Europe, East to India and Southeast Asia, and West (to Africa?): P.A. Underhill et al, "The Phylogeography of Y chromosomes binary haplotypes and the origins of modern human populations," ***Annals of Human Genetics*** 65 (2001): 43-62. See further J.R. Luis et al, "The Levant versus the Horn of Africa: Evidence for Bidirectional Corridors of Human Migrations," ***American Journal of Human Genetics*** 74 (2004): 532; Bernard Vandermeersch, "The Near Eastern Hominids and the Origins of Modern Humans in Eurasia," in Takeru Akazawa, Kenichi Aoki, and Tasuku Kimura (edd.), ***The Evolution and Dispersal of Modern Humans in Asia*** (Tokyo: Hokusen-sha, 1992): 29-38.

[32] Whalen and Peace, "Early Mankind in Arabia," 20, 23. On migration from Ethiopia to the south of Arabia, then north into the Levant see O. Bar-Yosef, "Pleistocene connexions between Africa and Southwest Asia: an archaeological perspective," ***The African Archaeological Review*** 5 (1987): 29-38 (30-31).

These early African expansionists likely belonged to the *Elongated type.*[33] This might account for the fact that in Arabia and Western Asia in general – lands which were among the African expansionists' earliest colonies – the indigenous populations are of this *Elongated* African variety. As U.P. and Susheela Upadhyaya explain:

> It is now generally accepted that in the Neolithic and early metal ages about 8th to 3rd millennia BC, the vast region of Western Asia with its extensions up to the Niles and Indus, was occupied by what may be called a blackish race with its local variations like Proto-Mediterranean, Mediterranean and Hamite. This race is characterized by blackish brown complexion, long head, long straight and narrow face, etc…In spite of some local differences like the Proto-Mediterranean type in Egypt and India, Hamitic type in East-Africa and Ibero-insular Mediterranean type from Anatolia to Western India, we can see, on the whole a fundamental racial and cultural unity in all this part of the ancient world which is rightly called the 'cradle of civilization'."[34]

It was no doubt this Black *Elongated type* which was the original population of the whole of Arabia and from which the dark-skinned southern Arab of today derived.[35]

---

[33] St. Clair Drake, ***Black Folks Here and There*** 2 vols. (Los Angeles: Center For Afro-American Studies University of California, 1987) I:121f: "Although some cogent reasons have been cited for believing that *homo habilis* and other African hominids *were* dark skinned, the oldest human fossils do not meet the anthropometric criteria for negroes, or any variety of modern man, for that matter. As to where and when the Negro type first appeared with the distinctive combination of skin-color, facial features, lip form, and hair type…modern physical anthropologys have no certain answer…Most anthropologists lean toward the view that the Negro physical type appeared late in the process of evolution in Africa, as a variation of a more generalized, probably dark-skinned human type." S.O.Y. Keita has noted that that stereotypical 'Negroid' morphology, the *Broad type*, actually "represents a microevolutionary extreme, not to be taken as a basal ideal type, just as very orthognathous blond northern European groups represent an extreme." "Studies of Ancient Crania," 44.

[34] U.P. Upadhyaya, "Dravidian and Negro-African (Ethnic and Linguistic Affinities)," in K.P. Aravaanan (ed.), ***Dravidians and Africans*** (Dakar: University of Dakar, 1997), 45f.

[35] Henry Field noted that "the Arabian Peninsula was once occupied by a people intermediate to the Somalis on the one hand and the Dravidian peoples of India on the

III. *White Invasions*

Whence cometh the white Arab? Bertram Thomas, historian and former Prime Minister of Muscat and Oman, reports:

> The original inhabitants of Arabia...were not the familiar Arabs of our time but a very much darker people. A proto-negroid belt of mankind stretched across the ancient world from Africa to Malaya. This belt...(gave) rise to the Hamitic peoples of Africa, to the Dravidian peoples of India, and to an intermediate dark people inhabiting the Arabian peninsula. In the course of time two big migrations of fair-skinned peoples came from the north...to break through and transform the dark belt of man beyond India (and) to drive a wedge between India and Africa...The more virile invaders overcame the dark-skinned peoples, absorbing most of them, driving others southwards...The cultural condition of the newcomers is unknown. It is unlikely that they were more than wild hordes of adventurous hunters.[36]

Among these white hordes were the Kassites (Figure 9), probably originating in the Zargos Mountains region in Iran, who invaded from the north and colonized eastern Arabia for about a century and a half (15th – 13th cent. BCE).[37] As François Lenormant recounts, the original 'Kushite' Arabians absorbed these 'coarse, white' invaders, Jectanides as he calls them. The latter eventually gained victory over the Arabian Kushites.[38] These white tribes settled among the original Black Arabians, learning their language and culture and becoming 'arabized' (*musta'riba*),[39] but

---

other": ***Ancient and Modern in Southwestern Asia*** (Coral Gables, Fl: University of Miami Press, 1956) 113.

[36] Bertram Thomas, ***The Arabs*** (London: Thornton Butterworth LTD., 1937) 355f.

[37] On the Kassites see D.T. Potts, "Elamites and Kassites in the Persian Gulf," ***JNES*** 65 (2006):111-119; W. Sommerfeld, "The Kassites of Ancient Mesopotamia: Origins, Politics and Culture," in J.M. Sasson (ed.), ***Civilizations of the Ancient Near East*** vol. 2 (New York, 1995) 917ff; Pierre Lombard, "The Occupation of Dilmun by the Kassites of Mesopotamia," in ***Bahrain, the Civilization of the Seas: From Dilmun to Tylos*** (Paris, 1999) 122-125.

[38] ***Histoire ancienne des Phéniciens*** (Paris: Lévy, 1890) 260-261; Diop, ***African Origin***, 123-125.

[39] On the civilizations of these *musta'riba* Arabs see Gus W. Van Beck, "The Rise and Fall of Arabia Felix," ***Scientific American*** 221 (1969): 36-48.

also changing the genetic and cultural makeup of the peoples they ruled.[40]

Figure 9
White invaders to Arabia in the second millennium BCE: Kassites

IV. *Afrabia and the Black Semites*

Al-**Ṭabarī** (d. 923), the famed Muslim historian and Qur'**ā**nic exegete, recorded in his ***Ta'rīkh al-rusul wa'l-muluk*** ("The History of the Messengers and Kings") the following on the authority of '**Abd Allāh b. 'Abbās,** the cousin of the prophet Mu**ḥ**ammad of Arabia:

> The Children of Sam (Shem) settled in the center of the Earth, which is between Satidma and the sea and between Yemen and Syria. Allah made the prophets from them, revealed the Books

[40] See e.g. Dr. Jivanji Jamshedji Modi, "The Physical Character of the Arabs: Their Relations with Ancient Persians," ***Anthropological Society of Bombay*** 11 (1919): 724-768.

> to them, made them beautiful, gave them a black complexion, and also gave them a black complexion with a light-brownish undertone…The children of Ham settled in the south..Allah gave them a black complexion and gave some of them a black complexion with a light-brownish undertone…The children of Japheth settled in Safoun toward the north…They are light-skinned and very fair-skinned.[41]

That the Semites, along with the so-called 'Hamites,' were originally a Black people is pretty clear. "Semitic" is properly a linguistic designation, not racial, and describes native speakers of one of the several living or dead Semitic languages. But Danna Reynolds observation here is critical: "the indigenous or 'black' tribes of Arabia were those who in ancient times migrated from Africa…and were the earliest purveyers and dispersers of the Semitic dialects."[42] The Semitic family of languages, the most widespread of which is Arabic, is a branch of a larger language phylum called Afroasiatic which consists of the Semitic, Ancient Egyptian, Berber, Cushitic, Omotic and Chadic families. While some scholars maintain that Afroasiatic originated in Asia,[43] most linguists now accept that it originated in Africa where five of the six generally recognized branches still reside.[44] Regarding the

---

[41] I have used here the translation by Tariq Berry, ***The Unknown Arabs: Clear, Definitive Proof of the Dark Complexion of the Original Arabs and the Arab Origin of the so-called African Americans*** (Morocco, 2002) 9.

[42] Reynolds, "African Heritage," 105.

[43] Jared Diamond and Peter Bellwood, "Farmers and Their Languages: The First Expansions," ***Science*** 300 (2003): 597-603; idem, "Response," ***Science*** 306 (2004) 1681; Werner Vycichl, "The Origin of the Hamito-Semitic Languages," in Herrmann Jungraithmayr and Walter W. Müller (edd.), ***Proceedings of the Fourth Internation Hamito-Semitic Congress, Marburg, 20-22 September, 1983*** (Amsterdam and Philadelphia: John Benjaminus Publishing Company, 1987) 109-121; Alexander Militariev, "Home for Afrasian: African or Asian," in ***Cushitic and Omotic Languages: Proceedings of the Third International Symposium, Berlin, March 17-19, 1994*** (Berlin, 1994) 13-32; "Evidence of Proto-Afrasian Cultural Lexicon (1. Cultivation of Land. II. Crops. III. Dwelling and Settlement)," in Hans G. Mukarovsky (ed.), ***Proceedings of the Fifth International Hamito-Semitic Congress*** (Wien, 1990) I: 73-85.

[44] John Huehnergard, "Afro-Asiatic," in Roger D. Woodard (ed.), ***The Ancient Languages of Syria-Palestine and Arabia*** (Cambridge: Cambridge University Press,

Semitic branch in particular, a number of scholars postulate an African origin of the linguistic family and its speakers.[45] Renowned Russian linguist Igor M. Diankonoff argued that the origin of the Afroasiatic family, including the Semitic languages, was in the north-western part of the modern Republic of the Sudan.[46] The Semites were said to have been a group of East Africans who branched off from the Proto-Afroasiatic stock in Africa and migrated to Syria-Palestine in 9th-8th millennium BCE. Later Diankonoff modified his position: still maintaining that North Africa is the origin of the Afroasiatic family in general, he moved the origin of the Proto-Semitic language to the area between the Nile Delta and Palestine, to where a group branched off from the parent Afroasiatic stock, migrated to the Levant area, and then became 'Semitized,' if you will.[47] Diankonoff points to the archaeological and architectural remains of the Jericho culture of 8th-7th millennium BCE Palestine as part of this early 'Common Semitic' culture. Earlier George A. Barton already spoke of the "African origin and

2008) 225; Christopher Ehret, S.O.Y Keita and Paul Newman, "The Origins of Afroasiatic," ***Science*** 306 (2004) 1680-1681; Carleton T. Hodge, "Afroasiatic: The Horizon and Beyond," in Scott Noegel and Alan S. Kaye (edd.), ***Afroasiatic Linguistics, Semitics, and Egyptology: Selected Writings of Carleton T. Hodge*** (Bethesda, Maryland: CDL Press, 2004) 64; ML Bender Upside Down Afrasian, Afrikanistische Arbeitspapiere 50 (1997): 19-34; Christopher Ehret, ***Reconstructing Proto-Afroasiatic (Proto-Afrasian): vowels, tone, consonants, and vocabulary*** (Berkeley: University of California Press, 1995) 487; Joseph H. Greenberg, "African linguistic classification," in Joseph Ki-Zerbo (ed.), ***General History of Africa, Volume 1: Methodology and African Prehistory*** (Berkeley and Los Angeles: University of California Press. 1981) 292–308. On the Africa vs. Asia AA Origin dispute see Daniel P. Mc Call, "The Afroasiatic Language Phylum: African in Origin, or Asian?" ***Current Anthropology*** 39 (1998): 139-143.

[45] See e.g. Gregorio del Olmo Lete, ***Questions of Semitic Linguistics. Root and Lexeme: The History of Research*** (Bethesda, Maryland: CDL Press, 2008) 115; Edward Lipiński, ***Semitic Languages: Outline of a Comparative Grammar*** (Leuven: Uitgeverij Peeters and Departement Oosterse Studies, 1997) 42-43; A. Murtonen, ***Early Semitic*** (Leiden: E.J. Brill, 1967), 74.

[46] "Earliest Semites in Asia," ***Altorientalische Forschungen*** 8 (1981)23-70.

[47] Igor M. Diankonoff, "The Earliest Semitic Society," ***Journal of Semitic Studies*** 43 (1998): 209-219.

Arabian cradle-land of the Semites,"[48] suggesting that the Afroasiatic (or to use the old term 'Hamito- Semitic') proto-language originated in Africa, from which a group migrated to Arabia forming the Semitic languages.[49] The final word on this matter is probably that of Peter Bellwood from the Australian National University: "Proto-Semitic is undoubtedly of Levant origin".[50] That is to say, a group of African Afroasiatic speakers migrated northeast into the Levant and there evolved the Proto-Semitic language, maybe as early as the 8th millennium BCE. It is appropriate to note here that Levantine populations, from the Natufians of the 11th millennium BCE to the Transjordan Kushites of the second, were Black peoples of the *Elongated* type.[51]

---

[48] George Aaron Barton, ***Semitic and Hamitic Origins: Social and Religious*** (Philadelphia: University of Pennsylvania Press, 1934) 8.

[49] George A. Barton, "The Origins of Civilization in Africa and Mesopotamia, Their Relative Antiquity and Interplay," ***Proceedings of the American Philosophical Society*** 68 (1929) 303-312: "As many of the linguistic phenomena which Hamites and Semites possess in common appear in the Hamitic languages in a more primitive form than in the Semitic, the one theory which satisfies the facts is that the Hamito- Semitic race originated in North Africa and the Sahara region, and that at a very early time-say 10,000 to 8000 B.C. or earlier-some of this stock migrated to Arabia-probably South Arabia via the Straits of Bab-el-Mandeb-where they spread over the peninsula in the course of subsequent millennia. As Arabia suffered desiccation, in common with North Africa, they were gradually forced to migrate in various directions in search of subsistence. It was under this pressure that, by migration and mingling with other races, the various Semitic nations of history, other than the Arabs, were formed."

[50] Peter Bellwood, ***First Farmers: The Origin of Agricultural Societies*** (Oxford: Blackwell Publishing, 2005) 209.

[51] On the Natufians of Palestine see Margherita Mussi, "The Natufian of Palestine: The Biginnings of Agriculture in a Palaeoethnological Perspective," ***Origini*** 10 (1976) 89-107; Sir Arthur Keith, "The Late Palaeolithi Inhabitants of Palestine," ***Proceedings of the First International Congress of Prehistoric and Protohistoric Sciences, London August 1-6 1932*** (London: Oxford University Press, 1934) 46-47; F.J. Los, "The Prehistoric Ethnology of Palestine," ***Mankind Quarterly*** 7 (1966): 53-59. On Natufian skeletal morphology see also A. Belfer-Cohen, L.A. Schepartz and B. Arensburg, "New Biological Data For the Natufian Populations In Israel," in Ofer Bar-Yosef and François R. Valla (edd.), ***The Natufian Culture in the Levant*** (International Monographs in Prehistory, 1991) 411-424. The ancient Egyptians themselves also depicted Syro-Palestinians as having "dark hair, brown complexions and Semitic features": Frank J. Yurco, "Were the Ancient Egyptians Black or White," ***BAR*** 15 (Sept/Oct 1989): 26. On the Black populations of the Levant see also Charles S. Finch III, "African and Palestine in Antiquity," in Runoko Rashidi and Ivan Van Sertima (edd.), ***African Presence in Early Asia***(New Brunswick: Transaction Publishers, 1999) 186-196. On the Transjordan Kushites of the second millennium BCE see below n. 110.

Now these were not wandering nomads: the Proto-Semitic lexicon does not present a necessarily nomadic group, but suggests sedentism.[52]

The Semitic languages, after evolving in *Afrabia*, reentered Africa proper. Semitic languages have been spoken in Ethiopia for at least four thousand years,[53] and "Most linguists agree that Proto-Ethiopian originated through contact between one group of South Semites, which settled on the Tigrean plateau, and local Cushitic populations."[54] While it is gong too far to say, as did W.F. Albright in 1918,[55] that ancient Egyptian is "a Semitic tongue," it is most certainly the case that

> the genetic relationship of Egyptian and the Semitic is solidly established…The regular phonological and semantic correspondences between the morphological systems of the Egyptian and the Semitic clearly demonstrate that these two language families are related.[56]

---

[52] Witold Tyloch, "The Evidence of the Proto-Lexicon for the Cultural Background of the Semitic Peoples," in James and Theodora Bynon (edd.), ***Hamitico-Semitica*** (The Hague: Mouton, 1975) 55-60.

[53] Philip Curtin, Steve Feierman, Leonard Thompson, Jan Vansina, ***African History*** (Boston: Little Brown and Co, 1978), 121; Grover Hudson, "Language Classification and the Semitic Prehistory of Ethiopia," ***Folia Orientalia*** 18 (1977): 119-166; Reynolds, "African Heritage," 101

[54] Rodolfo Fattovich, "The Afro-Arabian circuit: contacts between the Horn of Africa and Southern Arabia in the 3rd – 2nd millennium B.C.," in Lech Krzyzaniak, Michal Kobusiewicz, and Karla Kroeper, ***Interregional Contacts in the Later Prehistory of Northeastern Africa*** (PoznaÔ, 1996) 395; R. Hertzron, ***Ethiopic Semitic*** (Manchester: Manchester University Press, 1972); E. Ullendorff, ***The Semitic Languages of Ethiopia*** (London, 1955)

[55] "Notes on Egypto-Semitic Etymology," ***American Journal of Semitic Languages and Literatures*** 34 (1918): 81.

[56] Aaron D. Rubin, "An Outline of Comparative Egypto-Semitic Morphology," ***Egyptian and Semito-Hamitic (Afro-Asiatic) Studies*** (Brill, 2004): 454-486. See also Carleton T. Hodge, "An Egyptian-Semitic Comparison", ***Folia Orientalia*** 17 (1976): 5-28: "The language groups known as Semitic, Egyptian, Chadic and Berber are genetically related, deriving from a common proto-language …Egyptian…is closely related to Semitic." Thus, the relationship between Semitic and ancient Egyptian is not 'superficial' as suggested by Brunson, ***Predynastic Egypt***, 67.

IV.1. *Arabic, Language of Black Semites*

According to Muslim tradition the ancient peoples of *Afrabia* originally consisted of twelve tribes: **ʿĀd, Thamūd, Ṭasm, ʿImlīq, Immīm, Jāsim, Jurhum, ʿAbīl, Jadīs, ʿUṣ, Jāthir, Shālikh.**[57] These constitute the ***bāʿida*** or the now "extinct" Arabians. These tribes were the first to speak Arabic[58] and are therefore called ***al-ʿarab al-ʿāriba***, the "true Arabians," in contrast to *al-**ʿarab al-mustaʿriba*** "arabized Arabians", those foreign immigrants to Arabia who learned Arabic only after settling among "the true Arabs."[59] As al-**Ṭabarī** noted: "The Arabs called these nations the ***ʿāriba*** Arabs because the Arabic language was their original language, whereas they called the children of Ishmael b. Abraham the *mustaʿriba* Arabs because they only spoke these peoples' languages after they had settled among them."[60] The first to speak Arabic, we are told, was **ʿImlīq.**[61]

That these ***ʿāriba*** Arabs were Black is well documented in the Classical Arabic/Islamic sources.[62] Ibn Man**ẓū**r (d. 1311), author of the most authoritative classical Arabic lexicon, ***Lisān al-ʿarab***, notes the opinion that the phrase *aswad al-jilda*, 'Black-skinned,' idiomatically meant *khāliṣ al-ʿarab*, "the pure Arabs," "because the color of most of the Arabs is dark (*al-udma*)."[63] In other words, blackness of skin among the Arabs suggested purity

---

[57] John D. Baldwin, ***Pre-Historic Nations*** (New York: Harper & Brothers, Publishers, 1869) 78 Baldwin's list differs slightly from what we have here. For a different list *v.* ***EI²*** 10:359 s.v. **Ṭasm by** W.P. Heinrichs. On these various tribes and their dwellings *v.* al-**Ṭabarī**, ***Taʾrīkh al-rusul waʾl-muluk,*** vol. II edited and translated by William M. Brinner in ***The History of al-Ṭabarī: The Prophets and the Patriarchs*** (New York: State University of New York Press, 1986).

[58] ***EI²*** 10:359 s.v. **Ṭasm by** W.P. Heinrichs.

[59] See Philip Hitti, ***History of the Arabs*** (London: Macmillan, 1970), 32.

[60] Al-**Ṭabarī**, ***History***, 13f.

[61] Al-**Ṭabarī**, ***History***, 17f.

[62] See especially Berry, ***Unknown Arabs***.

[63] Ibn Man**ẓūr**, *Lisān al-ʿarab*, s.v. اخضر IV:245f; See also Edward William Lane, ***Arabic-English Lexicon*** (London: Williams & Norgate 1863) I: 756 s.v. خضر .

of Arab ethnicity. Likewise, the famous grammarian from the century prior, Muhammad b. Barrī al-'Adawī (d. 1193) noted that an *Akhḍar* or black-skinned Arab was "a pure Arab (*'arabī maḥḍ*)" with a pure genealogy, "because Arabs describe their color as black (*al-aswad*) and the color of the non-Arabs (*al-'**ajam***, i.e. Persians) as red (*al-**ḥu**mra*)."[64] Finally Al-Jahiz, in his *Fakhr al-s**ūdān** '**alā** '**l**-bidan*, ("The Boast of the Blacks over the Whites") declared: "The Arabs pride themselves in (their) black color, العرب تفخر بسواد اللون (*al-'arab tafkhar bi-saw**ā**d al-lawn*)"[65]

Jewish Rabbis of the 5th/6th centuries CE also knew the Arabs to be Black. Rabbi Akiba, famous first century Rabbi who is said to have visited Arabia, is presented in a 5th/6th century Jewish text commenting on Numbers 5:19, a passage dealing with how one knows if a wife has committed adultery. The Jewish (midrashic) text *Numbers Rabbah* says:

> The King of the Arabs put this question to R. Akiba: "I am black (*kûšī*) and my wife is black (*kûšīt*), yet she gave birth to a white son. Shall I kill her for having played the harlot while lying with me?[66]

As Jan Restö notes, while this midrash is probably completely legendary, it does give us a hint of Arabian ethnography, or what the views of the 5th/6th century redactors of this text were regarding Arabian ethnography at the time.[67] See also the *Targum Shir ha-Shirim* commenting on Song of Songs 1:5 ("I am

---

[64] Ibn Man**ẓūr**, ***Lisān al-'arab***, s.v. اخضر IV:245.

[65] Al-Ja**ḥiẓ**, ***Fakhr al-sūdān*** *'alā* ***al****-bidan*, 207. See also Ignaz Goldziher, ***Muslim Studies (Muhammedanische Studien)*** 2 vols. (London, Allen & Unwin, 1967-), 1:268 who notes that, in contrast to the Persians who are described as red or light-skinned (*a**ḥ**mar*) the Arabs call themselves black.

[66] *Num. R.* IX.34 (Soncino translation).

[67] Jan Retsö, ***The Arabs in Antiquity: Their History from the Assyrians to the Umayyads*** (London and New York: RoutledgeCurzon, 2003) 530. On the "rabbinic view of the Arab as dark-skinned" see further David M. Goldenberg, ***The Curse of Ham: Race and Slavery in Early Judaism, Christianity, and Islam (Jews, Christians, and Muslims from the Ancient to the Modern World)*** (Princeton: Princeton University Press, 2005), 122-24.

black and comely, O Daughters of Jerusalem, [black] as the tents of Qedar"):

> When the people of the House of Israel made the Calf, their faces became black like the sons of Kush who dwell in the tents of Qedar.

The Qedar was a Black Arab tribe, the most powerful Arab tribe of Syria and North Arabia who fought the Assyrians in the 7th century BCE.[68] Here they are identified with Kush. They were not active at the time of Rabbi Akiba's 5th/6th century CE redactors, but apparently their black memory was still alive and was transferred to the contemporary Black Arabs of the time. As Restö points out:

> The blackness of the Arabian king is due to his dwelling in the land of the Qedar whose inhabitants are black, according to the Song of Songs...Rabbi Aqiba's Arabia is thus identical with that of Qedar, which was the area between Egypt and Palestine.[69]

Thus, in the century or so prior to the rise of Prophet Muḥammad in Mecca, the Arabs were still known to be Black. It should be recalled that it is this very area – between Egypt and Palestine – that Diankonoff identified as the place of origin of the Semitic languages.

As late as the 19th century Black Arabs were still noted, though invasions, migrations, slavery, and miscegenation had severely

---

[68] The verbal root *qēdār* < *q – d – r* means "to be dark". As Marvin Pope informs us, "The root *qdr* itself carries the idea of darkness." ***Song of Songs: A New Translation with Introduction and Commentary*** (The Anchor Bible; Garden City, NY: Doubleday and Company, 1977) 319. See also Tremper Longman III, ***Song of Songs*** (Grand Rapids, Michigan and Cambridge: William B. Eerdman's Publishing, 2001) 97. Qedar is related to the Arabic root *kh-***ḍ***-r*, from which we get *akhḍar* "of blackish hue inclining to green, black-complexioned." See Jaroslav Stetkevych, ***Muḥammad and the Golden Bough: Reconstructing Arabian Myth*** (Bloomington and Indianapolis: Indiana University Press, 1996) 73.

[69] Restö, ***Arabs in Antiquity***, 530.

changed the complexion of the peninsula.[70] Muhammad Sadiq Bey, a Turkish photographer who traveled to Medina in 1861, noted that still, while there were light-skinned, almost white Medinese, the people were basically of "a dark, almost black complexion."[71] So too did John Lewis Burckhadt, Swiss traveler and Orientalist, describe in his ***Travels in Arabia*** Arabs whom he encountered as "very tall men, and almost black".[72] When adventurer and anthropologist Austin Henry Layard encountered in Hebron an Arab sheikh he noted that his complexion was "scarcely less dark than a negro."[73]

The original blackness of the Arabs is further supported by etymology. J.A. Loader argued in 1971 that the common Semitic root *ʿ–r-b* (from which we get the Arabic term *ʿarab*) meant primarily 'darkness' and wondered whether the Arabic *al-ʿarab*, "The Arabs", really meant 'the dark people.'[74] Loader had a hard time rectifying Semitic etymology with his very limited knowledge of Arabian ethnology, speculating: "But all Arabs are and were not of a conspicuously dark complexion, and therefore this explanation does not seem an attractive one…In any case the word is 'dark'."[75] But now we know that the original Arabs were dark, so Loader's etymological insight has been confirmed.[76]

---

[70] On which see Berry, ***Unknown Arabs***, Chapter 10; Reynolds, "African Heritage," 93-99.

[71] John De St. Jorre, "Pioneer Photographer of the Holy Cities," ***Saudi Aramco World*** (Jan-Feb 1999) 45.

[72] John Lewis Burckhardt, ***Travels in Arabia, comprehending an account of those territories in Hadjaz which the Mohammedans regard as sacred*** 2 vols. (London, H. Colburn, 1829) II:385.

[73] Austin Henry Layard, ***Early Adventures in Persia, Susiana and Babylonia: Including a Residence Among the Bakhtiyari and Other Wild Tribes Before the Discovery of Nineveh*** 2 vols. (London: John Murray, 1887) I:32.

[74] J.A. Loader, "The Concept of Darkness in the Hebrew Root ʿRB/ʿRP," in I.H. Eybers et al (edd.), ***De Fructu Oris Sui. Essays in Honour of Adrianus van Selms*** (Leiden: E.J. Brill, 1971) 99-144.

[75] Ibid., 107.

[76] Jan Restö, in his discussion of the etymology of the term 'Arab' did not consider this possible Common Semitic etymology: "The Earliest Arabs," ***Orientalia Suecana*** 38-39 (1989-1990): 131-139; idem, ***Arabs in Antiquity***, 105-113.

It is these Black Arabs, descendents of the original Kushite *Afrabians*, who are the original speakers of the Arabic language. University of Michigan Professor Emeritus George Mendenhall, one of the world's leading authorities on the Near East and Near Eastern languages, notes that "Arabic could not be a gift of the prophet Muḥammad, as many Islamic clerics claim, since its origins are in the early Bronze Age," over 3,000 years before Muḥammad.[77] Observing that the earliest segments of biblical Hebrew as a rule exhibit the highest percentage of Arabic cognates,[78] Mendenhall affirms that the further back we go, the closer Hebrew is to Arabic, thus strengthening De Goeje's opinion that "of all Semitic languages the Arabic approaches nearest to the original mother tongue."[79] Mendenhall has identified the "earliest identifiable Arabic-speaking social group" as the Midianites, an important political entity that came into existence suddenly in the 13th century BCE in northwest Arabia. This highly sophisticated culture spoke a language which is an

---

77 Quoted in interview by Jeff Mortimer, "Language of the Desert," ***Michigan Today***, Spring 1997 online version: http://www.ns.umich.edu/MT/97/Spr97/mta8s97.html accessed July 30, 2009.

78 George Mendenhall, "Arabic in Semitic Linguistic History," ***JAOS*** 126 (2006): 22-3.

79 Quoted in Samuel Marinus Zwemer, ***Arabia: The cradle of Islam: studies in the geography, people, and politics of the peninsula, with an account of Islam and mission-work*** (Oliphant, Anderson & Ferrier, 1912 [Revised edition]) 240. Nineteenth and early twentieth-century Semitists pretty much identified Arabic with Proto-Semitic. This is due to Arabic's extremely conservative evolution. Thus, Hitti (***Arabs***, 8) suggested: "(The Arab's) language, though the youngest among the Semitic group from the point of view of literature, has, nevertheless, conserved more of the peculiarities of the mother Semitic tongue-including the inflection-than the Hebrew and its other sister languages. It therefore affords us the best key for the study of the Semitic languages." This position, while not to be abandoned, must be modified by recent data. Arabic is indeed most conservative in terms of phonetics and derived models: it is said to preserve almost the complete original phonetic set of South Arabian and Ugatitic. Thus, for the most complete catalogue possible of the Proto-Semitic lexicon one should still start with the Arabic dictionary. In terms of semantic history, however, Arabic is quite innovative due to the great geographic extent travelled and cultures absorbed during the period of the Islamic empire. See del Olmo Lete, ***Questions of Semantic Linguistics***, 114-115; Federico Corriente, "The Phonemic System of Semitic from the Advantage of Arabic and its Dialectology," ***Aula Orientalis*** 23 (2005) 187-194; idem, "On the Degree of Kinship Between Arabic and Northwest Semitic," ***AIDA 5 Proceedings-Càdiz*** (2003): 187-194.

archaic ancestor of modern Arabic.[80] This is significant because, as David Goldenberg affirms: "Kush is the ancient name of Midian."[81] These Midianites, the earliest identifiable Arabic-speaking *social group*, are documented as a Kushite or Black Arabian tribe.[82]

[80] ***The Anchor Bible Dictionary***, ed. David Noel Freedman et al, 6 vols. (New York: Doubleday, 1992) 4:815 s.v. Midian by George E. Mendenhall.
[81] ***Curse of Ham***, 28. See also Restö, ***Arabs in Antiquity***, 139.
[82] "the people of Northwest Arabia (Midian) were called Kushites." Goldenberg, ***Curse of Ham***, 54.

Chapter Two

The Civilizations of Afrabia

"The Arabs are basically an AD people. There is no BC activity of consequence that can be attributed to them."
Dr. John Henrik Clarke, *The Rise of Islam in Africa.*

I. *Lost Civilizations*

It was popular among 19th century antiquarians to argue that there existed in remote antiquity a "widespread" civilization of Blacks extending over Africa, Asia, the Middle East, Europe, and the known world. These speculations were based largely on the observations of European adventurers who, in their world travels, discovered Black peoples everywhere an indigenous population.[83] The seat of this ancient Black civilization, they

---

[83] Sir Harry H. Johnston (1858-1927) thus noted:

> To this day dwarf Negro people survive in the Far East-the Samang in the forest of the Malay Peninsula and the Aeta in the Philippines. There are traces of the passage of a Negroid people through Sumatra and Borneo, in the island of Timor, and markedly in New Guinea...The existing population of Solomon Islands, of New Ireland, and of the New Hebrides, are much more Negro-Like in physical characteristics; in fact, most akin to the African Negros of all the Asiatic or Australasian peoples. Asiatic Negroes also seem to have entered Australia from New guinea and to have passed down to the eastern part of that continent till they reached the then peninsula of Tasmania...There is a Negroid (Melanesian) element in the Fiji, and as far west as the Hawaii Archipelago and among the Maoris of New Zealand; in much less degree also in Burma, Annam, Hainan, Formosa, the Riu-Kiu Islands, and Southern Japan..." (***The Negro in the New World*** [1910; rp. 1969: New York, Johnson Reprint Corporation], 25f.

See also Percy Sykes who wrote in ***History of Persia*** (London: Routledge and Kegan Paul, 1969) 51:

> Some years ago during the course of my travels, I was puzzled by the extremely dark populations of Baskakird and Sarhad, very remote and mountainous regions bordering on Persian Baluchistan. The solution may be that the whole country was originally peopled by Negritoes...who probably stretched along the northern shores of the Persian Gulf to India and that their descendants have survived in those distant parts.

speculated, was in Asia, either in India or on the Arabian Peninsula.[84] John D. Baldwin, member of the American Oriental Society, argued for example:

> Arabia, in very remote antiquity, was the seat of a brilliant civilization, which extended itself throughout Southwestern Asia, and spread its influence from the extreme east to the extreme west of the known world. The wonderful people of ancient Arabia-the revered and mysterious Ethiopians of ancient tradition-seem to have filled the world, as they knew it, with their commercial activity, their maritime enterprise, their colonies, and the light of their civilized life. Their traces are still found everywhere...The original country of the Cushite race...the original home where this culture had birth, and from which the Cushite colonies and influence went forth in every direction to spread civilization, and create such nations as Egypt and Chaldea...was the whole Arabian peninsula...We consider Egypt and Chaldea very old, but the culture and political organization of the Arabian Cushites were much older...[85]

That ancient Black Arabia was the seat of a civilization that rivaled that of Egypt and Mesopotamia was argued as well by African American historian Drusilla D. Houston, who argued in her ***Wonderful Ethiopians of the Ancient Cushite Empire***:

> To the Cushite race belonged the oldest and purest Arabian blood. They were the original Arabians and the creators of the ancient civilization, evidences of which may be seen in the stupendous ruins in every part of the country. At the time that Ethiopians began to show power as monarchs of Egypt about 3000 to 3500 B.C. the western part of Arabia was divided into two powerful kingdoms. In those days the princes of Arabia

---

[84] Godfrey Higgins, ***Anacalypsis*** 2 vols. (1836; New York: A&B Books Publishers, 1992), 1: 51ff; George and Henry Rawlinson, ***History of Herodotus*** (London: John Murray, 1858), 1:650; Baldwin, ***Pre-Historic Nations***; François Lenormant, ***Ancient History of the East*** 2 vols. (Philadelphia: J.B. Lippincott & Co., 1871), 1:58; Count Alam G. de Gurowski, ***America and Europe*** (New York: Books For Libraries Press, 1857), 175f; Rodgers, ***Sex and Race***, 263-264.
[85] Baldwin, ***Pre-Historic Nations***, 49.

belonged wholly to the descendants of Cushites, who ruled Yemen for thousands of year…3000 to 3500 B.C. Arabian civilization equaled that of Egypt and Babylon.[86]

As noted above Muslim tradition acknowledges twelve original tribes of ancient *Afrabia*. **'Ād** and, later, **Thamūd** are known from the Qur'**ā**n as the early civilizers of *Afrabia* who, having become proud and wicked, were destroyed.[87] According to a number of scholars the Adites were an empire of Kushites who ruled the whole of Arabia and the Middle East.[88] Wifred H. Schoff notes that "(The Plain of Dhofar in Southeastern Arabia), with its ancient capital, Saphar, was the center of the ancient Cushite empire (or Adite, from Ad, grandson of Ham) which included most of Southern Arabia and much of East Africa".[89] It has been suggested that **'Ād** originated around eight to ten thousand years ago in the "proto-Semitic homeland," that area in the north of the Arabian Peninsula (from northern Egypt to Syria).[90]

---

[86] Drusilla Dunjee Houston, ***Wonderful Ethiopians of the Ancient Cushite Empire*** (Baltimore: Black Classic Press Reprint, 1985) 120.

[87] On them *v.* ***EI***^{2} 1:169, s.v. **'Ād by** F. Buhl; ***EI***^{2} 10:436 **s.v.** Thamū**d by** Irfan Shahī**d**; al-**Ṭabarī, *History*,** 28-47.

[88] A.P. Caussin de Perceval, ***Essai sur l'histoire des Arabs avant l'Islamisme, pendant l'époque de Mahomet*** (Paris: Imprimeurs de l'enstitute, 1847) 7; Baldwin, ***Prehistoric Nations***, 78f. *See* also Diop, ***African Origin***, 123f; Houston, ***Wonderful Ethiopians***, 114. See also Dana Marniche, "When Arabia was Eastern Ethiopia (Part 4)"; "The Samudayt clan of the Mahra, from which came the Tsamud or Thamud, according to tradition were the 2nd Ad or remnant of the Adite whose power once extended from Sana'a in Yemen to Syria and Egypt." http://www.africaresource.com/rasta/sesostris-the-great-the-egyptian-hercules/when-arabia-was-eastern-ethiopia-part-4-by-dana-marniche/ accessed February 14, 2009. François Lenormant (***The Beginnings of History According to the Bible and the Traditions of Oriental Peoples*** [London: Sampson Low, Marston, Searle, and Rivington, 1885]) traces **'Ād**'s descent from Ham, the alleged progenitor of the Black populations of the world. Classical Islamic tradition preferred to make **'Ād** a descendant of Shem (al-**Ṭabarī, *History*,** 18), though the old Hamitic genealogy was remembered in the classic ***Arabian Nights***. There the Adites and Cushites were identified and connected to the Black children of Ham (Modern Library edition, 444, 465)

[89] Wifred H. Schoff, ***The Periplus of the Erythræan Sea*** (New York: Longmans, Green, and Co., 1912), 141f.

[90] Nicholas Clapp, ***The Road to Ubar: Finding the Atlantis of the Sands*** (Boston and New York: Mariner Books, 1999) 221.

Conceiving Arabia as the seat of ancient civilizations that rivaled the great civilizations which sprung up around the Nile and the Tigris and Euphrates is difficult, no doubt due to the 'tyranny of the desert'. Measuring 650,000 square kilometers (250,000 sq mi), the Rub al-Khali (Empty Quarter; Figure 10), Arabia's sea of sand, is the largest sand mass on earth. Its dominant position in terms of Arabia's modern geomorphic situation makes it difficult to imagine the peninsula as a once home of high civilizations. Desertification, however, is a relatively recent phenomenon for the peninsula. Formerly a 'tropical savanna', hyperaridity began in the area around 20, 000 years ago and desiccation around 6000 years ago.[91] Before the onset of the desserts the Empty Quarter was a fertile plateau, through which large streams carved deep and wide wadys.[92] There were then high civilizations on the peninsula. The remains of some of them are literally buried under this great dessert. This has been confirmed by a team of archaeologists, explorers and NASA scientists who discovered in 1992 the remains of the fabled ancient city Ubar/Iram under the sands of the Rub al-Khali.[93]

---

[91] D.T. Potts, ***The Arabian Gulf in Antiquity, I: From Prehistory to the Fall of the Achaemenid Empire*** 2 vols. (Oxford: Claredon Press, 1990) 16f.

[92] H.A. McCLure, "Al Rub' Al Khali," in S.S. Al-Sayari and J.G. Zötl, ***Quaternary Period in Saudi Arabia*** (Vienna and New York, 1978) I: 84.; J. McCorriston et al, "Holocene Paleoecology and Prehistory in Highland Southern Arabia," ***Paléorient*** 28 (2002): 64.

[93] John Noble Wilford, "On the Trail From the Sky: Roads Point to a Lost City," ***New York Times*** VOL. CXLI, Wednesday, February 5, 1992. A1; Runoko Rashidi, "Research Notes. Ancient Cities Beneath the Arabian Sands: Ubar and Saffara Metropolis," in Rashidi and Sertima, ***African Presence***, 312-313.

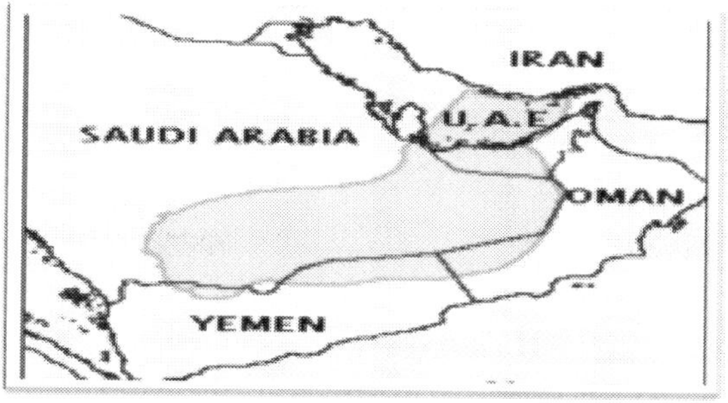

Figure 10
Rub al-Khali (Empty Quarter)

Ubar, called in the Qur'ān *Iram dhāt al-'Imād*, "Iram of the Pillars" (89:67) was a famed, fabulously wealthy trading center from around 3000 BCE – 200 CE in the area known today as the Empty Quarter (Rub al-Khali).[94] The people of Ubar were, according to tradition, a "tribe of blacks", the tribe of 'Ad, whose remnants today are the Shahra and Mahra tribes.[95] Some time between 300 and 500 CE Ubar was suddenly destroyed. According to Muslim tradition Ubar/Iram was built by Shaddād, the son of 'Ād as an 'imitation of Paradise' and was destroyed by a catastrophic punishment from God. It was lost to modern history and, thus, modern historians deemed it merely a fable because there was no trace of this 'lost city.' Lawrence of Arabia called it the "Atlantis of the sands." This all changed in 1992. NASA's Jet Propulsion Laboratory remote sensing satellites and ground penetrating radar, guided by photographs taken by Challenger Space shuttle in 1984, discovered remains of this lost city buried under the sands of the Empty Quarter in the Dhofar region of Southern Oman. The discovered ruins consist of octagonal walls with niches for eight pillars standing 30 feet high. The evidence indicates that its fate was indeed catastrophic: the city fell into a sinkhole created when an

[94] ***EI***[1] 3:519-520 s.v. Iram dhāt al-'Imād by A.J. Wensink; ***EI***[2] 3: 1270 s.v. Iram by W. Montgomery Watt.

[95] Clapp, ***Road to Ubar***, 98, 139.

underground limestone crater collapsed. The city became buried under sand. Nicholas Clapp, originator of the exploration project that led to Ubar's/Iram's discovery, explains:

> The legend of Ubar climaxed as the city 'sank into the sands.' It certainly did. Ubar wasn't burned and sacked, decimated by plague, or rocked by a deadly quake. It collapsed into an underground cavern. Of all the sites in all the ancient world, *Ubar came to a unique and peculiar end, an end identical in legend and reality*...
>
> At the outset of our search for Ubar, we scarcely imagined that we would find a reality that with a fair degree of accuracy validated the city's myth, but...it seemed we had. Whether by divine vengeance or the random happenstance of nature, Ubar came to an awful end...Strata and shards and carbon-14 dating have...given a new reality to the preaching of the prophet Muhammad.[96]

Figure 12
Reconstruction of Ubar based on discovered ruins

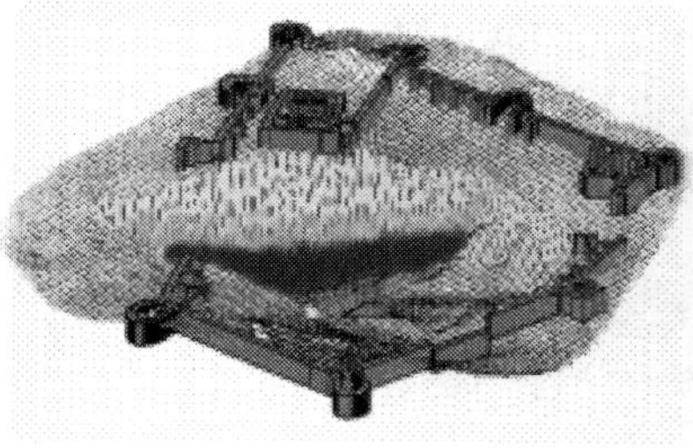

Figure 13
Reconstruction of Ubar Sinkhole

[96] Clapp, ***Road to Ubar***, 203, 259, 262.

That the people of Ubar were a Black people as claimed by tradition is supported by archeological evidence. Rock-art from the Rub al-Khali dated to the 4th – 2nd millennia BCE depict, according to renowned archeologist and Near Eastern ethnologist Emmanuel Anati, a "Cushite" or Black population of "oval-heads" who were a "beautifully built people of high stature, with elegant body features, slender and longs legs and harmonious shapes and movements."[97]

The discovery of the Ubar/Iram ruins under the sands of the Rub al-Khali should caution us against succumbing to the 'tyranny of the desert,' assuming that Arabia's current climate and geomorphic reality mitigates against the peninsula having played an important role in ancient civilizational experimentations. Nor are the Ubar/Iram ruins the only material evidence of civilization on the peninsula.[98] There were fortified towns in southwest Arabia, the other side of the peninsula, at the latest by 4000 BP.[99] In short, J. R. Wellsted's claim that "Arabia was among the first nations which felt the effects of civilization; and...it was here that the first large societies of men united themselves for mutual protection" cannot be dismissed.[100]

---

[97] Emmanuel Anati, ***Rock-Art in Central Arabia. Vol 1: The "Oval-Headed" People of Arabia*** (Louvain and Leuven, 1968) 180.
[98] Christopher Edens and T.J. Wilkinson, "Southwest Arabia During the Holocene: Recent Archaeological Developments," ***Journal of World Prehistory*** 12 (1998) 55-119; Rice, ***Archaeology***; Potts, ***Arabian Gulf***; ***The Temple Complex at Bahrain Barbar – A Description and Guide*** (Bahrain: Ministry of Information, 1990); Juris Zarins et al, "Preliminary Report on the Archaeological Survey of the Riyadh Area," ***ATLAL*** 6 (1982): 25-37; idem, "Rajājil-A Unique Arabian Site from the Forth Millennium B.C.," ***ATLAL*** 3 (1979): 73-77; Nabih Amin Faris, ***The Antiquities of South Arabia*** (Princeton: Princeton University Press, 1938).
[99] Edens and Wilkinson, "Southwest Arabia," 80, 92.
[100] J. R. Wellsted, ***Travels in Arabia*** (F.R.S, Indian Navy) I:355.

II. *Afrabia as Kusha Dwipa (Land of Kush)*

Based on a study of "mythologies, the ruins (archeology), the discoveries of linguistic science, and the general voice of tradition," John Baldwin concluded that "the original Ethiopia was not in Africa (but) the original home of the Cushites or Ethiopians, the starting point of their great colonizing and civilizing movements, was Arabia."[101] 'Ethiopia' is a Greek term meaning 'of burned face.' It is certain that the Greeks spoke of two Ethiopias or lands of burned face peoples: one west of the Red Sea in Africa, the other east of the Red Sea, as affirmed by Strabo (*Geography*, bk. I, ch. II):

> I assert that the ancient Greeks...designated as Ethiopia the whole of the Southern countries toward the ocean. And if the moderns have confined the appellation Ethiopians to those only who dwell near Egypt, this must not be allowed to interfere with the meaning of the ancients...The Ethiopians were considered as occupying all the south coasts of both Asia and Africa, and as 'divided' by the Red Sea into Eastern and Western, Asiatic and African.[102]

The Ethiopia or 'Kush' of Hebrew tradition is more geographically delimited: it is Arabia.[103] As Charles Foster clarifies in his ***Historical Geography of Arabia***:

> It is a matter of fact, familiar to the learned reader, that the names 'Ethiopia' and 'Ethiopians' are frequently substituted in

---

[101] Baldwin, ***Pre-historic Nations***, 21.

[102] Thus Sir E. Wallis Budge writes: "It seems certain that classical historians and geographers called the whole region from India to Egypt, both countries inclusive, by the name of Ethiopia, and in consequence they regarded all the dark-skinned and black peoples who inhabited it as Ethiopians. Mention is made of Eastern and Western Ethiopians and it s probable that the Eastern were Asiatics and the Western African." E. A. Wallis Budge, ***A History of Ethiopia, Nubia and Abyssinia (According to the Hieroglyphic Inscriptions of Egypt and Nubia and the Ethiopian Chronicles)*** 2 vols. (London, 1928: Methuen; republished in Oosterhout, the Netherlands, in 1966 in one volume by Anthropological Publications) I: 2. See also J.W. Gardner, "Blameless Ethiopians and Others," ***Greece and Rome***24 (1977): 185-193.

[103] Godfrey Higgins, ***Anacalypsis***, 2 vols. (New York: A&B Books, 1836, 1992), I: 52.

our English version of the Old Testament where the Hebrew preserved the proper name 'Cush.' And the name 'Cush', when so applied in Scripture, belongs uniformly, not to the African, but to the Asiatic Ethiopia, or Arabia.[104]

The biblical Table of Nations, particularly Gen. 10:7 describing the distribution of the sons of Kush, narrates an Arabian, not a continental African, genealogy,[105] and according to Fred V. Winnett these biblical Arabian genealogies "contain information of considerable value for the reconstruction of early Arabian history." He assumes these genealogies reflect the political and tribal situation in 6th cent BCE Arabia.[106] According to Jan Retsö these genealogies and other references in the Hebrew Bible are the "earliest attempt at a systematic description of peoples living on the (Arabian) peninsula,"[107] and these peoples are considered Kushites, black-skinned peoples (Jer 13:23).[108] Indeed, Kushites were the dominant ethnic group in Syria-Palestine in late 8th and 7th centuries BCE.[109] These were

---

[104] Charlse Forster ***Historical Geography of Arabia*** (London: Duncan and Malcom, 1844) I:12. See also Fritz Hommel, ***The Ancient Hebrew Tradition*** (London: Society for Promoting Christian Knowledge, 1897), 315 who notes: "Kush is a known Biblical designation of Central Arabia." Hommel theorized that the Arabian Cush and the North African Cush (Nubia) were colonies of Elam, the original Cush. These Elamite Cushites "were scattered over Arabia, and found there way to Africa (39)."

[105] Claus Westermann, ***Genesis 1-11: A Commentary*** (Minneapolis: Augsburg Publishing House, 1984) 511: "It is certain that the majority of the names describes peoples in Arabia."

[106] Fred V. Winnett, "The Arabian Genealogies in the Book of Genesis," in Harry Thomas Frank and William L. Reed (edd.), ***Translating and Understanding the Old Testament. Essays in Honor of Herbert Gordon May*** (Nashville and New York: Abingdon Press, 1970) 173 [art.=171-196].

[107] Retsö, ***Arabs in Antiquity***, 212. He says the biblical author here, called P, had in mind 7th century Arabia and "According to P, Kush encompasses the land on both sides of the Red Sea and…western Arabia consequently belongs to it."

[108] That Jer13:23 "speaks of the dark-skinned Cushites," is affirmed by Westermann, ***Genesis 1-11***, 510; Edward Ullendorff, ***Ethiopia and the Bible*** (London: Oxford University Press, 1968) 7. In Near Eastern, Greco-Roman, Biblical and Post-Biblical Jewish literature Kusites are noted for black skin: Goldenberg, ***Curse of Ham***, 113ff.

[109] On the Kushite presence in the Syro-Palestine region see Roger W. Anderson, Jr. "Zephaniah ben Cushi and the Cush of Benjamin: Traces of Cushite Presence in Syria-Palestine," in Steven W. Holloway and Lowell K. Handy (edd.), ***The Picture is***

no doubt *black* Syria-Palestinians. As Roger W. Anderson, Jr. notes: "The Cushites were probably dark-skinned or burnt-faced people, ones whom we would classify today as black."[110] William Foxwell Albright documented a district or tribe called Kush in southern Transjordan in the 19th century BCE and a ***Kûšân-rōm***, "high Kushan" in Northern Syria in 13th -12th cent BCE.[111] Even Arabic tradition records an Arabian Kush. Ibn al-Mujāwir in his ***Tārīkh al-mustabṣir*** records a tradition according to which the southern Tihāma (from Mecca southwards) was called Kush.[112]

The oldest Sanskrit geographical writings, such as the *Puranas*, describe Arabia as *Kusha-dwipa*, Land of Kush, one of seven main 'peninsulas' or lands (*Sapta-dwipa*).[113] Kusha-dwipa extends from the shores of the Mediterranean and the mouth of the Nile to Sirhind on the borders of India, i.e. the Arabian Peninsula (including Syria from the mouths of the Nile, Armenia, Tigris-Euphrates countries) and the region north of the Persian Gulf. In

---

Broken: Memorial Essays for Gösta W. Ahlström (JSOTSupp 190; Sheffield: Sheffield Academic Press, 1995) 45-70.

[110] Anderson, "Zephaniah ben Cushi," 68. But Anderson wants to connect these Syrian Kushites with the Nubian rulers of Egypt's 25th Dynasty who had some influence in the area. On the other hand Robert D. Haak has shown that this association is untenable. " 'Cush' in Zephaniah," in Holloway and Handy, ***Picture is Broken***, 238-251. On Kushites in the area see also Israel Eph'al, ***The Ancient Arabs: Nomads on the Borders of the Fertile Crescent 9th – 5th Centuries B.C.*** (Leiden: E.J. Brill, 1982) 78-79.

[111] Williams Foxwell Albright, ***Archaeology and the Religion of Israel*** (Baltimore: The John Hopkins Press, 1956) 205 n. 49. On the Kushite presence in North Arabia see also Goldenberg, ***Curse of Ham***, 20: "The existence of a Kushite people in the general area and references to it in the Bible have become well accepted in biblical scholarship."

[112] 83 [Eng. 109]

[113] According to the oldest tradition found in *Vayu* and *Bramanda Puranas* the Sapta-dwipa are:

1. Jambu-dwipa –center
2. Anga-dwipa – Northeastern Asia
3. Yama-dwipa – Ancient Chinese Empire
4. Yamala-dwipa – Southeastern Asian islands
5. Sancha-dwipa – Africa
6. Kusha-dwipa – Arabian Peninsula
7. Varach-dwipa – Europe

other words: *Afrabia* is Kusha-dwipa. In a later division found in Chapter IV, Book I of *Vishnu Purana*, six sub-dwipas are added, including a second Kusha-dwipa designated Kusha-dwipa *exterior* and contrasted with the original Kusha-dwipa, now called Kusha-dwipa *interior.* The second or exterior Kusha-Dwipa is located in Sancha-dwipa, i.e. Africa, beyond the straits of Bab-el-Mandeb (Upper Egypt). As Capt. Francis Wilford explained:

> Chusha-dwipa *without* is Abyssinia and Ethiopia, and the Brahmens account plausibly enough for its name, by asserting that the descendents of Cusha, being obliged to leave their native country, from them called Cusha-dwipa *within*, migrated into Sanc'ha'-dwip, and gave their new settlement the name of their ancestor (Cusha).[114]

Baldwin further notes: "All accounts agree in stating that this African Cusha-dwipa was created by emigration from Arabia and from countries connected with it…"[115] Thus, the Hebrews, Indo-Aryans, and Greeks (?) concurred in describing the same region as the *primary* Ethiopia/Kush: the Arabian peninsula, confirming Dana Marniche's observation: "as much as Arabia was an extension of Ethiopia, Ethiopia was considered Arabia."[116]

---

[114] "On Egypt and Other Countries Adjacent to the Cali River or Nile of Ethiopia from the Ancient Books of the Hindus," ***Asiatik Researches*** 3 (1896): 55 [art.=46-265]. See also François Lenormant, ***The Book of Genesis*** (Longmans, 1886) 77*:* "In the Puranas Cusha-dwipa, the Land of Cush, includes Arabia and other countries between the borders of India to the Mediterranean, while at a late period a second Cusha-dwipa, situated beyond the straits of Bab-el-Mandeb in Africa, was called Cusha-dwipa *without*, as having been colonized from Cusha-dwipa *within.*"

[115] Baldwin, ***Pre-Historic Nations***, 65.

[116] Dana Marniche, "The Afro-Arabian Origin of the Israelites and Ishmaelites."

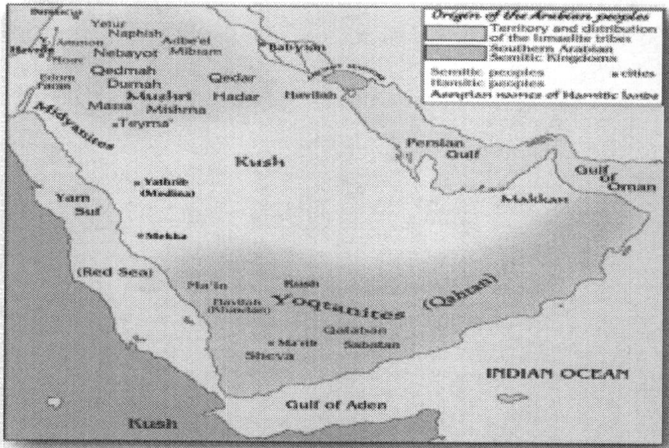

Figure 14
The Several 'Kush's' of antiquity

III. *Afrabia as Vagina Gentium*

Sir E.A. Wallis Budge, Egyptologist as well as Assyriologist, noted in ***The Gods of the Egyptians***:

> It is surprising…to find so much similarity existing between the primeval gods of Sumer and those of Egypt, especially as the resemblance cannot be the result of borrowing…and we are therefore driven to the conclusion that both the Sumerians and the early Egyptians derived their primeval gods from some common but exceedingly ancient source.[117]

The remarkable similarity between Sumerian/Mesopotamian and Egyptian civilizations has been frequently noted.[118] Highlighting the contemporary and similarly exceptionally fine quality of Ubaid (Sumerian) pottery and Badarian (Egyptian) pottery Michael Rice points out:

---

[117] Sir E.A. Wallis Budge, ***The Gods of the Egyptians*** 1:290.
[118] See e.g. discussion by John G Jackson, "Egypt and Western Asia," in idem, ***Ages of Gold and Silver*** (Austin: American Atheist Press, 1990) 65-85.

> This phenomenon, so unlikely in any event and doubly so with two apparently quite disparate peoples living relatively far from each other, is one of the most puzzling of the early, more or less simultaneous, developments of Egypt and Sumer... The apparently common factors which manifest themselves in Egypt and Sumer...are too many not to warrant some speculation about the possibility of their common, or at least related, origin.[119]

Equally remarkable are the parallels between Egypt and India. As Geeti Sen points out: "Neither historical events nor cross-cultural currents can explain the unique parallels in the myths and imagery of ancient Egypt and India."[120] Paul William Roberts opined that India and Egypt, as well as Babylon and Israel, were inheritors of the legacy of a lost civilization.

> There must have been one. There are too many similarities between hieroglyphic texts and Vedic ones, these in turn echoed in somewhat diluted form and a confused fashion by the authors of Babylonian texts and the Old Testament.[121]

Rice suggests that the common culture from which the Sumerians and Egyptians evolved was Arabian.[122] The Sumerians, those peoples who built the marvelous civilization by the Tigris and Euphrates rivers, were akin to the Dravidians, judging from the skeletal remains as well as linguistics.[123] We

---

[119] Michael Rice, ***Egypt's Making: The Origins of the Ancient Egypt 5000-2000 BC***, 2nd Edition (London: Routledge, 2003) 25.

[120] Geeti Sen, "The Lotus and the Seed," in Saryu Doshi and Mostafa El Abbadi (edd.), ***India and Egypt: Influences and Interactions*** (Bombay, India: Marg Publications, 1993) 3 [art.=3-13]. See also Sudhansu Kumar Ray, ***Prehistoric India and ancient Egypt; artistic, linguistic and political relations, revealed by the Bengali traditional documents*** (New Delhi: Cambridge Book and Stationery Store, 1956)

[121] Paul William Roberts, ***Empire of the Soul: Some Journeys in India*** (New York: Riverhead Books, 1997) 300.

[122] Rice, ***Egypt's Making***, 251.

[123] H.R. Hall, ***The Ancient History of the Near East: From the Earliest Times to the Battle of Salamis*** (London: Methuen, 1916) 173 notes: "And it is to this Dravidian

now know that these Sumerians originated in Arabia, as was early suspected.[124] The Sumerians point to Dilmun, the "archetypal Holy Land," as their place of origin.[125] This land is Eastern Arabia generally and (later) Bahrain in particular.[126] As P.V. Glob and T.G. Bibly state:

> Bahrain has proved to be the legendary Dilmun referred to in the cuneiform texts of Sumer, the bridge between that primary seat of urban revolution and the civilization of the Indus Valley in what is now Pakistan.[127]

Until about 3000 BCE inland Arabia was inhabitable. Already in the 4th millennium BCE Dilmun was a thriving center of trade[128] and Dilmun civilization dominated eastern Arabia until ca. 2000 BCE. The apex of this East Arabian civilization was during the Barbar period (third millennium BCE) and the remains of the Barbar temples exist today as a testament of this

---

ethnic type of India that the ancient Sumerian bears most resemblance". On the skeletal remains see Sir Arthur Keith, "Report on the Human Remains," in H.R. Hall et al, ***Ur Excavations, Volume I: Al-'Ubaid*** (London: Oxford University Press, 1927) 214-240; L.H. Dudley Buxton and D. Talbot Rice, "Report on the Human Remains Found at Kish," ***Journal of the Royal Anthropological Institute of Great Britain and Ireland*** 61 (1931): 57-119; Runoko Rashidi, "More Light on Sumer, Elam an India," in Rashidi and Van Sertima, ***African Presence***, 162-163. On the linguistic evidence see Paulinu Tambimutto, ***Europe and the Dravidians*** (London: P. Tambimutto, 1982) 14ff.

124 George A. Barton asked the question, "Whence Came the Sumerians? (***Journal of the American Oriental Society*** 49 [1929] 266) and answered: "they originated in Oman in eastern Arabia." See further idem, "The Origins of Civilization in Africa and Mesopotamia, Their Relative Antiquity and Interplay" ***Proceedings of the American Philosophical Society*** Vol. 68 (1929): 305-306; Henry Field, "The Ancient and Modern Inhabitants of Arabia," ***Open Court*** 46 (1932): 851-852; idem, "The Arabs of Iraq," ***American Journal of Physical Anthropology*** 21 (1936): 52.

125 Rice, ***Archaeology***, 11-12.

126 Rice, ***Archaeology***, 78; Potts, ***Arabian Gulf***, 86; Geoffrey Bibby, "The Origins of the Dilmun Civiliation," in Shaikha Haya Ali al Khalifa and Michael Rice (edd.), ***Bahrain through the ages: the Archaeology*** (London: KPI, 1986) 108-115.

127 P.V. Glob and T.G. Bibly, "A Forgotten Civilization of the Persian Gulf," ***Scientific American*** 203 (1960): 62-71.

128 Elisabeth C.L. During Caspers, "Sumer, Coastal Arabia and the Indus Valley in Protoliterate and Early Dynastic Eras," ***Journal of the Economic and Social History of the Orient*** 22 (1979): 121-135.

Kushite empire.[129] The eventual desiccation of the Arabian peninsula likely pushed these Arabian Kushites northward in search of a wetter environment.[130] As Michael Rice explains:

> In the sixth and fifth millennia BC, and perhaps from much earlier still, there was, all the evidence now suggests, a significant population in eastern Arabia and particularly in the south-eastern quadrant of the peninsula...It has been suggested that the people of this region were ancestral to the people who made Ubaid pottery...they in turn, were probably ancestral to the Sumerians. They were in all probability well established around the periphery of the Rub al-Khali and especially in what is now northern Oman. But gradually...the climate began to deteriorate and the desert, represented in Egyptian mythology by Set, the god of confusion and Lord of the East, began to move in towards the areas which had previously been able to support a population of men and animals...the people were forced to move, some eastwards and then north, others westwards along the edges of the dying lakes. These would reach the Red Sea: then the journey to Egypt would once more face the people of south-east Arabia as it had perhaps already faced some who had gone on the long sea route.[131]

We will discuss the westward, Nile-bound migrants below. These northward moving Arabians-turned-Sumerians brought with them a relatively high civilization. George A. Barton describes:

---

[129] On the Barbar temples see below.

[130] Henry Field, "The Ancient and Modern Inhabitants of Arabia," ***Open Court*** 46 (1932): 851-852: "Palaeolithic and Neolithic man inhabited North Arabia, while the climate was genial and the region well-watered. Some time before the historic period, the climate had changed to a marked degree and the inhabitants were forced to become nomads...or to migrate to water. Those who chose the latter course moved eastwards to the water and encamped beside the banks of the cool and refreshing Euphrates River. They were thus the first inhabitants of Mesopotamia."

[131] Rice, ***Egypt's Making***, 256.

> Certainly as early as 3,500 B.C. and perhaps as early as 4000 B.C., the Sumerians, pushing up the Persian Gulf from the south, made their way into Southern Babylonia...The memory of their coming is reflected in the myth of Oannes, recounted to us by Berossos, who taught men how to construct houses, till the earth, compile laws, and all other useful knowledge. It is clear that the Sumerians were highly civilized when they entered Babylonia; they knew the arts of agriculture by 3500 B.C.; they could make beautiful objects of gold and silver, surpassing in craftsmanship and beauty anything found in Egypt until centuries later; they could write; they had invented the principle of the real arch and dome; and they had invented the use of the wheel and had chariots.[132]

Carleton Coon suggested that, with the post-glacial desiccation of the Near East, Arabia served as a "*vagina gentium* ('womb of nations'), sending forth into other regions great numbers of inhabitants whom it could no longer support."[133] The Sumerians were such migrants from the Arabian interior, and the grandeur of the civilization that they established by the Tigris and Euphrates rivers witnesses to the level of skill and civilization that existed among the Arabian Kushites in remote antiquity, confirming the above conclusions of Baldwin and Houston. Of particular importance for this discussion is the fact that Sumerian religion derives from that of the Arabian Kushites.[134]

IV. *Afrabia as Ta-Neter*

We have seen that the evidence for Sumer/Mesopotamia evolving from an Arabian Kushite culture is significant, but Egypt too? R. Sayce and R. Peterson are sure that at least a portion of the Egyptian population originated in Arabia:

---

[132] "Origins of Civilization," 305-306.

[133] Carleton Coon, ***The Races of Europe*** (1939), 401.

[134] Langdon, ***Semitic Religion***, 3-4.

> Ancient Egyptian tradition pointed to 'the divine land' of Arabia Felix as that from which their principle deities had migrated...The 'divine land' was Southern Arabia...Botany...supports the tradition which brought the non-animistic divinities of Egypt from Arabia Felix.[135]

Sayce and Peterson's view is based on their identification of the fabled 'Punt' or 'Ta Neter', 'Divine Land', from which some Egyptian texts say the Gods and an ancestral race derived, as referring to Arabia.[136] Rice too has proffered interesting arguments for identifying the Divine Land, at least as described allusively in the Pyramid Texts and the inscriptions of the Horus Temple at Edfu, with Bahrain, Sumer's very own 'Divine Land' in eastern Arabia.[137]

The going opinion in late nineteenth and early twentieth century scholarship, due in large measure to the discussion by H. Brugsch,[138] was that the Egyptians' 'Punt' was located within southern Arabia. The tide turned, however, with the publication of R. Herzog's German monograph in 1968, ***Punt*** (Glückstadt: Augustin). Based on a study of the flora and fauna associated with Punt, Herzog placed it in Africa, in the region of the Upper Nile between Atbara and the confluence of the White and Blue Niles. The 'African hypothesis' was solidified in scholarly opinion, for the most part, by K.A. Kitchen, who argued extensively for a location in the area stretching from the Red Sea to the Nile, around the latitudes of Port Sudan and Massawa.[139]

---

[135] R. Sayce and R. Peterson, ***Race in Ancient Egypt and the Old Testament*** (1993) 65.

[136] W.M. Flinders Petrie, ***Making of Egypt*** notes that Punt was "sacred to the Egyptians as the source of their race." E.A. Wallis Budge, ***Short History of the Egyptian People*** (London: Dent, 1914) 10 says also: "Egyptian tradition of the Dynastic period held that the aboriginal home of the Egyptians was Punt."

[137] Michael Rice, " 'The island on the edge of the world'," in Al Khalifa and Rice, ***Bahrian***, 116-124; idem, ***Egypt's Making***, 242-263.

[138] ***Die Geographie des alten Ägyptens***, 3 vols. (Leipzig, 1857-1860) I:48-49, II:15-16, III:63-64. This is not to say that there was unanimity. A. Mariette demurred, arguing for an identification with Somalia: ***Les Listes géographiques des pylons de Karnak comprenant la Palestine, l'Ethiopie, le pays de Somal*** (Leipzig: Hinrichs, 1875) 60-66.

[139] "The land of Punt" in Thurstan Shaw et al (edd.), ***The Archaeology of Africa: Food, metals and town*** (London and New York: Routledge, 1993) 587-608; idem, "Further Thoughts on Punt and its Neighbours," in Anthony Leahy and John Tait (edd.),

Both the South Arabian and the East African theories have strengths and weaknesses and, in the end, fail to do justice to the entirety of the relevant material. Firstly, as both Johannes Dümichen and Edouard Naville pointed out, the evidence indicates that Punt clearly existed on *both* sides of the Red Sea.[140] Arguing for an exclusive location in south-eastern Africa or south-western Arabia falls victim to the 'tyranny of the Sea.' Rodolfo Fattovich's researches are important here. He has demonstrated the existence of an Afro-Arabian exchange circuit between peoples of the Horn of Africa, including the Ethio-Sudanese lowlands, and Southern Arabia starting in the 7th millennium BCE and firmly established by the 3rd – 2nd millennium BCE.[141] This circuit corresponds with the "Puntite-Egyptian" trade circuit outlined in some of the sources. Fattovich thus argues that "On the whole, the archaeological evidence from the Horn and Southern Arabia is quite consistent with the general picture of Put we can infer from the Egyptian sources."[142] That is to say, Punt/Ta-Neter included *both* East Africa and South Arabia. It is known that the highlands of the Ethiopian and Yemeni (South Arabian) regions form part of a wider region with very close geographical, climatic, zoological, botanical, and ethnological connections and Christopher Edens

---

Studies on Ancient Egypt in Honor of H.S. Smith (London: The Egypt Exploration Society, 1999) 173-178. See also Dr. Yosef A.A. ben-Jochannan, ***Africa, Mother of Western Civilization*** (Baltimore: Black Classic Press, 1988) 261.

140 Johannes Dümichen ***Geschichte des alten Aegyptens*** (Berlin: G. Grote, 1879) 102, 119-22; Edouard Naville, ***The Temple of Deir el Bahari: Its Plan, Its Founders, and Its First Explorers*** (London: The Egypt Exploration Fund, 1894) 22.

141 Rodolfo Fattovich, "The Afro-Arabian circuit: contacts between the Horn of Africa and Southern Arabia in the 3rd – 2nd millinium B.C.," in Lech Krzyzaniak, Michal Kobusiewicz, and Karla Kroeper, ***Interregional Contacts in the Later Prehistory of Northeastern Africa*** (Poznań, 1996) 395-402.

142 Rodolfo Fattovich, "Punt: the archaeological perspective," in Gian Maria Zaccone and Tomaso Ricardi di Netro (edd.), ***Sesto congresso internazionale de egittologia: Atti***, 2 vols. (Torino: Italgas. 1993) II: 399–405 (402). See further idem, "The Problem of Punt in the Light of Recent Field Work in the Eastern Sudan," in Sylvia Schoske (ed.), ***Akten des vierten internationalen Ägyptologen Kongresses, München 1985***, 4 Vols. (Hamburg: Helmut Buske Verlag, 1991) IV: 257–272 (258).

and T.J. Wilkinson have shown that southwest Arabia in the Bronze Age shows strong linkages with the Horn Africa.[143]

Herzog and Kitchen's African theses are based on a very limited selection of the relevant material.[144] Dimitri Meeks, Director of Research at the French Institute of Egyptology, is author of the most recent and most thorough look at the subject. Drawing on the full breadth of the source material Meeks concluded:

> Punt, we are told by the Egyptians, is situated – in relation to the Nile Valley – both to the north, in contact with the countries of the Near East of the Mediterranean area and also to the east or south-east, while its furthest borders are far away to the south. Only the Arabian Peninsula satisfies all these indications...The hypothesis of an African location for the land of Punt is based on extremely fragile grounds. It is contradicted by numerous texts and has become an established fact in Egyptology because no one has taken into account the full range of evidence on the subject regardless of place of origin or date. When all the evidence is assembled, the incoherent and implausible character of such an African hypothesis becomes self-evident. The only way to reconcile all the data is to locate Punt in the Arabian Peninsula.[145]

But this is an Arabian Peninsula that stretches westward across the Red Sea. As David M. Goldenberg documents:

> Today we see the Red Sea separating two distinct lands, Africa and Arabia. But in antiquity it was not seen that way. Indeed, in the world of classical antiquity, from Herodotus to Strabo, the term Arabia included the area across the Red Sea up until the Nile. It wasn't the Red Sea but the Nile that constituted the

---

[143] "Southwest Arabia During the Holocene."
[144] Dimitri Meeks, "Locating Punt," in David O'Connor and Stephen Quirke, ***Mysterious Lands*** (London: UCL Press, 2003) 53-80.
[145] Meeks, "Locating Punt,"58, 79.

boundary between Africa and Asia…These Greek and Roman…sources point to the same phenomenon as do the ancient Near Eastern sources – that the Red Sea did not serve as an ethnic boundary and land on both its sides shared the same name, whether that name was Arabia in the Greek sources or Kush in the Bible.[146]

Figure 15

Afrabia/Kusha-Dwipa/Ta-Neter (Punt) according to ancient Egyptian, Sanskrit and Greek sources

Identifying 'Punt' with the whole of the Arabian Peninsula including that portion on the African side of the Red Sea, rather than with just the south of the peninsula, is consistent with the meaning of *Ta-Neter*, 'God's Land.' As Abdel-Aziz Saleh has pointed out, the term covers a region of vast extent and means generally 'the Orient,' i.e., east of Egypt, north-east as well as south-east.[147] It is a synonym of and replaced the earlier Egyptian term *Akhit*, which meant "the far east".[148]

---

146 Goldenberg, ***Curse of Ham***, 18-19.

147 Abdel-Aziz Saleh, "Notes on the Ancient Egyptian *T:-NṮR* 'God' Land'," ***Bulletin du centenaire. Supplement*** (1981): 107-117.

148 M.Ch. Kuentz, "Autour d'une conception égyptienne méconnue: l'*Akhit* ou soi-disant horizon," ***BIFAO*** 17 (1920): 182, 189.

As Punt was "sacred to the Egyptians as the source of their race,"[149] at least *some* of their race, we are not surprised to discover that Arabian Kushites constituted some of the Pre-Dynastic population. This is not to revive that long-dead theory of the invasion of a so-called 'Dynastic Race' from the east[150]; this is now rightly rejected as there is no evidence of a military invasion into Egypt in the late pre-dynastic period.[151] It is also evident that the majority of the Egyptian population had a southern African origin.[152] There is, however, significant genetic and archaeological evidence of migrations into the Nile Valley early in the pre-historic period from Western Asia (*Afrabia*).

IV.1. *The Arabian Kushite (Semitic) Contribution to Egyptian Origins*

George Steindorff and Keith C. Seele offered this reconstruction of Egyptian origins in 1957:

> By approximately 6000 B.C. Egypt acquired much the same geographical countenance which it now exhibits. Its inhabitants, to judge by their language, had developed from at least two different strains...It is probable that Nilotic peoples poured in from the south, while from the east, by way of the Sinaitic peninsula or across the Red Sea, came Semitic tribesmen with their gift of agriculture. In the course of a few centuries these diverse elements became mingled until their original identity

---

[149] Petrie, ***Making of Egypt***, 77.

[150] Petrie, ***Making of Egypt***, 65ff; D.E. Derry, "The Dynastic Race in Egypt," ***Journal of Egyptian Archaeology*** 42 (1956) 80-85.

[151] David Wengrow, ***The Archaeology of Early Egypt: Social Transformations in North-East Africa, 10,000 to 2650 BC*** (Cambridge: Cambridge University Press, 2006) 111; Béatrix Midant-Reynes, ***The Prehistory of Egypt: From the First Egyptians to the Pharaohs*** (Massechusets: Blackwell, 2000) xiii.

[152] It is also likely that some of the southern populations that migrated northward had itself originated in Arabia, having crossed the Bab al-Mandab into Africa. Thus H.R. Palmaer appropriately affirms: "There is...no reason to doubt the tradition that at a period which may be placed between 5000-2000 BC, Asiatic nomad races, called Kushites, were driven first south of Arabia, and then across the Bab el-Mandeb into Africa." ***Sudanese Memoirs*** (Lagos, 1928) 2:2.

> was wholly lost. The result was a new race-the Egyptians-who were destined to give birth to the culture of the historical period.[153]

It is such a historical reconstruction that the Africentrist luminary Yosef A.A. ben-Jochannan fulminated against in his important work, ***The Black Man's North and East Africa*** (1971), arguing instead:

> the first of the foreign invaders from Asia – the Hyksos – arrived in northern Kamit (Egypt) as conquerors. Before this period in mankind's history, approximately c. 1675 B.C.E…there is no evidence suggestive of any major migration of so-called 'Semitic Peoples' from Asia moving into North or East Africa.[154]

Ben-Jochannan was loath to admit any significant 'Semitic' contribution to the origins of Nile Valley civilization.[155] Understandably so: he, like most writers on the subject in his day, took West Asian Semites to be a white ethnic group, and therefore the claim that Nile Valley civilization is indebted to a 'civilizing invasion' of white Semites from the east was but another version of the racist 'White Man's Burden' ideology.[156] Current data, however, forces a reconsideration of the whole question, with Steindorff and Seele's *basic* reconstruction vindicated but with critical modifications. For starters, the Semitic peoples of antiquity, we now know, were a Black group/groups. Semiticism undoubtedly evolved among African

---

[153] George Steindorff and Keith C. Seele, ***When Egypt Ruled the East*** (Chicago and London: University of Chicago, 1957) 9-10.
[154] Yosef A.A. ben-Jochannan and George Simmonds, ***The Black Man's North and East Africa*** (Baltimore: Black Classic Press, 2005 [1971] 19.
[155] Ben-Jochannan and Simmonds, ***Black Man's North and East Africa***, *passim*; Dr. Yosef A.A. ben-Jochannan, ***Africa: Mother of Western Civilization*** (Baltimore: Black Classic Press, 1988) 253, 273, 321, 350.
[156] Ben-Jochannan and Simmonds, ***Black Man's North and East Africa***, xii-xiii, I, 3; ben-Jochannan, ***Africa***, 350.

migrants to the Levant.[157] Ben-Jochannan is therefore right to reject the myth of a White Semitic North Africa in antiquity, but his (and his targets') equation of Semites with Caucasians is anachronistic.

Ben-Jochannan is also right to reject the myth of an early foreign invasion that stimulated Nile Valley civilization.[158] As noted above, no such *invasion* can be documented for Egypt's late Pre-Dynastic period. However, military invasion is not the only way to account for a Semitic presence in the area before the unification, and a Semitic presence, a *Black Semitic* presence (at least an *Afrabian* presence), is now indisputable. Even S.O.Y. Keita, in a number of meticulous studies, found that:

> The peopling of what is now the Egyptian Nile Valley, judging from archaeological and biological data, was apparently the result of a complex interaction between coastal northern Africans, "neolithic' Saharans, Nilotic hunters, and riverine proto-Nubians with some influence and migration from the Levant. The major variability of early 'Egyptians' is thus seen to have been mainly established in the *proto-predynastic period* by the settling of all these peoples.[159]

Keita notes that archaeology and historical sources attest to the "real presence" of Levantines/Middle Easterners in Predynastic Egypt.[160] Similarly Michael Rice accepts that "the founder population which formed the basis of the historic Egyptian community was the product of migrations of peoples seeking more amendable conditions after the deterioration of the climates of the North African littoral and the increasing aridity of

---

[157] See above.
[158] Ben-Jochannan, ***Africa***, 253.
[159] Keita, "Further Studies," 251; idem., "Studies of Ancient Crania," 36.
[160] S.O.Y. Keita, "Analysis of Naqada Predynastic crania: a brief report," in Lech Krzyzaniak; Micha Kobusiewicz (edd.), ***Interregional Contacts in the Later Prehistory of Northeastern Africa*** (Poznan: Poznan Archaeological Museum, 1996) 208.

the Arabian desert."[161] Cultural items suggest a connection between the Levant, that "Proto-Semitic homeland," and North Africa ca. 7000-6500 BP,[162] and Toby Wilkinson has demonstrated that 'Asiatics', peoples from the Levant, were resident in Egypt in the 4th millennium.[163] Flint tools and subterranean housing from Maadi and distinctive pottery from Buto all point to a resident (Black) Asiatic community from the Levant in Lower Egypt.

Paleoanthropological evidence indicates that *ca* 50-45 kya groups dispersed from the Horn of Africa region into Southern Asia and that a *back*-migration into Africa from the Levant into Egypt occurred *ca* 17.5-13.7 kya.[164] Christy G. Turner II, archeologist from Arizona State University, likewise presents results of diachronic comparisons of dental morphology in North/East African and Near Eastern samples evincing a migration into North Africa and the Nile Valley from the Near East *ca.* 10,000-7,000 years ago.[165] Turner and colleagues found that their was significant change in dental trait frequencies

---

161 ***Egypt's Making***, 27. See also Fekri A. Hassan, "The Predynastic of Egypt," ***Journal of World History*** 2 (1988): 158, 145.

162 Andrew B. Smith, "The Near Eastern connection II: cultural contacts with the Nile Delta and the Sahara," in Lech Krzyżaniak, Karla Kroeper and Michał Kobusiewicz (edd.), ***Interregional Contacts in the Later Prehistory of Northeastern Africa*** (Poznań, 1996) 29-35; David Wengrow, ***The Archaeology of Early Egypt: Social Transformations in North-East Africa, 10,000 to 2650 BC*** (Cambridge: Cambridge University Press, 2006) 35; Midant-Reynes, ***Prehistory of Egypt***, 219.

163 Toby Wilkinson, "Reality versus Ideology: The Evidence for 'Asiatics' in Predynastic and Early Dynastic Egypt," in Edwin C.M. van den Brink and Thomas E. Lewy, ***Egypt and the Levant: Interrelations From the 4th through the Early 3rd Millennium BCE*** (London: Leicester University Press, 2002) 514-520; Hassan, "Predynastic," 145, 160.

164 J.R. Luis et al, "The Levant versus the Horn of Africa: Evidence for Bidirectional Corridors of Human Migrations," ***American Journal of Human Genetics*** 74 (2004): 532.

165 "A dental anthropological hypothesis relating to the enthnogenesis, origin, and antiquity of the Afro-Asiatic language family," in John D. Bengtson (ed.), ***In Hot Pursuit of Language in Prehistory. Essays in the four fields of Anthropology in Honor of Harold Crane Fleming*** (Amsterdam and Philadelphia: John Benjamins Publishing Company, 2008) 17-23; C.G. Turner II and M.A. Markowitz, "Dental discontinuity between Late Pleistocene and recent Nubians: Peopling of the Eurafrican-South Asian triangle I," ***HOMO*** 41 (1990): 32-41.

between late Pleistocene (ended ca. 10,000 years ago) and Holocene (began ca. 10,000 years ago) North African populations: a more robust and complex dental morphology characteristic of West African 'Negroids' was followed by a simpler Near Eastern dentition similar to that of the Natufians of the Levant.[166] It was concluded that "the only way to explain these similarities and differences was to propose significant gene flow and/or actual migration from the Southern Levant into the Nile Valley at the end of the Pleistocene and continuing into the Holocene."[167]

While Turner and colleagues' studies support a significant (though not necessarily 'massive') pre-historic migration from the Levant into the Nile Valley, it does not – as he assumes – support a Levantine origin of the Afroasiatic language phylum.[168] Shomarka Omar Keita of the National Human Genome Center at Howard University, has looked at these questions of migration, Predynastic enthogenesis, and Afroasiatic origins in relation to published Y chromosome data.[169] Two Y chromosome markers studied by Keita are particularly significant: M35, which originated in eastern Africa and shows high frequencies among Afro-Asiatic speakers there (Cushitic, Egyptian, Berber) and M89, which originated in the Near East and shows high frequencies among Semitic speakers there. These distributions, according to Keita, give evidence of the Afroasiatic phylum having originated in the 'M35' region, from the Horn of Africa down the Nile Valley and to the Maghreb, and to the Semitic branch originating from an ancestral

---

166 J.D. Irish and C.G. Turner II, "West African dental affinity of Late Pleistocene Nubians. Peopling of the Eurafrican-South Asian triangle II," ***HOMO*** 41 (1990): 42-53.
167 Turner, "A dental anthropological hypothesis," 21.
168 Turner, "A dental anthropological hypothesis,"18.
169 Shomarka Omar Keita, "Geography, selected Afro-Asiatic families, and Y chromosome lineage variation. An exploration in linguistics and phylogeography," in John D. Bengtson (ed.), ***In Hot Pursuit of Language in Prehistory. Essays in the four fields of Anthropology in Honor of Harold Crane Fleming*** (Amsterdam and Philadelphia: John Benjamins Publishing Company, 2008) 3-16.

Afroasiatic group (a M35 bearing group) that migrated to Syria-Palestine before the Neolithic and there became 'Semitized,' if you will.[170]

Keita's study also gives evidence for a prehistoric back-migration into the Nile Valley from the Levant which is consistent with the dental studies of Turner and colleagues as well as the paleoanthropological evidence cited above. Of the Egyptian samples that Keita looked at, M35 was clearly the dominant marker, suggesting a biocultural affinity between the Nile Valley populations and East Africans further south. However, Keita's Egyptian samples also showed significant M89 frequencies: in two Egyptian samples the M89 marker was the majority.[171] This suggests migration into the Nile Valley of Near Eastern M89 bearers. More recently, Andrew Lancaster has brought together data from archaeology, comparative linguistics, and population genetics indicating that M35 bearers and Afroasiatic speakers originated around the Horn of Africa and migrated northward into the Levant, where Semitism will develop and later re-enter North Africa in the pre-historic period.[172] Thus, these data from diverse studies all converge to indicate that a part of the prehistoric Nile Valley populations originated in Western Asia, i.e. *Afrabia*.

IV.1.1. *The Badarians as Afrabians*

This 'Southern African' and 'Eastern Asiatic' *duality* of the prehistoric population of Egypt is reflected already in the earliest Upper Egyptian culture of the Predynastic period, the Badarian.

---

170 Keita, "Geography," 11. Keita does not use the term 'Semitized.' Instead he suggests that the ancestral M35 group from Africa, upon arriving in Syria-Palestine, encountered there and was "adopted" by a M89 bearing population.

171 Keita, "Geography," 8.

172 Andrew Lancaster, "Y Haplogroups, Archaeological Cultures and Language Families: a Review of the Possibility of Multidisciplinary Comparisons Using the Case of E-M35," ***Journal of Genetic Genealogy*** 5 (2009): 35-65.

> without any doubt the basic agricultural and pastoral complex of the Badarian culture, the occurrence of the first painted pottery and the first copper, together with some important ideological conceptions (e.g. about the Great Mother or of the Procreative Power), have Middle Eastern roots...other evidence points to African origins. This cultural duality is a...*parallel* to the ascertained biological duality of the population.[173]

The Badarian culture of Middle Egypt, evidenced by around 600 'wealthy' graves, was excavated in 1924-29 by the British School of Archeology in the region of El-Badari on the east bank of the Nile.[174] Thermolumenescence tests give a date of 5000 BCE,[175] though most writers prefer the 'lower' radiocarbon dates of 4400-4000 BCE.[176] The Badarians were a highly cultured and civilized group, "bearing witness to a complex and technologically advanced society".[177] Their pottery, evidence of a high level of pyrotechnology, is particularly fine, unmatched by anything produced by subsequent Egyptians.[178] Badarian culture is especially important in that it is the *Urgemeinde* ("proto-community") out of which Dynastic Egypt eventually evolved.[179]

---

[173] Eugen Strouhal, "Evidence of the Early Penetration of Negroes into Prehistoric Egypt,"***Journal of African History*** 12 (1971) 7 [art.=1-9].

[174] Guy Brunton and Gertrude Caton-Thompson, ***The Badarian Civilization and Predynastic Remains Near Badari*** (London: British School of Archaeology in Egypt, 1928); Guy Brunton, ***Mostagedda and the Tasian Culture*** (London: Bernard Quaritch Ltd., 1937)

[175] Stan Hendrickx and Pierre Vermeersch, "Prehistory: From the Palaeolithic to the Badarian Culture (c. 700,000-4000 BC)," in Ian Shaw (ed.), ***The Oxford History of Ancient Egypt*** (London: Oxford University Press, 2000) 39.

[176] Diana Holmes and Renée Friedman, "Survey and test excavations in the Badari region," ***Proceedings of the Prehistoric Society*** 60 (1994): 105-142; Hassan, "Predynastic," 140-141, 153.

[177] Jean Leclant in Midant-Reynes, ***Prehistory of Egypt***, xii.

[178] Hendrickx and Vermeersch, "Prehistory," 40-41; Brunton and Caton-Thompson, ***Badarian Civilization***, 41.

[179] Shomarka O.Y. Keita notes that "The Badari-Naqada continuum formed the cultural core of later Egyptian civilization": "Analysis of Naqada," 208.

While some early biometric studies saw a homogenous Badarian community,[180] the excavators of this culture clearly noted the heterogeneity of the population.[181] The community seems to have consisted of two basic types: gracile and robust.[182] Most of the Badarians were short, around 5 feet tall with minimal muscular development.[183] "In fact," said anatomist Grafton Elliot Smith, "there is a suggestion of effeminate grace and frailty about his bones".[184] The Badarian bones are so effeminate, Brenda N. Stoessiger informed us, "skulls are extremely difficult to sex, being all of a frail and feminine type."[185] Their crania have, we are told, a strange blend of "Caucasoid" and "Negroid" traits.[186] The skull is long and

---

[180] Brenda N. Stoessiger, "A Study of the Badarian Crania Recently Excavated by the British School of archaeology in Egypt," ***Biometrika*** 19 (1927): 110-150; G.M. Morant, "A Study of predynastic skulls from Badari based on measurements taken by Miss B.N. Stoessiger and D.E. Derry," ***Biometrika*** 27 (1935): 293-309. See also G. Elliot Smith, "The People of Egypt," ***The Cairo Scientific Journal*** 3 (1909): 56.

[181] Brunton and Caton-Thompson, ***Badarian Civilization***, 20. See also Hendrickx and Vermeersch, "Prehistory," 42: "It seems obvious that the Badarian culture did not appear from a single source"; Midant-Reynes, ***Prehistory of Egypt***, 164.

[182] Elise J. Baumgartel, "Predynastic Egypt," in I.E.S. Edwards, C.J. Gadd, N.G.L. Hammond (edd.), ***The Cambridge Ancient History*, Volume I: *Prolegomena and Prehistory***, 3rd Edition (Cambridge: Cambridge University Press, 1970) 473; Strouhal, "Evidence," 4.

[183] Sonia R. Zakrzewski, "Variation in Ancient Egyptian Stature and Body Proportions," ***American Journal of Physical Anthropology*** 121 (2003) 219-229.

[184] Grafton Elliot Smith, ***The Ancient Egyptians and the Origins of Civilization*** (Freeport: Books For Libraries Press, 1923) 56ff; idem, "The Influence of Racial Admixture in Egypt," ***The Eugenics Review*** 7 (1915): 163-183; idem, "The People of Egypt," ***The Cairo Scientific Journal*** 3 (1909): 51-63.

[185] Stoessiger, "Study of the Badarian Crania," 124. See also Morant, "Study of predynastic skulls from Badari," 299. A. Caroline Berry, R.J. Berry and Peter J. Ucko, "Genetical Change in Ancient Egypt," ***Man*** NS 2 (1967) 551 describe the Badarians as a "mysterious delicately formed race".

[186] Strouhal, "Evidence," 5 notes that of the 117 skulls that he examined, most (94) "showed mixed Europoid-Negroid features in different combinations". See further Ernest Warren, "An Investigation on the Variability of the Human Skeleton: With Especial Reference to the Naqada Race Discovered by Professor Flinders Petrie in his Explorations in Egypt," ***Philosophical Transactions of the Royal Society of London. Series B, Containing Papers of a Biological Character*** 189 (1897) 191; Cicely D. Fawcet and Alice Lee, "A Second Study of the Variation and Correlation of the Human Skull, with Special Reference to Naqada Crania," ***Biometrika*** 1 (1902): 436. But cf. Keita, "Further Studies," 248. On the relation of Naqada I and Badarian cultures see MC Nutter, "An Osteological Study of Hominoidea," unpublished dissertation, Cambridge University, 1958 who demonstrated that Badarian and Naqada I crania were

narrow (dolichocephalic), showing "no sign of the characteristic Negro broadness in the facial area."[187] Hair is wavy or straight (Euplocomic or Euthycomic), "never kinky".[188] On the other hand the nose is broad (platyrrhine) and the face is protruding in the lower jaw (prognathic), giving "a more generally Negro appearance".[189] Also, the Badarian small frame is of a "Negroid," even "super-'Negroid'" or tropical African body plan.[190] This set of characteristics clearly points to the *Elongated type*,[191] particularly the Eastern articulation of this type. Several commentators have noted its resemblance to the Indian (Dravidian) type.[192] It is thus certain that these proto-Egyptians

---

almost identical; Keita notes that "Naqada culture primarily derived from Badari": "Analysis of Naqada Predynastic crania," 203. Rice, ***Egypt's Making***, notes also: "The Naqada I people were almost certainly the direct descendents of the earlier settlers and their culture really represents a more advanced phase of the Badarian (30)." See further Midant-Reynes, ***Prehistory***, 170; Hassan, "Predynastic," 159.

[187] J.M. Crichton, "A Multiple Discriminant Analysis of Egyptian and African Negro Crania," ***Papers of the Peabody Museum of Archaeology and Ethnology*** 57 (1966):62; Stoessiger, "Study of the Badarian Crania," 144; Fawcet and Lee, "Second Study," 434; Smith, ***Ancient Egyptians***, 56.

[188] Patricia V. Podzorski, ***Their Bones Shall Not Perish: An Examination of Predynastic Human Skeletal Remains from Naga-ed-Dêr in Egypt*** (Surrey: SIA, 1990) 85; Smith, ***Ancient Egyptians***, 56; Brunton and Caton-Thompson, ***Badarian Civilization***, 20.

[189] Crichton, "Multiple Discriminant Analysis," 62; G.M. Morant, "A Study of Egyptian Craniology from Prehistoric to Roman Times," ***Biometrika*** 17 (1925) 10; idem, "Study of predynastic skulls from Badari," 307; idem, "The Predynastic Skulls from Badari and Their Racial Affinities," in Brunton, ***Mostagedda*** 66; Sonia R. Zakrzewski, "Population Continuity or Population Change: Formation of the Ancient Egyptian State," ***American Journal of Physical Anthropology*** 132 (2007): 506; Podzorski, ***Their Bones Shall Not Perish***, 92.

[190] Zakrzewski, "Variation," 227-8; Michelle H. Raxter et al, "Stature Estimation in Ancient Egyptians: A New Technique Based on Anatomical Reconstruction of Stature," ***American Journal of Physical Anthropology*** 136 (2008): 151; Morant, "Egyptian Craniology," 10.

[191] Keita, "Further Studies," 250 notes: "The modal phenotype in archaic and early Old Kingdom Egyptian art seems to be Elongated African."

[192] Brenda N. Stoessiger noted in her 1927 craniometric study: "When we compare the Badarian race with others outside of Egypt, it is not to the Mediteranean or any Negro type which it resembles most closely but the primitive Indian, the Dravidian and the Veddah." Stoessiger, "Study of the Badarian Crania," 147; Brunton and Caton-Thompson, ***Badarian Civilization***, 68; Petrie, ***Making of Egypt***, 7; Andrzej Wierciński, "The Analysis of Racial Structure of Early Dynastic Populations in Egypt," ***Materiały I Prace Antropologiczne*** 71 (1965): 3-47; A.C. Berry, "Origins and Relationships of the Ancient Egyptians. Based on a Study of Non-metrical Variations in

were *not* the Twa or Bushmen as Sir E.A. Wallis Budge and others assumed.[193]

Coexisting with this 'gracile' type was a more massive, rugged or robust type.[194] Some individuals reached 6 ft tall; some were strong and muscular.[195] While only a minority, this type may have accounted for one quarter of the Badarian population.[196] Eugen Strouhal, in his study of 117 Badarian crania, found that 24 were of the so-called 'pure' gracile *Elongated type* (which he labels with the out-dated and misleading terms "Europoid" and "Mediterranean"). Ninety-four (80.3 %) were of "mixed Europoid-Negroid" character: thus, the 'typical' Badarian mix of long, narrow head on the one hand and broad nose and protruding jaw on the other. Fourteen skulls were found to be robust (6) or 'purely' Negroid (8), i.e. the *Broad type*.[197] Strouhal's examination of a number of crania with hair produced five samples that were flattened in the cross-section (*Eriocomic*, "wooly"), showing "the Negroid influence among the Badarians."[198] Thus, he concludes, "the Negroid (read: *Broad type*) component among the Badarians is anthropologically well based."[199] Strouhal is therefore convinced that the Badarians are the "ultimate evidence" of the prehistoric biological contact

---

the Skull," ***Journal of Human Evolution*** 1 (1972): 199-208; Drake, ***Black Folk***, I:154. On the other hand, V. Giuffrida-Ruggeri saw these Predynastic Egyptians as Ethiopians: "Were the Pe-Dynastic Egyptians Libyans or Ethiopians?" ***Man*** 15 (1915): 51-56; idem, "A Few Notes on the Neolithic Egyptians and the Ethiopians," ***Man*** 16 (1916) 87-90.

193 On Budge and others see discussion in James E. Brunson, ***Predynastic Egypt: Before the Unification. An African-centric View*** (Dekalb, Illinois, 1991) 31-32.

194 J. Lawrence Angel, "Biological Relations of Egyptians and Eastern Mediterranean Populations during Pre-dynastic and Dynastic Times," ***Journal of Human Evolution*** 1 (1972) 310; Strouhal, "Evidence," 4; Wierciński, "Analysis of Racial Structure," 42.

195 Brunton and Caton-Thompson, ***Badarian Civilization***, 20.

196 Strouhal, "Evidence," 4. See also Cheikh Anta Diop, "Origin of the Ancient Egyptians," in G.Mokhtar (ed.), ***UNESCO General History of Africa* II: *Ancient Civilizations of Africa*** (Heinemann, California: UNESCO, 1981) 28-31 (abbreviated reprint in Ivan van Sertima [ed.], ***Egypt Revisited*** [New Brunswick: Transaction Publishers, 1989] 9-11).

197 Strouhal, "Evidence," 5.

198 Strouhal, "Evidence," 5. See also Crawford, "Racial Identity," 62.

199 Strouhal, "Evidence," 5. See also Crawford, "Racial Identity," 62.

between the Asiatic *Elongated* and African *Broad* types in the Nile Valley.[200] On the other hand, S.O.Y. Keita sees both types as indigenous African varieties which "united very early by a developing common culture."[201] These two positions can be reconciled by recognizing *Afrabia*, i.e. the Arabian Peninsula's status as the northeastern extremity of Africa.

While Keita is certainly correct in his recognition of the *Elongated* and *Broad* types as indigenous African varieties,[202] he goes too far in his claim that "data from physical anthropology, archaeology and linguistics do not suggest a primary origin external to Africa for the early Nile Valley peoples."[203] This statement is certainly true for most of the historic peoples that will converge to produce the "ancient Egyptian" race; it is true for *all* of the peoples only if we employ the broader, more natural definition of 'Africa' which includes *Afrabia*. Toby Wilkinson's measured statement is no doubt more appropriate:

> Recent evidence suggests that it is time to re-appraise the extent and nature of Egypt's early contacts with the rest of the Near East. From the Predynastic period, foreigners...seem to have settled in Egypt...It seems increasingly likely that, during the fourth and early third millennia BCE, the eastern Mediterranean in general, and the area encompassing the Nile Delta, the north Sinai and southern Palestine in particular, witnessed *significant mixing of people and ideas*...Foreign cultures and foreign people may, after all, have played a role in the early development of Egyptian civilization...The picture that is emerging from archaeology is not of Egypt as a civilization apart. Rather, there seems to have been a high degree of

---

[200] Strouhal, "Evidence," 6.
[201] "Further Studies," 251.
[202] "Further Studies," 246.
[203] "Analysis," 206. See also idem, "Early Nile Valey Farmers From El-Badari: Aboriginals or 'European' Agro-Nostratic Immigrants? Craniometric Affinities Considered With Other Data," ***Journal of Black Studies*** 36 (2005): 191-208.

contact – both direct and indirect – between the peoples of the ancient Near East, at all periods." [204]

The evidence suggests that the Badarian culture consisted of Black 'Asiatics' and Africans. The culture's characteristic Rippled pottery and shell fishhooks have been connected with that of the Khartoum Neolithic culture of the Sudan.[205] This was a robust and very Negroid (*Broad*) culture,[206] and may thus account for the robust, Negroid element among the Badarians. On the other hand, the Badarian's Western Asiatic connection is even more substantial.[207] L. Krzyzaniak places the ultimate origin of these turban-wearing Badarians in Southwest Asia, stressing the fact that the characteristic rippling effect on Badarian pottery was practiced ca. 4500 BCE already in Jericho, Byblos, southern Anatolia and northern Mesopotamia.[208] The wheat, barley and flax found in Badarian settlements come from West Asia, as does no doubt the sheep, goats, first copper, and the Great Mother, all associated with this culture.[209] As James Mellaart puts it:

---

[204] Wilkinson, "Reality versus Ideology," 518-19.

[205] A.J. Arkell and Peter J. Ucko, "Review of Predynastic Developments in the Nile Valley," ***Current Anthropology*** 6 (1965): 150-151. On the Khartoum Neolithic see Midant-Reynes, ***Prehistory***, 126ff.

[206] Arkell and Ucko, "Review," 148; Strouhal, "Evidence," 6.

[207] On Badarian contacts with West Asia see also Sava P. Tutundžić, "The problem of foreign north-eastern relations of Upper Egypt, particularly in Badarian period: an aspect," in Lech Krzyżaniak and Michał Kobusiewicz (edd.), ***Late Prehistory of the Nile Basin and the Sahara*** (Poznań, 1989) 255-260.

[208] ***Early Farming Cultures of the Lower Nile: The Predynastic Period in Egypt*** (Warsaw, 1977) 81. On the evidence of turban-wearing among the Badarians see Baumgartel, "Predynastic Egypt," 469.

[209] B.G. Trigger, "The Rise of Civilization in Egypt," in J. Desmond Clark (ed.), ***The Cambridge History of Africa,* Volume I:*From the Earliest Times to c. 500 BC*** (Cambridge: Cambridge University Press, 1982) 495, 545: "current evidence favours an Asian origin for all of the principle Egyptian cultigens...While the possibility that certain plants and animals may have been domesticated locally cannot be ruled out, food production in Egypt, from Predynastic times on, was clearly an extension of the south-west Asian patter." Baumgartel, "Predynastic Egypt," 473; Arkell and Ucko, "Review," 147.

> Neither the wild ancestors of wheat, barley, etc., nor those of sheep and goat (as against cattle and pig) are native to North Africa, and their presence in Egypt is artificial and man-made...These northern contributions show that the Egyptian development was not a completely African affair.[210]

Similarly the Badarians worshipped the god Set, who was considered "the Lord of Asia and the lands east of Egypt".[211] This evidence at least partly supports the early claim that "it is to Asia, and not to Africa or Europe, that we should look for the source of the Badarian people."[212] This is likely the case for part of the Badarian population; some of it no doubt came from further south in Africa. It must be emphasized that what is proposed here is not a "mass migration" or "wholesale settler colonization of the Nile Valley by a community of alien origin," perspectives that "(deny) indigenous in situ evolution and culture to supra-Sahara and Saharan Africa" and in effect "de-Africanizes a part of Africa due to outmoded non-evolutionary theories."[213] The evidence clearly suggests that historic Egypt developed out of a predominantly southern African culture that

---

[210] James Mellaart, "Comments to A.J. Arkell and Peter J. Ucko, 'Review of Predynastic Developments in the Nile Valley'," ***Current Anthropology*** 6 (1965) 161. See also Rice, ***Egypt's Making***, 26: "The strains of domesticated goats and sheep which were known to the earliest settlers in the Nile Valley are thought to be of western Asiatic origin...It may not be without significance that on some predynastic pots, goats, sheep and sometimes even bovines are shown standing in boats, as though this was a deliberate attempt to preserve the memory of their journey, from wherever they came, to the Valley." See further David Wengrow, ***The Archaeology of Early Egypt: Social Transfrmations in North-East Africa, 10,000 to 2650 BC*** (Cambridge: Cambridge University Press, 2006) 16, 23; Elise Baumgartel, "Comments to A.J. Arkell and Peter J. Ucko, 'Review of Predynastic Developments in the Nile Valley'," ***Current Anthropology*** 6 (1965) 157; idem, ***The Cultures of Prehistoric Egypt*** (London: Oxford University of Press, 1947) 23.

[211] Rice, ***Egypt's Making***, 249.

[212] Petrie, ***Making of Egypt***, 7. See also Wierciński, "Analysis," 42: "the core of the most ancient known Egyptian populations is not of African origin but probably had been created by the two main migratory waves in the Predynastic period coming from the Northern and Southern parts of Western Asia through Sinai to Lower Egypt and, through Bab El Mandeb and Nubia to Upper Egypt."

[213] Keita, "Early Nile Valey Farmers From El-Badari," 192, 205.

absorbed a smaller north-eastern African, i.e. *Afrabian* culture. Archaeologist/linguist Peter Bellwood summarizes it best:

> the striking fact remains that the Nile Valley cannot be demonstrated to have been settled by agriculturalists until about 5500-5000 BC, at which time a full agropastoral economy with pottery was introduced from Southwest Asia…When agriculturalists first entered the Nile Valley at about 5500 BC, other people who made pottery, collected wild sorghum, and, according to some authorities, herded cattle, had already been living at Nabta Playa and Bir Kiseiba in Egypt's Western Desert for possibly 3,000 years, during periodic and brief phases of wetter climate…Mid-Holocene dessication of the Sahara with retraction of the summer monsoon finally led to virtual abandonment of Nabta Playa and other oasis settlements by about 4000 BC, and this might have led to a kind of refuge movement into the Nile Valley, where Saharan people would have met and mixed with the descendents of the Southwest Asian Neolithic population responsible for the introduction of the Southwest Asian agricultural tradition into the Nile Valley about 1,500 years earlier. The resulting amalgam was later to develop into one of the most remarkable civilizations of the ancient world, a true synthesis of the Oriental and the African.[214]

It is to be noted again that all of these actors in this historic drama were Black peoples.

VI.1.2. *Afrabia and the Anu*

Art historian James E. Brunson has identified the Amratian (Naqada I) culture that emerged out of the Badarian as the historic race of the Anu.[215] This may or may not be the case. The

---

[214] ***First Farmers***, 101.

[215] James E. Brunson, ***Before the Unification: Predynastic Egypt, An Afrocentric View*** (Dekalb, Il: KARA Publishing, 1989) 3.

Anu, first discovered by French Egyptologist Abbe Émile Amélineau,[216] are considered the aboriginal or 'Old Race' of Egypt, the "first Blacks to inhabit Egypt".[217] According to Amélineau the Anu were a southern race that came slowly down the Nile founding and shutting themselves within fortified cities for defensive purposes: Esneh, Erment, Qouch and Heliopolis.[218] They were an agricultural people raising cattle on a large scale along the Nile. Significantly, to the Anu are attributed the rudiments of Egyptian civilization.

> To this people we can attribute, without fear of error, the most ancient Egyptian books, *The Book of the Dead* and the *Texts of the Pyramids*, consequently, all the myths or religious teachings. I would add almost all the philosophical systems then known and still called Egyptian. They evidently knew the crafts necessary for any civilization and were familiar with the tools those trades required. They knew how to use metals, at least elementary metals. They made the earliest attempts at writing, for the whole Egyptian tradition attributes this art to Thoth, the great Hermes an Anu like Osiris, who is called Onian in Chapter XV of *The Book of the Dead* and in the *Texts of the Pyramids*. Certainly the people already knew the principal arts; it left proof of this in the architecture of the tombs at Abydos, especially the tomb of Osiris and in those sepulchers objects have been found bearing unmistakable stamp of their origin.[219]

This is remarkable, considering that the Anu were *not* the "pharaonic" race of Dynastic Egypt. In fact, they were the *conquered enemy* of the latter. As Flinders Petrie remarked, the

---

[216] ***Nouvells Fouilles d'Abydos*** (Paris: Paris Press, 1899); ***Prolegomenes a l'etude de la religion egyptienne*** (Paris: Ed. Leroux, 1916).
[217] Diop, ***African Origins***, 105; Hall, ***Ancient History***, 96; Petrie, ***Making of Egypt***, 68. On the Anu as a Black race see also St. Clair Drake, ***Black Folk Here and There***, I:163; Diop, "Origins (UNESCO)," 31-34 [=Sertima, 12-15]
[218] Amélineau, ***Prolegomenes***, II:124; Diop, "Origin (UNESCO)," 32; idem, ***African Origins***, 77.
[219] Amélineau, ***Prolegomenes***, II:124 .See also Diop, ***African Origins***, 77.

falcon-bearing tribe of Horus (the Dynastic Race) were "the natural enemy of the Aunnu, the Set-bearing tribe."[220] While Petrie sought the home of the 'conquering' race in Elam (Persia), Bruce Williams and James E. Brunson have made a strong case for identifying this group with the earlier Nubian civilization of Ta-Seti.[221] Thus, the story of the so-called 'Dynastic Conquest' is that of one Black group (Nubians) conquering another (the Anu).[222] And according to Amélineau "The conclusion to be drawn from these considerations is that the conquered Anu people guided its conquerors at least along some of the paths to civilization and the arts."[223]

Whence came this 'Old Race' of predynastic Egypt? Amélineau thought they were Africans from the south. On the other hand, H.R. Hall suggested that the Anu were a 'proto-Semitic' race that entered the Nile Valley from the Arabian Peninsula through the Isthmus of Suez.[224] Drusilla Dunjee Houston likewise suggested that "The ancient inhabitants of Arabia Petrae were the 'Anu' of the Old Race of Egypt,"[225] and Cheikh Anta Diop too describes "Arabia Petraea, land of the Anu, Blacks who founded Northern On (Heliopolis) in historical times."[226] There is evidence supporting an Arabian provenance. Pliny the Elder (d. 79 CE) noted that Heliopolis (On, the city of

---

[220] W.M.F. Petrie, ***The Making of Egypt*** (London, 1939) 70.; V. Giuffrida-Ruggeri, "A Few Notes on the Neolithic Egyptians and the Ethiopians," ***Man*** 16 (1916): 88.

[221] Bruce Williams, "The Lost Pharaohs of Nubia," in Sertima, ***Egypt Revisted***, 90-104; Brunson, ***Predynastic Egypt***, 75-112.

[222] Susan Wise Bauer notes also that "The Scorpion King," whom she assumes to be the Dynastic conqueror of 3200 CE, "was a descendent of an African people who had once lived on either side of the Nile valley." ***The History of the Ancient World: From the Earliest Accounts to the Fall of Rome*** (New York and London: W.W. Norton, 2007) 22.

[223] Amélineau, ***Prolegomenes***, II:124. See also Petrie, ***Making of Egypt***, 77: "Some of the most obvious public works of the Ist dynasty were the carrying on of earlier undertakings (of the Annu). The great historical maces, and the irrigation works, had been developed under the Scorpion king of the Aunu, and both may have originated much earlier."

[224] ***Ancient History***, 89-91.

[225] Houston. ***Wonderful Ethiopians***, 112.

[226] ***African Origins***, 109.

the Anu) was founded by Arabs. Diop objects to this on the basis of the late appearance on the historical scene of the "mulatto" Semitic Arabs, and because Heliopolis/On was elsewhere said to have been founded by the Anu, a Black people.[227] But this objection to Pliny's note lacks force in that the early Arabians were not the mulatto Semites of later history, but a Kushitic people, as demonstrated above. We have no reason to assume that Pliny did not mean these true, Black "Arabs" when he spoke of the city's founding. The profile and headdress of the Anu as depicted on the Tara-Neter tile recalls the same profile and headdress of the Kushite Asiatic depicted on the Tomb of Shabataka, XXV Dynasty (Figure 16).

Figure 16
Depiction of the Anu on Tara-Neter tile (left) and Kushite Asiatic as depicted on Tomb of Shabataka (right)

Also significant is the fact that the Anu seem to have been depicted red in contrast to their black-depicted Nubian

[227] ***African Origins***, 73.

conquerors. Petrie calls attention to a number of depictions of black men overcoming red men, and these have been connected with the Dynastic festival commemorating the "Slaughter of the Anu."[228] If the conquering race were Nubians of Ta-Seti, as seems likely, their depiction as Black men makes good sense. Why would the Anu then be depicted red[229]? Dana Reynolds, I believe, hit on the answer with this anthropological insight:

> The early desert populations of Arabia and Africa were for the most part derived from Africans who seem to have undergone a specialized physical development having evolved in hot, dry regions in the late stone age. Many of the Eritrean-looking men of Arabia and those in Africa...are often found in areas where temperatures soar above 120 degrees .They tend to be very slender with gracile bones and attenuated limbs. The skin, though dark-brown or black-brown, tends to have a strong reddish hue, which is thought, also, to be due to the ecological pressures of the environment in which they evolved...These characteristics...are now attributed, by some population biologists and geneticists, to the ancient adaptation of Africoids to certain specific, ecological factors including the change to a

---

[228] Petrie, ***Making of Egypt***, 66, 667. On this festival of the 'Slaughter of the Anu" see Giuffrida-Ruggeri, "Few Notes," 88; Brunson, ***Predynastic Egypt***, 55.

[229] In a brief discussion James Brunson ("Ancient Egyptians: 'The Dark Red Face Myth'" in Sertima, ***Egypt Revisited***, 53-54) argued, unconvincingly, that the red depiction of the Egyptians symbolized the Egyptian male as "the blood of life" and possessor of spirit after death, qualities denied non-Egyptians who were thus portrayed in their natural colors. This argument has a number of weaknesses to it, especially as an explanation of the Anu's red depiction. First, in as much as the Egyptian woman was considered possessor of spirit after death, the choice to depict her yellow in stead of red causes problems for this interpretation. Also, since this 'symbolic' red was reserved for the Dynastic Egyptians and not their foreign 'enemies,' one is at a loss to explain the redness of their arch-enemies, the Anu. As David O'Conner has documented, the foreigner was the chaotic and evil 'other' according to Egyptian national ideology, and even native Egyptians, when they in some way rebeled against the order of Ma'at in society, take on the attributes of the foreign 'other' ("Egypt's Views of 'Others'," in John Tait [ed.], ***'Never Had the Like Occurred': Egypt's view of its past*** (London: UCL Press, 2003) 155-157. Thus, as historic 'enemies of the state,' the Anu's depiction in the this allegedly 'symbolic native red' makes Brunson's interpretation difficult to accept here.

neolithic diet in combination with dwelling in exceeding hot, dry habitats.[230]

This would tend to disqualify the 'red' Anu as an equatorial race (i.e. Twa), and a post-desiccation Arabian habitat certainly best matches the ecological characteristics noted by Reynolds. The very name 'Anu' seems also to point to Arabia. James E. Brunson has documented 'Anu' peoples in Sumer and in India, designated with the characteristic "three pillars" as in Egypt.[231] We recall that the Sumerians originated in eastern Arabia, and tell of their migration northward in the myth of the civilizing fish-man, Oannes, which is related to the term Anu.[232] This means that the Sumerian "Anu" were an East Arabian group. The further association with India is consistent with the linguistic and genetic evidence that points to the Dravidians having entered Northern India from the Middle East/Western Asia/*Afrabia*.[233] We thus likely have the following situation: a group of eastern Arabians (Anu) migrated north becoming the Sumerians. Some of these continued into India. Another group travelled west into the Nile Valley. This Arabian/Indian/Egyptian nexus no doubt lies behind the fact that at various times all three shared the same names: Ethiopia, India and Arabia, each applied to all three areas interchangeably.[234] As Philip Mayerson documents, Byzantine authors after the 4th century indiscriminately apply the name 'India' to South Arabians, Ethiopians, and sub-continental

---

[230] Dana Reynolds, "The African Heritage & Ethnohistory of the Moors," in Ivan van Sertima, ***Golden Age of the Moor*** (New Brunswick: Transaction Publishers, 1992)104.
[231] ***Before the Unification***, 5-6; ***Predynastic Egypt***, 45.
[232] ***Predynastic Egypt***, 43.
[233] Partha P Majumder, "Ethnic Populations of India as seen from an evolutionary perspective." ***Journal of Bioscience*** 26 (2001): 541: "The northern exit route of humans from Africa to India was through the Middle East and west Asia."
[234] Dana Reynolds (now Dana Marniche) observes: "It must be said that early Greeks and Romans did not usually distinguish ethnically between the people called Saracens and the inhabitants of southern Arabia (the Yemen) which was called India Minor or Little India in those days, nor southern Arabians from the inhabitants of the Horn of Africa...Strabo, around the first century B.C., Philostratus and other writers, speak of the area east of the Nile in Africa as 'Arabia'." "African Heritage," 105.

Indians.[235] It is no doubt in this context as well that we are to understand and accept Grafton Elliot Smith's observation:

> The balance of probability is strongly in favour of the view that the Arabs and the Proto-Egyptians were sprung from one and the same stock, the two divisions of which living in the territories separated by the Red Sea, had become definitely specialized in structure, in customs and beliefs, long before the dawn of the period known as Predynastic in Egypt…the linguistic evidence…according to many scholars, points to a similar conclusion.[236]

Also A. Sayce and R. Peterson: "In color (dark red), form and features (gracile) the inhabitants of Arabian Punt resembled the inhabitants of Egypt."[237] At least *some* of the inhabitants of Egypt.

---

[235] "A Confusion of Indias: Asian India and African India in the Byzantine Sources," ***JAOS*** 113 (1993) 169-174.
[236] Grafton Elliot Smith, ***The Ancient Egyptians and the Origins of Civilization*** (Freeport: Books For Libraries Press, 1923), 101-102; idem, "The Influence of Racial Admixture in Egypt," ***The Eugenics Review*** 7 (1915): 163-183; idem, "The People of Egypt," ***The Cairo Scientific Journal*** 3 (1909): 51-63 (56).
[237] ***Race in Ancient Egypt***, 65.

Chapter Three

The Religion of Afrabia

I. *The Neolithic and the Birth of a New Religion*

In 1994 French archaeologist Jacques Cauvin published what I consider to be a profoundly important monograph, *Naissance des divinités, Naissance de l'agriculture: La Révolution des Symboles au Néolithique* ("Birth of the Gods, Birth of Agriculture: The Symbolic Revolution in the Neolithic").[238] In it Cauvin cogently argued that the Neolithic revolution *ca* 10,000 BCE was preceded by a 'revolution of symbols.' That is to say, even before the change in subsistence strategies that defined the neolithisation of the Near East, there occurred an equally dramatic and consequential change in the collective 'psycho-culture' of the still hunter-gatherers of the Epipaleolithic, a change evidenced most clearly in a new symbolism as reflected in the art forms. The former symbolic art of the Epipaleolithic was primarily zoomorphic, with animals represented 'democratically,' if you will: no hierarchical organization is evident and no animal personality is made prominent. Thus, while selection of animals depicted may reflect a sense of 'religious awe' on the part of our primitive artists, no animal species stands out as an 'animal god' or a theriomorphic representation of 'God'.[239] This all changed on the eve of the Neolithic. For some reason a new and rather coherent symbolic system, or as Cauvin calls it 'a new religion', emerged wherein the divine is represented through two primary symbols: a bull and a woman. Originating in the Levant – the area where Semiticism is thought to have originated – this new religion and its two symbols will dominate theological expression in the Near East throughout the whole Neolithic and Bronze Age periods:

---

[238] (CNRS Publications, Paris. Second, revised edition, 1997). English translation, ***The Birth of the Gods and the Origins of Agriculture*** (Cambridge: Cambridge University Press, 2000).
[239] Cauvin, ***Birth of the Gods***, 68.

> The Woman and the Bull of the Neolithic appeared in the Levant as divinities whose emergence in the tenth millennium (BCE) is followed by their diffusion throughout the ancient Near East. The Goddess, flanked by her male partner assimilated by the bull, will be the keystone of a whole religious system...[240]

This symbolic/theological revolution was accompanied by a geometrical/architectural change: the change from circular (or oval) semi-subterranean houses (pits) to above-surface rectangular homes. Speaking on the 'language of geomorphic shapes,' Cauvin observes:

> In the universal language of simple forms, the circle (or the sphere) signifies both that which transcends man and remains beyond his reach (the sun, the cosmic totality, 'God')...On the contrary, the rectangle, examples of which are rare in our everyday observations of nature, requires human initiative for its existence: the stone is not cubic or rectangular unless so fashioned. *The square and the rectangle denote then the manifest, the concrete, that which has been realized*...the 'square house,' generally built on the surface, is witness to a different mental attitude (emphasis mine-WM).[241]

The work of classical scholar and antiquarian Richard Payne Knight further illuminates this 'geometrical revolution.' In his important work, ***The Symbolic Language of Ancient Art and Mythology***, Knight points out that in the traditions of antiquity fire and water are the primary symbols of the active and passive productive powers of the universe. Fire, the active power, was masculine and represented by a circle, while water was the feminine passive power represented by the square or

[240] Cauvin, ***Birth of the Gods***, 69.
[241] Cauvin, ***Birth of the Gods***, 132.

rectangle.[242] The ancients understood that productivity resulted from the interaction of the two, the solar and the aquatic, and this interaction was hieroglyphically represented as a circle (or asterisk) within a square. This is the origin of the designation for the goddess as 'the Place of the Gods' or the House of God[243]: the solar has indwelled within the aquatic. This 'geometrical revolution' of the Neolithic therefore, in as much as it is related to the symbolic/theological revolution, seems to have signaled a theological refocusing: from the transcendent to the immanent aspects of deity. The anthropomorphic (woman) and theriomorphic (bull) symbolism signaled the same. It is not at all clear what social, economic or cultural changes might have stimulated this psychological and, indeed, paradigm shift, but it was of profound and lasting consequence for the history of religion from that point till today. How does the Bull and the Woman of this Epipaleolithic/Neolithic 'new religion' signal divine immanence?

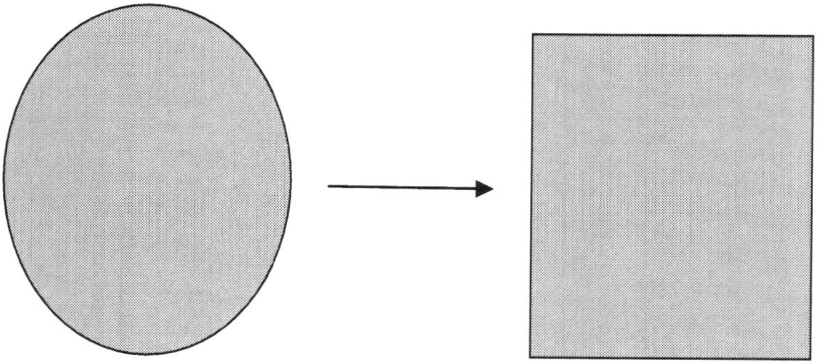

Figure 17
The Geometric/Architectural Revolution

[242] Richard Payne Knight, ***The Symbolic Language of Ancient Art and Mythology. An Inquiry*** (New York: J.W. Houton, 1876) 25-28, 60-64.
[243] Knight, ***Symbolic Language***, 64.

The Goddess: In the History of Religions water, that amorphous cosmic material from which life emerges, often assumes a feminine character.[244] Thus, as Marjia Gimbutas amply demonstrates, the primary symbolism of the goddess is aquatic – water, zig-zags, M's, aquatic birds, ect. – associating her with the cosmic waters which are her element and her sphere.[245] As the cosmic womb of life she is depicted as a cow and black.[246] This black goddess represents divine imminence. As Gimbutas states: "The goddess is immanent rather than transcendent and therefore physically manifest."[247] The role of the Woman in this ancient mythic scheme was eloquently elaborated by François Lenormant in 1874 in his ***Magie chez les Chaldéens et les origines accadiennes*** ("The Chaldean Magi and Akkadian Origins"). Discussing the Mesopotamian and Levantine religious tradition, or "Kushito-Semitic" tradition, Lenormant affirms that these religions "show the same fundamental ideas, and have the names of the great majority of the gods in common".[248]

> The idea of the Divine Being one, and universal, *who mingles himself with the material world*, which has emanated from his substance and not been created by him, is met with everywhere at the basis of belief…Cause and proto-type of the visible world, a nature-god has necessarily a double essence; he possesses the two principles of all terrestrial generation, the active principle and the passive principle, male and female; it is a duality in unity, a concept which, in accordance with the doubling of the symbols, has given birth to the idea of female divinities. The

---

[244] ***Encyclopedia of Religion, New Edition*** 14: 9702 s.v. Water by Jean Rudhart.
[245] Marjia Gimbutas, ***The Language of the Goddess*** (New York: Thames & Hudson, 2001) xxii, 3, 25, 29.
[246] Ibid., xix. In the ***Ṛg*** *Veda* the cosmic waters are cows (e.g. 4.3.11; 3.31.3; 4.1.11) and in *Pañcaviṃśa-Brāmana* 21.3.7 the spotted cow Śabalā is addressed: "Thou art the [primeval ocean]." On water and cows in Indic tradition see further Anne Feldhaus, ***Water and Womanhood. Religious Meanings of Rivers in Maharashtra*** (New York and Oxford: Oxford University Press, 1995) 46-47.
[247] Ibid., 316.
[248] François Lenormant, ***Magie chez les Chaldéens et les origines accadiennes*** (Paris: Maissonneuvee, 1874) 106

goddess, in the religions of the Euphratico-Syrian [Kushito-Semitic] group is entitled the 'manifestation' ['reflection' rather] of the male god to whom she corresponds. She does not differ from him essentially…Thus is Chaldea and Babylonia, as in Syria and Phoenicia, every god is necessarily accompanied by a goddess who corresponds to him. These divine personages are not imagined separately, but in couples; and each of these couples forms a complete unity, a reflection of the unity. When the god has a solar character, the goddess has a lunar nature; if the one presides over the day, the other presides over the night; if one personifies the elements regarded as active, fire, and air, the other personifies the passive elements, water and earth (emphasis mine-WM).[249]

Figure 18
Enthroned Goddess, flanked by felines, giving birth to child who emerges between her legs. Central Anatolia, 6000 BCE.

[249] Ibid., 117, 129.

The Bull: As the "fecundator *par excellence*, indeed the proto-type of male fertility,"[250] the Bull is the paramount 'attribute animal' of the Creator God in the ancient world.[251] This Divine Bull, that is to say the bull used to represent the all-powerful male creator-god, was a black bull, in particular the now extinct (sic) *Bos primigenius* or aurochs bull.[252] Standing two meters to the shoulders, weighing upwards of a ton, with a meter-wide spread of horns, the *Bos primigenius* was an immense beast, a contemporary of the other megaforms: the mammoth and huge Irish elk. This bull had powerfully developed and coordinated flesh, muscle and bone, making him the paragon of power and nobility. As Michael Rice writes in his study of the ancient and wide-spread bull-cult:

> The essential and distinctive elements in the bull's status in antiquity are the recognition of his nobility as a lordly beast…and his concentrated, highly coordinated power…the

---

[250] Jack Randolph Conrad, ***The Horn and the Sword. From the Stone Age to modern times – the worship of the Bull, God of power and fertility***. (New York: E P Dutton and Company Inc., 1957) 85.

[251] The bull represented potency, fecundity, and primordial materiality, all essential characteristics of the creator-deity. On the creator deity and the bull *v.* René L. Vos, "Varius Coloribus Apis: Some Remarks of the Colours of Apis and Other Sacred Animals," in Willy Clarysse, Antoon Schoors and Harco Willems (edd.), ***Egyptian Religion: The Last Thousand Years, Part 1. Studies Dedicated to the Memory of Jan Quaegebeur*** (Leuven: Uitgeverij Peeters en Departement Oosterse Studies, 1998) 709-18; Harold Bayley, ***The Lost Language of Symbolism: An Inquiry into the Origin of Certain Letters, Words, Names, Fairy-Tales, Folklore, and Mythologies*** 2 vols. (London: Williams and Norgate, 1912) I:323-4. On the symbolism of the bull see further Michael Rice, ***The Power of the Bull*** (London and New York: Routledge, 1998); Conrad, ***The Horn and the Sword***; Mircea Eliade, ***Patterns in Comparative Religion***, trns. Rosemary Sheed (1958; Lincoln and London: University of Nebraska Press, 1996) 82-93; ***DDD*** s.v. "Calf," by N. Wyatt, 180-182. 'Attribute Animals' were fauna that symbolically represented particular attributes or characteristics of the anthropomorphic gods. See True Islam, ***The Truth of God: The Bible, The Qur'an, and The Secret of the Black God*** (Atlanta: All-In-All Publishing, 207) 23-28. On the 'attribute animal' in ancient Near Eastern (hereafter ANE) religion see Erik Hornung, ***Conceptions of God in Ancient Egypt: the One and the Many*** (Ithaca: Cornell University Press, 1982)109-25; P. Amiet, ***Corpus des cylinders de Ras Shamra-Ougarit II: Sceaux-cylinres en hematite et pierres diverses*** (Ras Shamra-Ougarit IX; Paris: Éditions Recherche sur les Civilisations, 1992) 68.

[252] Rice, ***Power of the Bull***, 23-24.

bull is the epitome of cheiftaincy, hence of kingship…The bull is always portrayed in all his vigour, potency and beauty.[253]

The beauty of the aurochs bull has much to do with its distinctive dense black coat with a white stripe running down its spine and white curly tuft between its horns. In the ancient bull-cult this black bull-hide is associated with the black primordial waters and signals the black skin of the creator-god who emerged out of those waters and produced therefrom an earthly body.[254] According to this 'Myth of the Black God' the creator-deity emerged from these waters as a so-called 'sun-god,' initially possessing a body of brilliant white or golden light, but later chose to cloak this fiery, *transcendent* body with a more accessible, tolerable (for his creatures) black body, made out of the matter of the primordial waters.[255] It is this aquatic black body that is represented by the black bull. In geometrical terms, the 'sun-god'

---

[253] Ibid., 274.

[254] See e.g. the black skin of the Egyptian deity Min, the 'creator god *par excellence*." Robert A. Armour, ***Gods and Myths of Ancient Egypt*** (Cairo and New York: The American University in Cairo Press, 1986, 2001) 157; Veronica Ions, ***Egyptian Mythology*** Middlesex: The Hamlyn Publishing Group Ltd., 1968) 110. While Min was associated with a white bull in New Kingdom Panopolis and Coptos at an earlier period in Heliopolis he was associated with the black bull Mnevis. See G.D. Hornblower, "Min and His Functions," ***Man*** 46 (1946): 116 [art.=113-121). On Min and black bovines see also H. Gauthier, ***Les personnel du dieu Min*** (Le Caire, 1931; IFAO. Recherches d'Archéologie 2) 55-57. On the mythological significance of the black bovine skin see especially Vos, "Varius Coloribus Apis." On the black bovine, Creator-god, and primordial waters see Asko Parpola, "New correspondences between Harappan and Near Eastern glyptic art," ***South Asian Archaeology*** 1981, 181 who suggests that 'the dark buffalo bathing in muddy water was conceived as the personification of the cosmic waters of chaos". See also W.F. Albright who noted that "the conception of the river as mighty bull is common": "The Mouth of the Rivers," ***AJSL*** 35 (1991): 167 n.3 [art.=161-195]. The black bull (*k" km*) of Egypt, Apis, personified the waters of the Nile which was regarded as a type of Nu, the dark, primeval watery mass out of which creation sprang (See Émile Chassinat, "La Mise a Mort Rituelle D'Apis," ***Recueil de travaux relatifs a la philology et a l'archeologie egyptiennes et assyriennes*** 38 [1916] 33-60; E.A. Wallis Budge, ***The Egyptian Book of the Dead (The Papyrus of Ani). Egyptian Text Transliterated and Translated*** [New York: Dover Publications, Inc. 1967] cxxiii). See also the Babylonian Enki, called ***am-gig-abzu***, 'black bull of the Apsû (primordial waters)." See Albright, "Mouth of the Rivers," 167. On the black bull and the black waters of creation see also Vos, "Varius Coloribus Apis," 715, 718.

[255] On this 'Myth of the Black God' in ancient tradition see Appendix.

with his transcendent luminous body is analogous to the circle,[256] while the immanence of the rectangle is analogous to the aquatic black body, theriomorphically represented by the black bull and anthropomorphically represented by the Black Goddess. In other words, both the black bull and the black goddess represent the physical immanence of the creator-god in the world. What then is the relation between these two symbols?

Figure 19
Reconstituted *Bos primigenius*

Rice noted "the curious combination of the Goddess cult…with the cult of the bull," for which he could find no explanation. [257] But I believe he hit on the explanation of this relationship when he points out that, according to the myth associated with the ancient bull-cult "The bull…is a creature of

[256] On this 'transcendent' luminous body in ancient tradition and the Semitic religions see Jean-Pierre Vernant, "Dim Body, Dazzling Body," in Michel Feher, Ramona Naddaff and Nadia Tazi (edd.), ***Fragments for a History of the Human Body: Part One*** (New York: Zone, 1989): 19-47; A. Leo Oppenheim, "Akadian *pul(u)***ḫ***(t)u* and *melammû*," ***Journal of the American Oriental Society*** 63 (1943): 31-34. Wesley Williams, "A Body Unlike Bodies: Transcendent Anthropomorphism in Ancient Semitic Tradition and Early Islam," forthcoming in the ***Journal of the American Oriental Society*** 128 (2009).

[257] Rice, ***Power of the Bull***, 82-83.

the Mother,"[258] i.e. the black body is the product of the primordial aquatic matter, symbolically personified in the Woman. In a very real sense, the 'new religion' was about *Corpus dei*, the Body of God. The Goddess is the *matrix*. The aquatic black body of the creator-deity derives from the primordial black waters, personified in and symbolized by the black Mother Goddess. This is why the Mother Goddess is usually depicted with the youthful male god on her lap or emerging from her womb (Figures 18 and 20).[259] To fully comprehend this theme, we must disentangle the motif of the Cosmic Mother as both wife (primarily) and mother (secondarily) of the creator-god. Jack Randolph Conrad notes:

> In Egyptian theology, Ra, the sun, the Bull of Heaven, reproduced himself...by copulating with his mother. He is described as the "bull of his mother, who rejoices in the cow, the husband impregnating with his phallus"...Such gods were called Kamutef, or "bull of his mother".[260]

The mythic motif behind these expressions is as follows: in the form of a luminous divine man (sun-god) the creator-god emerges out of the primordial waters, the latter personified as a cow and described as his 'mother'.[261] Because the sun-god 'went back into' his mother, the primordial waters, to produce a new body – the black body – he is said to have 'copulated' with her, who is now also described as his 'wife'. This copulation, however, produced him all over again, reborn through her but now as the immanent Black God, with a black body from the primordial

---

[258] Rice, ***Power of the Bull***, 102.
[259] See below.
[260] ***Horn and the Sword***, 86.
[261] See for example the Egyptian image of a mighty cow rising up out of the waters bearing the sun-disk between her horns. The cow is the "mother of the sun god"; Erik Hornung, ***Idea into Images: Essays in Ancient Egyptian Thought*** (Timken Publishers, 1992) 41.

black mater. Edmund Leach, in his essay "The Mother's Brother in Ancient Egypt," explains this theological concept:

> Total deity is conceived as a bisexual triad – God the Father, God the Son, and God the 'Mother of God' – but the theology insists that God is consubstantial-coeternal from the beginning, (so) the system by which God the Father 'begets' God the Son through the body of the Mother of God replicates itself indefinitely, so that the Mother of God is also the Spouse of God, the Sister of God, and even the Daughter of God.[262]

The 'new religion' is not a "female monotheism"[263] or a "Goddess-centered religion."[264] The Goddess's role in this myth is not as singular 'life-creating power' nor is the male bull-god 'ephemeral and mortal' in relation to her.[265] As Conrad documents, "for millennia the bull-god, the father-god of strength and fertility, stood unchallenged as the supreme god of the ancient Near East."[266] The Goddess in this myth is a *matrix*, that *prima material* out of which life emerged, but the role of Creator of the cosmos is reserved for the male god, the Bull God. The goddess appears as the god's complement and, symbolically, as the personification of the aquatic substance of the god's earthly body. This mystery of the union of the masculine Sun God and the aquatic primordial matter, personified as the Mother Goddess, is at the heart of the 'new religion', as evidenced by the later mystery systems that will evolve out of it.[267] This is the alchemical *coniunctio oppositorum* or "synthesis of opposites," the synthesis of the male element (fire, sun, right) and

---

[262] Edmund Leach, "The Mother's Brother in Ancient Egypt," ***Royal Anthropological Institute News*** 15 (1976): 19.
[263] Cauvin, ***Birth of the Gods***, 32.
[264] Gimbutas, ***Language***, xvii.
[265] Gimbutas, ***Language***, 316, 175.
[266] Conrad, ***Horn and the Sword***, 112.
[267] On which see Appendix below.

female element (water, moon, left).[268] As Wendy Doniger O'Flaherty informs us:

> The image of fire in water is the ultimate resolution of opposites; held in suspended union, each retains its full power and nothing is lost in the compromise, but there is complete balance.[269]

This is why the mythological family of Egypt was always a tri-unit consisting of father, mother, and *boy*-child.[270] The mother and father represented differentiation, the young boy the unity of the two, the *coniunctio oppositorum*. The child is a boy because this child is the creator of the material world reborn. The 'new religion,' through its symbolism of Bull and Woman, is focused on the male god in his imminent black body rather than in his transcendent, fiery aspect.

Figure 20
Black Madonna and
Child of Einsiedeln

[268] Willibald Kirfel, ***Die fünf Elemente unsbesondere Wasser und Feur: Ihre Bedeutung für den Ursprung altindischer und altmediterraner Heilkunde*** (Walldorf-Hessen, 1951) 17; Manley P. Hall, ***Melchizedek and the Mystery of Fire*** (Los Angeles: Philosophical Research Society, 1996) 9; idem, ***The Hermitic Marriage*** (Los Angeles: Philosophical Research Society, 1996) 42.

[269] Wendy Doniger O'Flaherty, "Submarine Mare in the Mythology of Śiva," ***JRAS*** (1971): 9.

[270] Françoise Dunand and Christiane Zivie-Coche, ***Gods and Men in Egypt: 3000 BCE to 395 CE*** (Ithaca and London: Cornell University Press, 2004) 30-1.

II. *Ancient Cult Centers of the New Religion*

This 'new religion' of the Bull and the Goddess seems to have originated in the (black) Levant which, as Rice reminds us, is really just an extension of Arabia, despite the modern political boundaries.[271] While evidence of this new religion is found as far back as 10,000 BCE (e.g. aurochs skulls with horns buried in houses), we have a good amount of material evincing a cult center in the ninth millennium BCE in 'Ain Ghazal, a Neolithic village located near present day Amman, Jordan and dated ca. 8300-6000 BCE (calibrated dates). One of the largest Neolithic villages of the ancient Near East, archaeologists have unearthed multi-roomed rectangular structures. Along with remains yielding information about diet and subsistence economy, archaeologists have found human and animal figurines, some of which hint at the religious life of the villagers. The most frequent animal figurine is the bull. Expressing 'the numinous', the bull figurine "conveyed force, vitality, dynamism."[272] In one home a stone bin containing aurochs bones and a bull figure has been found.[273]

According to G.O. Rollefson, one of the lead excavators of 'Ain Ghazal, this material "project(s) a strong picture of intensive attention to politico-religious ceremony and ritual."[274] Along with the bull figurines, a remarkable stone statuette of a pregnant woman has been recovered. Denise Schmandt-Besserat has made a strong case for interpreting this piece as a pregnant goddess, "a stone metaphor" to "express the mysteries of

---

[271] Rice, ***Power of the Bull***, 193, speaking of Syria and Jordan, "extensions of the great Arabian Desert" and thus "share many of the same cultural characteristics and much of the same form of society."

[272] Denise Schmandt-Besserat, "Animal Symbols at 'Ain Ghazal," ***Expedition*** 39 (1997): 49, 52.

[273] Ibid., 52; Rice, ***Power of the Bull***, 194.

[274] G.O. Rollefson, "Ritual and Ceremony at Neolithic Ain Ghazal (Jordan)," ***Paléorient*** 9 (1983): 30 [art.=29-38]. See also idem., "Neolithic 'Ain Ghazal (Jordan): Ritual and Ceremony, II," ***Paléorient*** 12 (1986): 45-52.

origins".[275] Indeed, but it undoubtedly concerns the mystery of the origin of the immanent black body (represented by the bull) of the creator of the cosmos.

Being that genetic evidence indicates a migration from Western Asia (*Afrabia*) into Northern India in the pre-historic period, we are then not surprised to learn that in the oldest Neolithic site unearthed thus far on the subcontinent of India evidence of the cult of the Bull and Woman has been found. Mehrgarh, dated to 7000-3200 BCE, is located on what is now the Kachi plain of today's Baluchistan, Pakistan. Four thousand years its successor, the Indus Valley civilizations undoubtedly evolved out of this early community. Evidence for the earliest practice of dentistry has been found here as the drilling of human teeth *in vivo* (*i.e.* in a living person) is indicated in the remains of nine adults found in the Mehrgarh population.[276] Most importantly for our discussion, figurines have been recovered – bull and woman figurines predominating.[277] Interestingly, we meet the motif that will only later appear in Egypt – the Mother (Goddess) with child on her lap, reminiscent of Isis and Horus. The child and the bull are no doubt two different representations of the male god born from the primordial matrix, the Mother Goddess.

Without question, the most elaborate, extensive cult center for this new religion was in Mehrgarh's Anatolian contemporary, Çatal Hüyük (6500-5700 BCE). As Rice notes:

> Catal Hüyük represents a high point in the development of the bull-cult; so much does the worship of the bull dominate the remains of the settlement that many of the aspects of later bull-

---

[275] Denise Schmandt-Besserat, "A Stone Metaphor of Creation," ***Near Eastern Archaeology*** 61 (1998): 109-117.

[276] A. Coppa, et al, "Early Neolithic tradition of dentistry: Flint tips were surprisingly effective for drilling tooth enamel in a prehistoric population," ***Nature*** 440 (April, 2006): 755-756.

[277] Gregory L. Possehl, ***The Indus civilization: a contemporary perspective*** (Rowman Altamira, 2002) 177-180.

worship seem to have their origin there, though they may reappear in times and places far distant from the sixth millennium on the Konya plain (Turkey)…what is certain is that, whilst the Catal Hüyük community disappeared around 5600 BC…many of the characteristics of the bull-cult developed on the plains of Anatolia were to be reproduced in Sumer, Elam, Egypt and Crete, in some cases thousands of years after the proto-city at Catal Hüyük was abandoned.[278]

Figure 21
Excavation Report drawing of Bull Shrine VII, 8. Çatal Hüyük.

Çatal Hüyük in Anatolia, Turkey is a highly developed 'proto-city' in what Marjia Gimbutas has described as 'Old Europe,' that Europe prior to the coming of the Indo-Europeans. 'Old Europeans' were a Black people.[279] According to Bernard Vandermeersch, modern humans in Europe originated in West Asia and migrated north into Europe.[280] West Asia was a part of

[278]Rice, ***Power of the Bull***, 75, 83.
[279] See especially Ivan Van Sertima (ed.), ***African Presence in Early Europe*** (New Brunswick: Transaction Publishers, 1985) and C. Loring Brace et al, "The questionable contribution of the Neolithic and the Bronze Age to European craniofacial form," ***Proceedings of the National Academy of Sciences, USA*** 103 (2006): 242-247.
[280] Bernard Vandermeersch, "The Near Eastern Hominids and the Origins of Modern Humans in Eurasia," in Takeru Akazawa, Kenichi Aoki, and Tasuku Kimura (edd.), ***The Evolution and Dispersal of Modern Humans in Asia*** (Tokyo: Hokusen-sha, 1992): 29-38.

the 'Black Belt' during this period. The human depictions on the walls at Çatal Hüyük show a decidedly dark people.[281] It is likely that this Anatolian cult of the Bull and Woman diffused from the Levant,[282] the black or Afrabian Levant. Çatal Hüyük was not a center of goddess worship[283]: both the anthropomorphic male god and female goddess are depicted enthroned.[284] It is not the case, as Cauvin and Gimbutas claim, that the male deity represented by the bull, due to his filial relationship with the goddess, is secondary or subordinate to her.[285] Rather, at Çatal Hüyük "the bull is a paramount figure; indeed the shrines...represent a sort of cathedral consecrated to the bull" (Figure 21).[286]

The central myth of the Çatal Hüyük cult is no doubt hinted at by an important and well known find: a clay figurine of a corpulent woman sitting on a throne flanked by two leopards (Figure 18).[287] This figure has been interpreted as a 'birth-giving Goddess' sitting on a 'birth-throne,' an infant's head "emerging from her ample thighs".[288] While not everyone shares this interpretation of the figure,[289] it is supported by other imagery at the proto-city. On walls of a domestic sanctuary a figure is

---

[281] See wall painting reproduced in Ian Hodder, ***The Leopard's Tale: Revealing the Mysteries of Çatalhöyük*** (New York: Thames & Hudson, 2006) 31.
[282] Cauvin, ***Birth of the Gods***, 29.
[283] See Cynthia Eller, ***The Myth of Matriarchal Prehistory: Why an Invented Past Won't Give Women a Future*** (Boston: Beacon Press, 2000) 142-147; Ian Hodder, "Introduction," ***Çatalhöyük 2005 Archive Report*** at http://catalhoyuk.com/archive_reports/2005/ar05_01.html accessed June 26, 2009; idem, ***Leopard's Tale***, 208-214.
[284] James Mellaart, "Çatal Hüyük, a Neolithic City in Anatolia," ***Proceedings of the British Academy*** 50 (1965): 202-246, esp. Plates LXXXa (male god); Hodder, ***Leopard's Tale***, Plate 24.
[285] Cauvin, ***Birth of the Gods***, 32; Gimbutas, ***Language***, 266. See also Mellaart, "Çatal Hüyük," 207.
[286] Rice, ***Power of the Bull***, 8.
[287] Ian Hodder, current excavator of the site, has argued that these images not isolated symbols, but embedded in myths that circulated widely in Anatolia and the Middle East prior to Çatal Hüyük. ***Leopard's Tale***, 142, 164, 202.
[288] Gimbutas, ***Language***, 107; Cauvin, ***Birth of the Gods***, 29; Rice, ***Power of the Bull***, 77.
[289] Hodder, ***Leopard's Tale***, 261.

depicted, arms and legs spread, concentric circles drawing attention to the belly (Figure 22). While the figure is likely a bear or a bear-human hybrid rather than a woman as initially thought,[290] the bear is still an ancient symbol of the mother-goddess.[291] Underneath this bear figure are bucrania (bull heads) and the whole scene suggests that the 'bear-goddess' is "giving birth to bulls...whose sculpted bucrania, set below her, seem to emanate from her".[292] This combination of sanctuary and image of mother-goddess giving birth to the bull-god, the Black God, is vitally important. We will encounter it again in Mecca, Arabia.

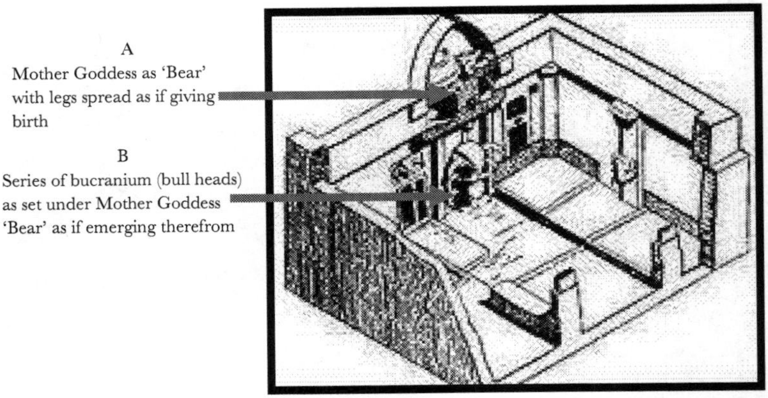

Figure 22
Çatal Hüyük Shrine

[290] Hodder, ***Leopard's Tale***, 142, 201.
[291] Gimbutas, ***Language***, 116-119. See also Hodder, "Introduction," who acknowledges that "it remains possible that the figures are 'mother bears' and representative of a female divinity."
[292] Cauvin, ***Birth of the Gods***, 29. Rice, ***Power of the Bull***, 79 interprets this wall scene similarly: "the bull is depicted being born of the Goddess who is shown on the walls...bringing forth a bull's..head."

III. *Proto-Semitic Religion and the Black God*

The Proto-Semites are believed to have been the speakers of that language (Proto-Semitic) from which the various Semitic languages derived (Arabic, Hebrew, Ugaritic, Akkadian, etc.).[293] It has been suggested that these Proto-Semites originated in the Levantine area (the northern portion of the Arabian Peninsula) and began diverging into separate 'Semitic' languages maybe around 5000 BCE. As these Proto-Semites will eventually evolve into the Semites (Arabs, Hebrews, Canaanites, Akkadians, etc.), Proto-Semitic religion will make an important contribution to the development of the Semitic religious tradition, even the Semitic monotheistic traditions (i.e. the so-called 'Religions of the Book'- Judaism, Christianity, and Islam). As we will see, it is of some consequence that the Semitic tradition is believed to have evolved in the same area where the 'new religion' of the Black Bull and Black Goddess, i.e. the religion of the Black God, evolved.

According to the Proto-Semitic lexicon as it has been reconstructed from the various Semitic languages, the name of God in Proto-Semitic religious tradition consisted of two letters, *'ḷ*.[294] These letters are conventionally vocalized as *El* or *Il*, but this is only an old Western convention out of ignorance of the true phonetics. More recent data allows us to be more precise. It is the second letter which is actually the 'nucleus' of the divine

---

[293] While the linguistic-historical reality of a 'Proto-Semitic' language has been recently challenged, most notably by Mario Liverani ("Semites" in G.W. Bromiley et al (edd.), ***International Standard Bible Encyclopedia*** [Grand Rapids: Zondervan, 1988] IV: 388-392), it has been strongly defended: del Olmo Lete, ***Questions of Semitic Linguistics***, 111-113; Lipiński, ***Semitic Languages***, 41-42; William Sanford LaSor, "Proto-Semitic: Is the Concept No Longer Valid?" ***MAARAV*** 5-6 (Spring, 1990): 189-205.

[294] ***TDOT*** 1:243 s.v. אל by F.M. Cross; A. Guillaume, ***Islam*** (London: Penguin Books, 1956) 7: "The oldest name for God used in the Semitic word (*sic*) consist of but two letters, the consonant 'l' preceded by a smooth breathing".

name,[295] the Proto-Semitic phoneme ***ḷ*** which was a "dark" *l* (velarized alveolar lateral approximant), a quite heavy *l* written ***ḷ***.[296] As an oral consonant, air is allowed to escape through the mouth, producing a thick "*lah*" sound when pronounced. The first letter (ʾ), a glottal stop, was a consonantal sound – a smooth breathing – produced when the vocal cords are constricted to interrupt the flow of air and then released. The sound of the released air – an 'ah' sound – is the consonantal sound, transliterated simply as an initial '*a*.'[297] Thus, the vocalization of the Proto-Semitic divine name ***ʾḷ*** is ***A-ḷah,***[298] which eventuated in the Hebrew *אלה* ***ʾAlāh***, the Syriac ܐܠܗܐ ***ʾAlāhā*ʾ** and the Arabic الله ***Aḷḷāh.***[299]

[295] Benjamin Walker, ***Foundations of Islam: The Making of a World*** (London and Chester Springs: Peter Owen, 1998) 41 notes that "*al*, 'god'…is based on the phoneme *l*, the nucleus of the divine name in many Semitic languages." See also ***EI2*** 3:1093 s.v. *Ilāh* by D.B. Macdonald.

[296] On this Proto-Semitic letter see Alice Faber, "On the Nature of Proto-Semitic **l*," ***JAOS*** 109 (1989): 33-36.

[297] On the initial "A" in this Proto-Semitic divine name see Werner Daum, ***Ursemitische Religion*** (Stuttgart; Berlin; Köln; Mainz: Verlag W. Kohlhammer, 1985) 77-78.

[298] Alice Faber points out that the name ***Aḷḷāh*** is the lone surviving example in Arabic of this Proto-Semitic phoneme (*****ḷ***). "Nature of Proto-Semitic **l*".

[299] Frank Moor Cross has argued that Proto-Semitic *ʾl* is an archaic bilateral that was extended to a trilateral by the Western Semites (Ugaritic, Hebrew, Aramaic, Arabic) with the orthographic addition of an *h* (*ה* / ***ﻫ***). ***TDOT*** 1:242 s.v. **אל** by Cross; ***DDD2*** s.v. Eloah **אלה** by D. Pardee, 285. On the other hand LaSor ("Proto-Semitic," 205) suggests that both *ʾl* and *ʾlh* were part of the Proto-Semitic lexicon. In the dialects of epigraphic Arabian one finds both *ʾl* and *ʾlh* (S.D. Ricks, ***Lexicon of Inscriptional Qatabanian*** [StP 14; Rome, 1989] 10-11). On *Alah* as an ancient variant of *Allah* see Patricia Turner and Charles Russell Coulter, ***Dictionary of Ancient Deities*** (New York: Oxford University Press, 2001) 37 s.v. Allah. On *Allah*'s relation to *ʾl* and the Ugaritic "El" see also Finn O. Hvidberg-Hansen, "Fra El til Allah," in Frede Løkkegaard, Egon Keck, Svend Søndergaard, Ellen Wulff (edd.), ***Living waters: Scandinavian orientalistic studies presented to Frede Løkkegaard on his seventy-fifth birthday, January 27th 1990*** (Copenhagen: Museum Tusculanum Press, 1990) 113-127.

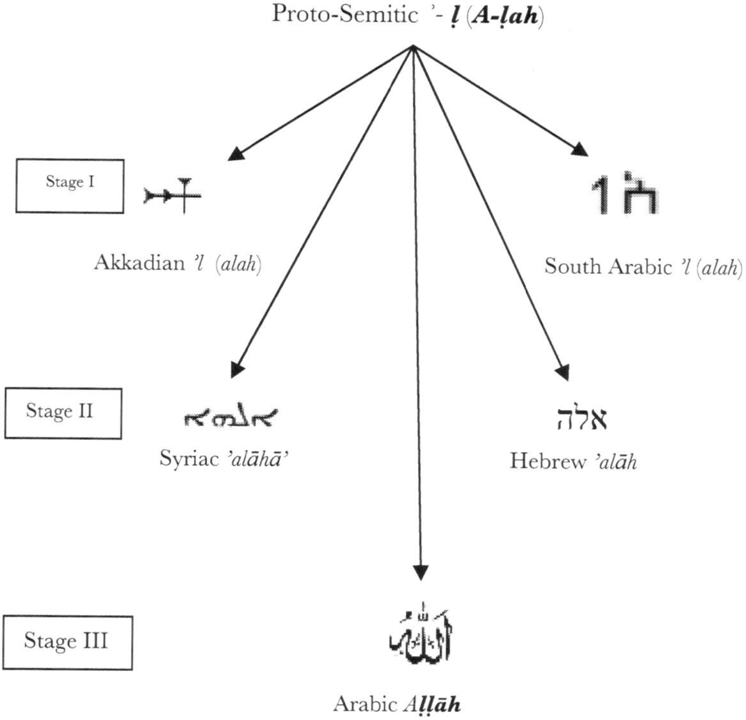

What do we know of this Proto-Semitic ***ʾḷ* (*Aḷah*)**? He was the almighty Creator God. He appears as such in both Ugaritic and Old South Arabian,[300] thus in the north and the south of the peninsula. But we can say more. Ancient Middle Eastern religion has been described as a broad and languid river which from time to time and in different places splits into a multiplicity of side-channels, later reunited, and always moving in the same direction.[301] One side-channel that is most characteristic of the

---

300 Ulf Oldenburg, "Above the Stars of El: El in Ancient South Arabic Religion," ***ZAW*** 82 (1970): 195; Johannes C. De Moor, "El, The Creator," in Gary Rendsburg and Cyrus H. Gordon (edd.), ***The Bible World: Essays in Honor of Cyrus H. Gordon*** (New York: Ktav Pub Inc, 1980) 171-187.
301 John E. Healey, ***The Religion of the Nabataeans: A Conspectus*** (Leiden: Brill, 2001) 1.

'general flow' of Afrabian religion is the South Arabian religious tradition. Stephen Langdon, in his discussion of Semitic mythology, assumed that South Arabia was the original home of Semitic religion and remains the place where 'pure and undefiled' Semitic religion may be examined.[302] More recently Werner Daum has argued that it is in South Arabia, the two Yemens in particular, which is "still that part of the Middle East which most vividly retains the manners and customs of ancient Arabia."[303] South Arabia, therefore, "conveys Arabia's yesterworld," religiously as well as culturally.

The epigraphic evidence confirms that *'l*, also written *'lh*,[304] was the supreme creator-god all over southern Arabia.[305] While later deities such as 'Attar the moon-god will replace *'l* as the most important South Arabian deity, he, Shams the sun-goddess and others arrived on the scene only later, brought south by Mesopotamian immigrants. *'l/ 'lh* is eventually 'crowded out' by these nature deities.[306] In Old South Arabian he was also the paragon of righteousness, as Ulf Oldenburg informs us:

> The numerous theophorous names composed with the proper name of *'El* [read: ***Aḷah***] illuminate the distinct character of El and his original glory. He was called 'the first' and 'exalted', the king above all, and therefore his title *the King* became another name for El. He was characterized by his strength...As the

[302] Langdon, ***Semitic Religion***, 3-6.

[303] Werner Daum, "A Pre-Islamic Rite in South Arabia," ***Journal of the Royal Asiatic Society*** (1987): 5.

[304] S.D. Ricks, ***Lexicon of Inscriptional Qatabanian*** (StP 14; Rome, 1989) 10-11.

[305] Javior Teixidor (***Pagan God***, 83 n.46) notes regarding the Semitic inscriptional evidence in Arabia: "An important feature of the entire pre-Islamic onomastics is the overwhelming popularity of the element *'l* and *'lh* in Arabic proper names." See also Oldenburg, "Above the Stars of El," 195; G. Ryckmans, ***Les noms propres sud-sémitiques*** (Lorvain, 1934) I:1, II: 2ff; James A. Montgomery, ***Arabia and the Bible*** (Philadelphia: University of Pennsylvania, 1934) 149, 153.

[306] Oldenburg, "Above the Stars of El," 193; D.H. Müller, "Über אל und אלה im Sabäischen," in ***Actes du sixième congrès international des orientalistes*** (Leide: E.J. Brill, 1885) 465-472; Wendell Phillips, ***Oman: A History*** (Logmans, 1967) 2-3; ***Encyclopedia Britannica*** [2004] s.v. Arabian Religion by Jacques Ryckmans.

> almighty king of creation he ruled in righteousness, and *Righteousness* became the name of El, by which he is invoked in the oldest class of personal names; it reveals El as the author and standard of righteousness. He was the great judge of all men, who in his infinite wisdom pronounced righteous judgment rendering to every one according to his deeds and severely punished iniquity. But above all he was known for his great love and mercy as he willingly pardoned sin and blessed his creatures with health and long life...The terms of kinship 'father, uncle, brother', which are so abundant in the oldest names reflect a patriarchal social organization typical of nomadic tribes. El belonged to the clan as head of it, and his function was that of a guardian defending the rights of its members...Another important name of El was *Savior*."[307]

Aḷah had a feminine complement, *Alat*,[308] and the two are the same as the Allah and Allat (or: al-Lāh and al-Lāt) of later Arabic orthography. "Just as the highest god," Ditlef Nielsen informed us, "was simply known as Il or Ilah 'God', so the wife of this god was simply known as 'the goddess,' Ilat or Ilahat."[309] She is the 'Queen of Heaven' and 'Mother of the Gods.' In Ugaritic texts dated prior to 1200 BCE she is called *'ṯrt ym.*, "She Who Strides (*'ṯr*) on the Sea (*yam*)," later shortened to Athirat (*'ṯrt*). She is thus an *aquatic* Mother Goddess, as we would expect. This attribute sheds further light on the nature and character of the divine feminine complement. According to Oldenberg the name Athirat is also related to the noun *'ṯrt* which means 'sanctuary.'[310] E. Lipiński points out that the Hebrew cognate of the Ugaritic term, *'ašērā*, which is the name of the Hebrew Mother Goddess, likewise means 'shrine, holy place.'[311] This theme, which we have

---

307 Oldenburg, "Above the Stars of El," 195-196, 197.
308 ***ER*** 3:37 s.v. Canaanite Religion; Marvin H. Pope, ***El in the Ugaritic Texts*** (Leiden: E.J. Brill, 1955) 7.
309 Ditlef Nielsen, ***Der dreieinige Gott in religionshistorischer Beleuchtung: Die Drei Göttlichen personen*** (Gyldendalske boghandel, Nordisk forlag, 1922) volume I: 317.
310 ***The Conflict between El and Baal*** (Leiden: Brill, 1969) 28 n. 1.
311 "The Goddess Aṯirat in Ancient Arabia, in Babylon, and in Ugarit," ***Orientalia Lovaniensia Periodica*** 3 (1971): 111-116.

already encountered, will have great significance for us later: the aquatic female complement of the male god is identified as *his temple or shrine*. Below we shall see just how the ancients understood the male god to 'inhabit' the feminized 'temple'.

In 1985 German scholar Werner Daum published an important monograph, ***Ursemitische Religion*** ("Proto-Semitic Religion"). Daum suggests that our best evidence for reconstructing the 'Ursemitische Religion' comes from southern Arabia. By a close study of ancient South Arabian inscriptions and modern Yemeni folktales and ritual practices, Daum was able to produce a convincing reconstruction of proto-Semitic Religion, or at least important aspects thereof. The most important observation for our purposes is that, according to Daum's reconstruction, ***'ḷ*** the high god of the proto-Semites was *a black god.* This Proto-Semitic black deity was depicted as an old, bearded man and associated with the black rain cloud and the black bull (and ibex, the "bull-goat"[312]). These, Daum tells us, "symbolisiert den dunklen 'Il (‚symbolized the dark 'Il')."[313] He was called *shaība*, „old man."[314] Thus, *the Proto-Semitic God* ***Aḷah*** *is the god of the 'new religion' of the Levant, the Black God* symbolized by the Black Bull!

The British historian Julian Baldick followed up and expanded upon Daum's research with ***Black God: The Afroasiatic Roots of the Jewish, Christian and Muslim Religions***.[315] Baldick's research suggested that, just as there is an 'Afroasiatic' language group indigenous to North Africa and Arabia, there is likewise an 'Afroasiatic' religious tradition indigenous to the same area and peculiar to the same groups. This 'Afroasiatic' religious tradition is characterized by a dualistic logic which emphasizes the male-female dichotomy and by a divine triad consisting of a Black rain god, a goddess, and a young hero god. Among the Oromo of southern Ethiopia, e.g. God is called *Waqa Quracca* meaning Black (*Quracca*) God

[312] The ibex is a wild mountain-goat, genus *Capra*, whose Latin name is akin to the Old Spanish *bezerro*, "bull."
[313] Daum, ***Ursemitische Religion***, 99.
[314] Ibid., 68-70.
[315] New York: Syracuse University Press, 1997.

(*Waqa*).[316] He rides the dark clouds, has red eyes representing his anger, and is the Creator. The Oromo sacrifice Black sheep to him hoping to procure rain.

Figure 23
Canaanite representation of their supreme god El (***Alah***), the Black God. Statuette was excavated at Megiddo, Israel, in 1935-1936.

IV. *Afrabia and the Religion of the Black God*

In the 1950's and 60's a Danish expedition unearthed a remarkable system of temples in Barbar, Bahrain, the ancient Dilmun of Sumerian lore (Figure 27). Called the 'Barbar Temples' in today's literature, they are three successive temples built one on top of the other over time, the first raised anywhere from 3000 to 2200 BCE, the last maybe around 1800 BCE.[317]

---

[316] Baldick, ***Black God***, 114.
[317] On the Barbar Temples see Rice, ***Archaeology of the Arabian Gulf***, esp. 156-172; Potts, ***Arabian Gulf in Antiquity*** 1: 168-172, 201-207; Ministry of Information, ***The Temple Complex at Bahrain Barbar – A Description and Guide*** (Bahrain: Ministry of Information, 1990)

These temples are notable for their antiquity as well as their architecture. As Rice notes, they are "[among] the most ancient of buildings… for the earliest of them…must have been erected not long after the first centuries of the invention of stone architecture itself."[318] The architecture of the Barbar temples, he says, "reveals a high standard of technical competence."[319] This architecture is similar to and thus suggests some connection with the earliest Sumerian temple architecture (Figure 27).[320] The fine quality of the recovered objects indicates that a high culture flourished there. And even though these temples are considered the most important ancient structures in the entire gulf region thus far identified, they do not represent the beginning of Afrabian civilization and high culture; the Barbar period only represents the high point of a civilization that had already flourished for millennia prior.[321]

Who was the resident deity at Barbar? While a number of suggestions have been made,[322] we can only guess his identity.[323] His character is clear however from the recovered artifacts and seals. Most important is the remarkable copper bull head, indicating that we have here a temple of the bull god (Figure 24).[324] This is confirmed by the collection of seals uncovered from the Dilmun region in general where the bull and the ibex are prominently represented.[325] One seal is of particular significance: it depicts an anthropomorphic deity with a crown of bull horns on, enthroned on a bull (Figure 25).[326] The bull-god of Barbar had aquatic associations: the heart of the temple is a

---

318 Rice, ***Archaeology of the Arabian Gulf***, 149.
319 Ibid., 171.
320 ***Temple Complex***, 9, 28; Rice, ***Archaeology of the Arabian Gulf***, 149.
321 Caspers, "Sumer, Coastal Arabia and the Indus Valley"; ***Temple Complex***, 44.
322 On which see Potts, ***Arabian Gulf in Antiquity*** 1: 17-172.
323 Rice, ***Archaeology of the Arabian Gulf***, 1.
324 Rice, ***Power of the Bull***, 168-171.
325 Ibid.; ***Temple Complex***, 38-42.
326 Robert G. Hoyland, ***Arabia and the Arabs: From the Bronze Age to the Coming of Islam*** (London an New York: Routledge, 2001) 196, Pl. 31.

sacred well which may represent what was thought to be an entrance to the underground primordial waters.[327]

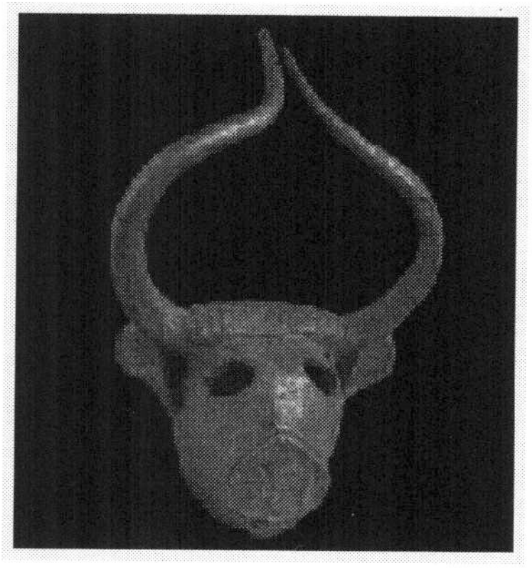

Figure 24
Barbar Temple Bull head

Figure 25
Dilmun Seal with enthroned
Bull god

[327] ***Temple Complex***, 7, 13.

Figure 26
Excavated ruins of Barbar Temple

Figure 27
Reconstructed Barbar Temple. Notice the black bull statues and sacred pool.

All of this, plus the obvious connections with Sumer, has convinced many scholars that the resident deity at Barbar was none other than the Sumerian deity Enki who likely entered the Mesopotamian area from Dilmun, i.e. from the Arabian Gulf.[328] In other words, the god that would become the important Sumerian/Akkadian deity Enki/Ea probably originated in eastern Arabia. His myth sheds light on the central myth of the 'new religion' as it spread far and wide after originating in the Levant. Understanding the character of this god therefore gives us great insight into the religion of ancient *Afrabia*, the matrix of Islam.

IV.1. *'Enki' and the Religion of the Black God*

Figure 28
Enki enthroned in rectangular, watery shrine, donning the characteristic mark of divinity, the bull-horned cap

[328] Ibid., 11; Rice, ***Archaeology of the Arabian Gulf***, 163, 168; Khaled Al Nashef, "The Deities of Dilmun," in Al Khalifa and Rice, ***Bahrain through the ages***, 340-366.

The earliest evidence of this deity is likely the reed hut shrine unearthed in Eridu (Mesopotamia) dated ca. 5000 BCE, which is likely dedicated to this god.[329] Enki was the supreme, creator god of ancient Mesopotamia,[330] and he was the Black God, the Bull God, *par excellence*.[331] He personified the primordial black waters (*abzu/apsû*),[332] and was himself personified in the black bull and the ibex.[333] As the creator god, he personified male reproductive power,[334] signaled by his 'phallocentrism' in Sumerian myth.[335]

---

329 Rice, ***Archaeology of the Arabian Gulf***, 90; Tony Nugent, "Star-god: Enki/Ea and the biblical god as expressions of a common ancient Near Eastern astral-theological symbol system," unpublished dissertation, Yale University,1982, 29; H.W.F. Saggs, ***The Greatness that was Babylon*** (1962) 39-40.

330 Most discussions of Mesopotamian religion see the pantheon as topped by a triad: (1) An, the god of heaven, the highest god; (2) Enlil, the god of 'wind', of second rank; (3) and Enki/Ea, god of earth and the subterranean waters, of third rank. Samuel Kramer even thought Enki's subordination to Enlil produced in the former an 'inferiority complex' ("Enki and his Inferiority Complex," ***Orientalia*** 39 [1970]: 103-110). However, it has been cogently argued that this situation did not prevail in the earliest period. According to Piotr Steinkeller "Enki undoubtedly was the original head of the pantheon." Steinkeller suggests that Enlil was a secondary development in the Sumerian Pantheon: "On Rulers, Priests and Sacred Marriage: Tracing the Evolution of Early Sumerian Kingship," in Kazuko Watanabe (ed.), ***Priests and Officials in the Ancient Near East: Papers of the Second Colloquium on the Ancient Near East--the City and its Life held at the Middle Eastern Culture Center in Japan (Mitaka, Tokyo), March 22-24, 1996*** (Heidelberg: Universitätsverlag C. Winter, 1999) 113-114. Piotr Michalowski agrees that Enlil was a late comer to the Sumerian pantheon and usurped the prime position of Enki, "THE male player" of the pantheon: "The Unbearable Lightness of Enlil," in Jiri Prosecky (ed.), ***Intellectual Life in the Ancient Near East: Papers Presented at the 43rd Rencontre assyriologique internationale, Prague, July 1-5, 1996*** (Prague: Academy of Sciences of the Czech Republic, Oriental Institute, 1998) 241.

331 He is called *am-gig-abzu*, "black bull of the *apsû*"; *am-an-ki*, "wild bull of heaven and earth"; *dara-abzu* "ibex of the *apsû*." See W.F. Albright, "The Mouth of the Rivers," ***AJSL*** 35 (1991): 167; Nugent, "Star-god: Enki/Ea," 21.

332 Albright, "Mouth of the Rivers," 165. The Sumerian text *Enki and the World Order* refers to the "great majestic black water flood of the deep [Sum. engur = Akk. *Apsû*]." See discussion in Richard E. Averbeck, "Myth, Ritual, and Order in 'Enki and the World Order'," ***JAOS*** 123 (2003): 761 n. 13.

333 Rice, ***Power of the Bull***, 90; idem, ***Archaeology of the Arabian Gulf***, 137.F.A.M. Wiggermann, "Extensions of and Contradictions to Dr. Porada's Lecture," in Edith Porada, ***Man and Images in the Ancient Near East*** (Wakefield, Rhode Island: Moyer Bell, 1995) 88-90; Michalowski, "Unbearable Lightness of Enlil," 245.

334 Steinkeller, "On Rulers, Priests and Sacred Marriage" 113 describes him as: "Enki, a personification of male reproductive power, the god of fresh water and creative intelligence."

335 Jerrold S. Cooper, "Enki's Member: Eros and Irrigation in Sumerian Literature," in Hermann Behrens, Darlene Loding, and T. Roth (edd), ***DUMU-E2-DUB-BA-A:***

Now the deity An (Sumerian ^{d}AN, Akkadian *Anu*) is actually presented in the literature as *the* creator and supreme head of the Sumerian pantheon, Enki being a son.[336] But An seems to have created only half of the cosmos, at least *as An*. The other half, the 'lower' half, was created by his first born son, called in Sumerian texts Enki and in Akkadian texts Ea.[337] The relation of Enki to An appears, however, to be much more complex and intimate than that of father and son. In the *Enūma eliš*, the famous Babylonian creation account, Ea (Enki) is created by Anu (An) as his "likeness,"[338] indicating that, as Richard J. Clifford perceives, "Ea is equal to Anu".[339] "Equal" here, however, means *identical.* This is indicated by the mystical numbers the Mesopotamians attributed to their deities. Each of the major gods was given a mystical number from the sexagesimal (base-sixty) counting system. In Akkadian Anu has two mystical numbers, 1 and 60, denoting not only that he is the supreme god of the pantheon, but also that he is "the first (god), the heavenly father, the greatest one in heaven and earth, (and) the one who *contains* the entire universe".[340] As Simo Parpola explains: "As 'One and Sixty' Anu's number comprised the mystic numbers of *all other gods*: he was the Alpha and the Omega".[341] According to Parpola the Mesopotamian pantheon can be reduced to "mere aspects of a few 'great gods,' and these again to mere aspects or powers of a

Studies in Honor of Ake W. Sjoberg (Philadelphia: University Museum / Babylonian Section, 1989) 87-89.

336 ***ER*** (New Edition) 1: 301-303 s.v. An by Silvia Maria Chiodi; Herman Wohlstein, ***The Sky-God An-Anu*** (Jericho, New York: Paul A. Stroock, 1976).

337 In two late Babylonian temple ritual texts (ca. 500 BCE) which seem to preserve this old joint creation motif, the *kalû* priest recited: "After Anu engendered heaven, (And) Ea had founded earth/*apsû*". As Richard J. Clifford (***Creation Accounts***, 71) notes: "Creation here is entirely the work of Anu and Ea", "each creating his half of the world." Enki is *dumu sag*, 'first-born son' of An. See Nugent, "Star God Enki/Ea," 89.

338 Clifford, ***Creation Accounts***, 88.

339 Ibid., 89.

340 Knut Tallqvist, ***Akkadische Gotterepitheta*** (1938), 254,

341 Simo Parpola, "The Assyrian Tree of Life: Tracing the Origins of Jewish Monotheism and Greek Philosophy," ***JNES*** 3 (1993): 184 n. 89. Parpola cites texts identifying Anu with both the crescent moon=first god=1 and the full moon=all gods=60.

single universal God". This indicates "a sophisticated monotheistic system of thought sharply deviating from the current simplistic notion of Mesopotamian religion and philosophy."[342] In other words, all of the gods can be reduced to aspects or attributes – manifestations, if you will – of the one god An/Anu.[343] Enki/Ea's case is particular in that he, like Anu, has two mystical numbers: 1 and 60, An/Anu's exact numbers.[344] Thus Enki, An's 'first-born', is actually An himself at a secondary stage of manifestation. This is why, though only one supreme deity can actually be the "creator of everything," "father of the gods," "archetype of the creation of heaven and earth," etc, both An and Enki are so called.[345]

The iconography helps us to better understand the 'stage' that Enki represents *viz-à-viz* An. Enki is famously depicted inside a rectangular shrine made of water (Figure 28). This represents the god inside his temple which is identified with the abzu/*apsû*, also written ENGUR in Sumerian. The abzu/*apsû* is the black primordial waters, out of which Enki built his ziggurat temple called É-sira, "House of the neter-sea" and É-engurra, "House of the ENGUR (*Abzu*)."[346] Tony Nugent insightfully brings to our attention the fact that this iconography mirrors the original cuneiform ideogram for ENGUR: the ^{d}An sign (star) enclosed within a rectangle 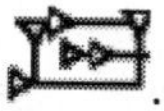.[347] An is a luminous god, his ideogram

---

[342] Ibid., 184 n. 90.

[343] See also Stephen Herbert Langdon, ***Semitic Mythology*** (Mythology of the All Races, Volume V; Boston: Marshall Jones Company, 1931) 93: "In the minds of the earliest Sumerians *dingir* Enlil, *dingir* Enki, etc., really means An-Enlil, An-Enki ,etc.; that is, Enlil, Enki, ect., are only aspects of the father Anu."

[344] Parpola, "Assyrian Tree of Life," 190.

[345] Tallqvist, ***Akkadische Gotterepitheta*** , 254; Nugent, "Star God: Enki/Ea," 43-44. On Enki as "primordial agent of the creation of the world" see E.C., "Mesopotamian Cosmogony," in Y. Bonnefoy and Wendy Doniger (edd.), ***Mythologies***, 2 vols. (Chicago and London: The University of Chicago Press, 1991) I: 156.

[346] S. Langdon, "Two Sumerian Hymns from Eridu and Nippur," ***American Journal of Semitic Languages and Literatures*** 3 (1923): 161, 162; Nugent, "Star God: Enki/Ea," 274.

[347] Nugent, "Star God: Enki/Ea," 32.

being the asterisk, a cuneiform star with eight points (written DINGIR), later modified to a wedge cross.[348] Enki, who is called the "bright light in the heaven" and "Great Light of the *Apsû*,"[349] is thus identified with the god An: he is the god An *enclosed within the watery temple.*[350] As An is the 'star-god' *par excellence*, Enki is the "star-god of the waters," to use Nugent's terms.[351]

What does "star-god of the waters" actually indicate or imply? It indicates that the luminous god of heaven, An, *incarnated within* a black, aquatic body produced from the primordial waters, the *Apsû*, becoming thereby Enki. In Mesopotamian tradition "Water endows the being with form".[352] This is further confirmed by the

---

[348] The AN ideogram underwent the following evolution:

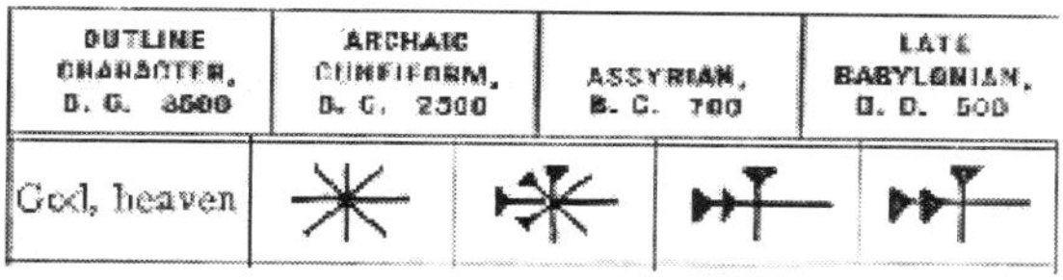

[349] Nugent, "Star God: Enki/Ea," 269; Andrew George "Babylonian texts from the folios of Sidney Smith, Part Two: prognostic and diagnostic omens." ***Revue d'assyriologie***, 85 (1991): 152 [art.=137-167]

[350] This is undoubtedly the motif behind the enigmatic reference in one Sumerian hymn to Anu having "sat in the *kimaḫḫu* (the lower world)" [Langdon, "Two Sumerian Hymns," 172] and his temple having "descended fro heaven" (see Å.W. Sjöberg and E. Bergmann, ***The Collection of the Sumerian Temple Hymns*** [Locust Valley, NY, 1969] 29). On allusions in the literature to the motif of the fall of An to the underworld see further Jan van Dijk, "Sumerische Religion," in J.P. Asmussen et al (edd.), ***Handbuch der Religionsgeschechte*** (Göttengen: Vandenhoeck and Ruprecht, 1971) I: 452. In light of the ontological identity of An and Enki, the descent of An may be described in the narrative which Thorkild Jacobson calls "The Descent of Enki" (a portion of the composition known as "Gilgamesh, Enkidu and the Netherworld"), which narrates Enki's descent to and enslavement with the aquatic underworld of Ereshkigal. See Thorkild Jacobson, "The Descent of Enki," in Mark E. Cohen, Daniel C. Snell and David B. Weisberg, ***The Tablet and the Scroll: Near Eastern Studies in Honor of William W. Hallo*** (Bethesda, Maryland: CDL Press, 1993) 120-123.

[351] Nugent, "Star God: Enki/Ea," 286.

[352] Richard J. Clifford, ***Creation Accounts in the Ancient Near East and the Bible*** (CBQ Monograph Series 26; Washington, D.C.: Catholic Biblical Association of America, 1994) 33. See for example the Sumerian text *Nammu and Enki,* where the 'waters in the belly' of Nammu, feminine personification of the primordial waters, is said to "give form to the limbs" of the new creature (man) there developing. See Herbert Sauren, "Nammu and Enki," in Mark E. Cohen, Daniel C. Snell and David B. Weisberg, ***The Tablet and the Scroll: Near Eastern Studies in Honor of William W. Hallo*** (Bethesda, Maryland: CDL Press, 1993) 202.

'temple theology' of Mesopotamia and the ancient Near East.[353] The temple was considered an architectonic icon: an image in stone of the god. As Mark S. Smith puts it, speaking of the West Semitic tradition: "temples tell not only where the deities are, but also what and how they are."[354] In particular, the temple architecture symbolically reflects the anthropomorphic body of the god and 'houses' the story of how this divine body emerged out of the primordial waters.[355] Thus, the seven levels of the Mesopotamian ziggurat or stepped-pyramid represent the seven stages of the divine descent from the highest heaven into material enmeshment (incarnation; Figure 29). [356] The temple is thus the link between heaven and earth, dur-an-ki, its top portion

---

[353] John M. Lundquist has documented the existence of a 'common temple theology' in the ancient Near East, a common ritual and mythic -number of shared motifs. See John M. Lundquist, "The Common Temple Theology of the Ancient Near East," in T.G. Madsen (ed.), ***The Temple in Antiquity*** (Provo: BYU Press, 1984) 53-76; idem, "Temple Symbolism in Isaiah," in by Monte S. Nyman (ed.), ***Isaiah and the Prophets: Inspired Voices from the Old Testament*** (Provo: BYU Press, 1984) 33-55.

[354] Mark S. Smith, "Like Deities, Like Temples (Like People)," in John Day (ed.), ***Temple and Worship Biblical Israel*** (London/New York: Clark, 2005) 21.

[355] Andrzej Wierciński, "Pyramids and Ziggurats as the Architectonic Representations of the Archetype of the Cosmic Mountain," ***Occasional Publications in. Classical Studies*** 1 (1978): 69-110; I.W. Mabbett, "The Symbolism of Mount Meru," ***History of Religions*** 23 (1983) 64-83; Mohiy wl-Din Ibrahim, "The God of the Great Temple of Edfu," in John Ruffle, G.A. Gaballa and Kenneth A. Kitchen (edd.), ***Orbis Aegyptiorum Speculum: Glimpses of Ancient Egypt. Studies in Honour of H.W. Fairman*** (Warminster, 1979) 170-171; Ragnhild Bjerre Finnestad, ***Image of the World and Symbol of the Creator: On the Cosmological and Iconological Values of the Temple of Edfu*** (Wiesbaden: Harrassowitz, 1985); Stella Kramrish, "The Temple as Purusa," in Pramod Chandra (ed) ***Studies in Indian Temple Architecture*** (American Institute of Indian Studies, 1975) 40-46. Erik Hornung, ***Idea into Image: Essays on Ancient Egyptian Thought*** (Timken Publishers, 1992) Chapter 6;

[356] Mabbett, "Symbolism of Mount Meru," 64i; Amar Annus, "The Soul's Ascent and Tauroctony: On Babylonian Sediment in the Syncretic Religious Doctrines of Late Antiquity," in Thomas Richard Kämmerer (ed.), ***Studies on Ritual and Society in the Ancient Near East. Tartuer Symposien 1998-2004*** (Berlin and New York: Walter de Gruyter, 2007) 1-53; Pirjo Lapinkivi, ***The Sumerian Sacred Marriage in the Light of Comparative Evidence*** (Helsinki: The Neo-Assyrian Text Corpus Project, 2004) 146.

touching heaven, its bottom reaching deep into the Abzu.[357] The lowest level of the ziggurat and the exterior walls of the temple present the external body of the god, which is associated with the primordial waters: thus the undulating course of the bricks on the external walls of the Egyptian temple are designed to imitate the waves of Nun, the primordial waters in Egyptian cosmogonic thought.[358] Enki's 'dark house' made from the black primordial waters thus signals his dark bodily appearance.[359] This black appearance, lastly, is associated with the Bull.[360]

---

[357] D.O. Edzard, "Deep-Rooted Skyscrapers and Bricks: Ancient Mesopotamian Architecture and its Imagery," in M. Mindlin, M.J. Geller and J.E. Wansbrough (edd.), ***Figurative Language in the Ancient Near East*** (London: University of London, 1987) 13-24.

[358] A.J. Spenser, "The Brick Foundation of Late-Period Temples and their Mythological Origin," in John Ruffle, G.A. Gaballa and Kenneth A. Kitchen (edd.), ***Orbis Aegyptiorum Speculum: Glimpses of Ancient Egypt. Studies in Honour of H.W. Fairman*** (Warminster, 1979) 133; Dunand and Zivie-Coche, ***Gods and Men in Egypt***, 88; Hornung, ***Idea into Image***, 119. On the cosmic/cosmogonic symbolism of the Egyptian temple see also John Baines, "Temple Symbolism," ***RAIN*** 15 (1976): 10-15.

[359] On Enki's "dark (Sum. kukku) house" see Wolfgang Heimpel, "Anthropomorphic and Bovine Lahmus," in Manfried Dietrich and Oswald Loretz (edd.), ***dubsar anta-men: Studien zu Altorientalistik. Festschrift fur Willem H. Ph. Romer zur Vollendung seines 70*** (Münster: Ugarit-Verlag, 1998) 148 n. 41. That this architectual darkness reflects somatic (soma= „body") darkness is indicated in a particularly significant text cited by Thorkild Jacobsen (*TC*, V, 47, 1.2.): "Ea resembles the *apsû*, the *apsû* resembles the sea, the sea Ereshkigal" (Thorkild Jacobsen, "Sumerian Mythology: A Review Article," ***JNES*** 5 [1946]: 141). Enki/Ea himself thus has the appearance of the black primordial waters.

[360] In hymns Enki's temple is compared to a bull and it was topped by bovine horns. Wayne Horowitz, ***Mesopotamian Cosmic Geography*** (Winona Lake, Indiana: Eisenbrauns, 1998)124; S. Langdon, "Two Sumerian Hymns from Eridu and Nippur," ***American Journal of Semitic Languages and Literatures*** 3 (1923): 164, 165, 169.

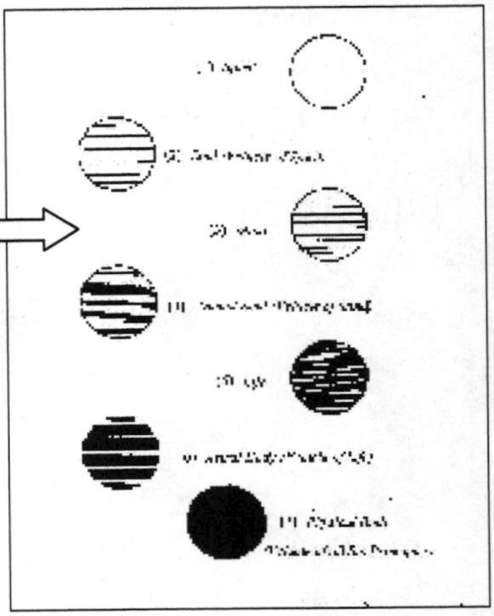

Figure 29
Mesopotamian seven-level ziggurat and the seven-stage divine descent from spirit to coarse matter

IV.1.1. *Enki as* Coniunctio oppositorum

We have here the means to reconcile the two contrasting descriptions of Enki: on the one hand as "bright light in the heavens," "Great Light of the *Apsû*," who "radiantly appears in heaven and earth"[361]; and on the other hand as "black bull of the *Apsû*" whose appearance resembles the black waters of the underworld.[362] We see that Enki is a composite deity: the union of the star-god *par excellence*, An, with the primordial waters produced Enki, the Black Bull of the *Apsû*.[363] He is the *Coniunctio oppositorum* personified. This is confirmed by an Archaic Period Mesopotamian seal. Enki is depicted bearded and enthroned, crowned with bull-horned cap. Fishes are depicted swimming up

---

361 Nugent, "Star God: Enki/Ea," 269.

362 Albright, "Mouth of the Rivers," 167; Jacobsen, "Sumerian Mythology," 141.

363 On Enki's/Ea's association with aquatic bovines in Mesopotamian myth see Wolfgang Heimpel, "Anthropomorphic and Bovine Lahmus," in Manfried Dietrich and Oswald Loretz (edd.), ***dubsar anta-men: Studien zu Altorientalistik. Festschrift fur Willem H. Ph. Romer zur Vollendung seines 70*** (Münster: Ugarit-Verlag, 1998) 129-156.

non-existent streams toward his knees – a representation of the god's aquatic nature – and flames spring up from his shoulders – the mark of a solar character.[364] In an Assyrian seal the god is depicted in his characteristic rectangular, watery shrine with the sun disk.[365] This equally resolves the apparent conflict between the descriptions of An himself as the luminous star deity of heaven and his own close association with the black bull. Indeed, An can be considered the Bull God *par excellence*: his characteristic attribute animal was the black bull (Figure 30).[366] Besides the cuneiform star, An's other particular emblem is the cap with bull horns, which became the mark of divinity in Mesopotamian iconography.[367] Not only is An ritualistically identified with a bull "black as asphalt," but the black hide of the bull is identified with the divine skin of An/Anu.[368] Lastly, this might explain why An, the star-god, can be associated with jugs of water.[369]

---

[364] van Buren, ***Flowing Vase***, 34. The rays that are often depicted emanating from the shoulders of deities in Mesopotamian iconography are a sign of their *melammu*, their brilliant luminous being. See F.A.M. Wiggermann, "Extensions of and Contradictions to Dr. Porada's Lecture," in Edith Porada, ***Man and Images in the Ancient Near East*** (Wakefield, Rhode Island: Moyer Bell, 1995) 86; E. Cassin, ***La Splendeur Divine*** (Paris and the Hague: Mouton, 1968); A. Leo Oppenheim, ***Ancient Mesopotamia*** (Chicago: University Press, 1964) 98; idem, "Akadian *pul(u)ḫ(t)u* and *melammû*," *JAOS* 63 (1943): 31-34.

[365] William Hayes Ward, ***The Seal Cylinders of Western Asia*** (Washington D.C.: Carnegie Institute, 1910) 217 fig. 656; Van Buren, ***Flowing Vase***, 39.

[366] Daum, ***Ursemitische Religion***, 204; E. Ebeling, ***Tod und Leben nach den Vorstellungen der Babylonier*** (Berlin-Leipzig, 1931) 29; C. Bezold, ***Babylonisch-assyrisches Glossar*** (Heidelberg: C. Winter, 1926) 210 s.v. sugugalu; Georgia de Santillana and Hertha von Dechend, ***Hamlet's Mill: An essay on myth and the frame of time*** (Boston: Gambit, Inc., 1969) 124.

[367] On this horned crown see E. Douglas van Buren, "Concerning the Horned Cap of the Mesopotamian Gods," ***Orientalia*** NS 12 (1943): 318-327.

[368] In one description of the Babylonian *kalû*-ritual the slaying and skinning of the sacrificial bull, 'black as asphalt,' is mythologized as the god Bēl's slaying and flaying of the god Anu, whose characteristic attribute animal was the black bull. See Alasdair Livingstone, ***Mystical and Mythological Explanatory Works of Assyrian and Babylonian Scholars*** (Winona Lake, Indiana: Eisenbrauns, 2007) 117 (VAT 10099).

[369] E. Douglas van Buren, ***The Flowing Vase and the God with Streams*** (Berlin, 1933) 9.

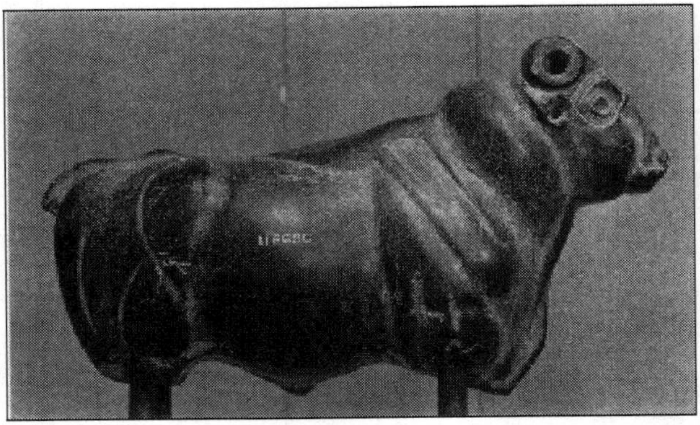

Figure 30

Image of Sacrificial Bull, "black as asphalt" used to represent the Sumerian/Akkadian king of the gods, An/Anu (From Elizabeth Lansing, ***The Sumerians: Inventors and Builders*** [New York: McGraw-Hill Book Company, 1971])

The paradigmatic *Coniunctio oppositorum* involves a union of masculine and feminine principles. This is true in this case as well. It seems that in the early Uruk period of Mesopotamian religion, when Enki was the chief deity of the pantheon, he was paired in most city-states with a female complement.[370] At this time, Piotr Michalowski suggests, "the Mesopotamian pantheon was headed by a couple associated primarily with fertility: Enki and Ninhursag. Their names may have changed over the centuries, but that is a small matter."[371] Ninhursag indeed was just one of the names by which Enki's female complement was known, and Thorkild Jacobsen traces her "straight back to the neolithic precursor of the *potnia theron*, 'the Great Goddess of Life, Death, and Regeneration,' to use Marjia Gimbutas's term for

[370] Steinkeller, "On Rulers, Priests and Sacred Marriage," 113-114.
[371] "Unbearable Lightness of Enlil," 244.

her."[372] In other words, Enki's female complement is the goddess of the 'Woman and Bull' religion of the Levant.

The primordial waters are feminine in Mesopotamian tradition.[373] In fact, they are Nammu, Enki's mother. Nammu is the "universal primordial mother" and Enki is her first born son.[374] Most significantly Enki's aquatic temple É-engurra, "House of the ENGUR (*Abzu*)," and thus his black body, is identified with Nammu.[375] This equation is critically important: Nammu (dark primordial mother/waters) = Enki's dark, rectangular aquatic temple = Enki's black, anthropomorphic *male* body. Thus in the incantation text *An Address to the River of Creation* we read:

> Incantation: You, River, creatress of everything,
> When the Great Gods dug you,
> They placed good things on your banks,
> Within you, Ea, the king of the Apsu, built his home.[376]

What these equations signify is that the aquatic temple (É-engurra) represents a black body made from the feminine substance of the primordial waters (Nammu) within which divine luminance (i.e. An) incarnated or indwelled. That this male, anthropomorphic black body is symbolized by a feminine rectangular black shrine will take on greater importance as we discuss the Ka'ba cult of Mecca.

---

372 "The Eridu Genesis," ***JBL*** 100 (1981): 514 n. 5.

373 Rice, ***Archaeology of the Arabian Gulf***, 130 also points out: "The Sumerian cosmology held that in the beginning was the primeval sea, represented as female".

374 J. Bottéro, "Intelligence and technical function of power in the structure of the Mesopotamian pantheon: the example of Enki/Ea", in Y. Bonnefoy and Wendy Doniger (edd.), ***Mythologies***, 2 vols. (Chicago and London: The University of Chicago Press, 1991) I:148; Jacobsen, "Sumerian Mythology," 141.

375 Nammu is written with the ENGUR sign and in the *Yale Syllabary* Nammu is equated with Abzu. See Jacobsen, "Sumerian Mythology,"130.

376 Horowitz, ***Mesopotamian Cosmic Geography***, 338. On "River as cosmic water (*apsû*)" see Clifford, ***Creation Accounts***, 58-59.

The significance of the divine feminine in the Mesopotamian articulation of the 'new religion' must be further explored in order to understand the divine feminine in later articulations, such as in Egypt and Mecca. Two myths that give us great insight in this regard are called *Nammu and Enki* and *Enki and Ninhursaq*. *Nammu and Enki* recounts the creation of man and woman by Nammu and Enki. Enki is here "the creator of all myriads in existence." These two, Nammu and Enki, are coexistent from the beginning in this myth.[377] However Nammu, as mother of the gods, is also Enki's mother, he being called her 'son' (*dumu*). Yet, Enki takes her in marriage - she is now his wife - and impregnates her, apparently with the gods and the cosmos. Enki brought forth from Nammu's womb man and woman. What is significant is how the marriage of Enki and Nammu is described. Theirs is a particular type of marriage with implications for understanding later developments of the myth associated with the 'new religion': it is an *entrance marriage* in which the husband enters the house and family of the wife. The children take the woman's name and perpetuate only this family name.[378] The husband who enters the wife's house and takes her family name is analogous to the male god, An, entering the black body (temple made from primordial matter/mother, *Apsû/Nammu*) and thence forth known by her family names (En-ki, "Lord of the *earth*," rather than En-an, "Lord of Heaven").

That this 'marriage' has somatic (*soma* = body) significance and actually alludes to the divine male *incarnating* within a 'feminine' body (substance-wise) is confirmed by the myth known as *Enki and Ninhursaq*. In this narrative Enki's relations with seven

---

[377] Herbert Sauren, "Nammu and Enki," in Mark E. Cohen, Daniel C. Snell and David B. Weisberg, ***The Tablet and the Scroll: Near Eastern Studies in Honor of William W. Hallo*** (Bethesda, Maryland: CDL Press, 1993) 203.
[378] Ibid., 204.

or eight female characters are recounted.[379] These female character's all seem to be variants of Enki's commonly recognized wife, called in this myth Damgalnuna,[380] herself likely a form of Nammu. Damgalnuna, called the 'birth-goddess of the great gods' and 'Great Lady of the Waters,' seems to be a form of the primordial mother-goddess. *Enki and Ninhursaq* opens with Enki and Ninsikilla – Damgalnuna's first guise – 'asleep' within the primeval 'city' before the creation of the 'real' world. In the cosmogonic texts 'city' is a way of metaphorically describing the pre-creation period.[381] It is thus not surprising to find the male and female principles asleep – inactive – during this time.[382] Once the merely virtual primeval city is transformed by Enki into a real city – the beginning of creation – he enters into sexual relations with Damgalnuna and her various guises. These relations, as Keith Dickson suggests, are tantamount to partial (temporary) returns to the 'womb' from which Enki himself came originally,[383] the primordial waters.

This series of relations climaxes with Enki's full, bodily – not just phallic – incorporation into the body of Ninhursaq, Damgalnuna's main guise in this myth.[384] Ninhursaq means 'Lady of the mountain', and this is quite apt. 'Mountain' is a metaphorical description of the temple and the anthropomorphic body of the god,[385] thus Enki's full, bodily incorporation into the body of Ninhursaq means the same thing as Enki entering and

---

[379] On this mythic narrative see especially Keith Dickson, "Enki and Ninhursaq: The Trickster in Paradise," ***JNES*** 66 (2007): 1-32; idem, "Enki and the Embodied World," ***JAOS*** 125 (2005): 499-515.

[380] Bendt Alster acknowledges the identity of most of these women, but distinguishes – unjustifiably – Damgalnuna from them: "*Enki and Ninhursag*: The Creation of the First Woman," ***Ugarit-Forschungen*** 10 (1978): 25 [art.=15-27]. Rather see Dickson, "Enki and Ninhursag," 10; Clifford, ***Creation Accounts***, 36.

[381] See Clifford, ***Creation Accounts***, 18-19.

[382] Bendt Alster ("*Enki and Ninhursag*," 16) argues that, while cosmogony is not the main theme, this does seem to be a myth of creation from a very specific point of view.

[383] "Enki and Ninhursag," 30.

[384] Ibid., 28-29.

[385] See especially Wierciński, "Pyramids and Ziggurats"; Mabbett, "Symbolism of Mount Meru."

residing in his temple: incarnation in a material body. With Enki "lodged within" Ninhursag's body they are able together to bring forth gods and cosmic order and stability.[386] While this 'creation process' is the result of the collaborative efforts of the male and female deities, and the former is incorporated within the latter, it is important to point out that in this narrative Enki is still the lone creator.[387] Even the birth metaphor that is used here returns to Enki: he is the one who, inside the body of the birth-goddess, is 'pregnant' with the creations.[388] Indeed, the main emphasis of *Enki and Ninhursag* is the *body* of Enki, which is the lone guarantor of cosmic stability.[389] "The acts and tribulations," Dickson informs us, "of Enki's body traversing, modifying, and being modified by female bodily space have in a sense been the subject of the myth all along."[390] Enki's [read: An's] luminous body has indeed been modified: it is now incarnated within a black, aquatic body. This is undoubtedly the mythic motif behind his designation, 'the first god to walk/ride the waves.'[391]

IV.1.2. *Enki and the Myth of the Black God*

The Mesopotamian version of the 'Myth of the Black God' is therefore the following:

The 'beginning' began with an inchoate state of undifferentiation.[392] This dark, aquatic undifferentiated mass,

---

386 Dickson, "Enki and the Embodied World," 508, 512; idem, "Enki and Ninhursag," 31.

387 Alster rightly points that "it is the mothergoddess who urges Enki to act. It is Enki who has the power to create, but the female deities who urge him to use his power." "*Enki and Ninhursag*," 17.

388 Dickson, "Enki and Ninhursag," 30.

389 Dickson, "Enki and the Embodied World," 508, 512; idem, "Enki and Ninhursag," 31.

390 Dickson, "Enki and Ninhursag," 32.

391 Nugent, "Star-god: Enki/Ea," 281.

392 On the various primary sources, themes and important secondary discussions of Mesopotamian creation myths see Clifford, ***Creation Accounts***, Chapters 2 and 3.

considered feminine and personified as a cow, was uncreated.[393] Within this there existed a luminous, masculine numen.[394] At some point this numen produced in the primordial waters a 'seed,' mythological language for the primordial atom or the first distinct particle of matter.[395] Out of this 'seed' the divinity grew, this growth leading eventually to the separation of heaven *(an)* and earth *(ki)* out of this mass.[396] This separation is the first act in the cosmogonic process.[397] What this 'separation' seems to mean is that the luminous numen – heaven *(an)* personified in the god An (ᵈAn) – emerged out of this 'seed (atom)' and separated from the dark watery mass. The god An apparently created a 'heavenly' realm, luminous and 'pure,' but arid, virtual and full of dormant potentiality rather than being vibrant and 'real.'[398]

---

393 Horowitz, ***Mesopotamian Cosmic Geography***, 335 notes: "No Sumerian text preserves an account of the creation of the Apsu or the separation of the Apsu from heaven and earth in early times. This apparently indicates that the Sumerians conceived the Apsu to be a primordial element". Rice, ***Archaeology of the Arabian Gulf***, 130 also points out: "The Sumerian cosmology held that in the beginning was the primeval sea, represented as female". The Babylonian Tiamat (primordial salt-waters) seems also to have been presented as a bovine in the *Enūma eliš*: see B. Landsberger and J.V. Kinnier Wilson, "The Fifth Tablet of Enuma Elis," ***JNES*** 20 (1961): 175 [art.=154-179]. See also Clifford, ***Creation Acc.ounts***, 26.

394 See texts and discussion in ibid., 28, 62-63, 86-89; Frans Wiggermann, "Mythological Foundations of Nature," in Diederik J.W. Meijer (ed.), ***Natural Phenomena: Their Meaning, Depiction and Description in the Ancient Near East*** (North-Holland, Amsterdam, 1992) 282.

395 Clifford, ***Creation Accounts***, 29. On the atom in cosmogonic myth see True Islam, ***Truth of God***, 140-144 and below.

396 In one presargonic text we read: "The divine lord (ᵈEN) was coming of age, Heaven and earth, (still) together, were screaming – in those days Enki and Nunki (sic) were not yet alive, Enlil was not yet alive, Ninlil was not yet alive." Frains Wiggerman remarks: "I take this to mean that the divine lord (ᵈEN), the active, procreative element in the god name ᵈEN-ki, grows inside Heaven and Earth still united, and starts the painful process of separation"; "Mythological Foundations of Nature," 282. On the other hand Horowitz and Bendt Alster take the "divine lord (ᵈEN)" here as An: Horowitz, ***Mesopotamian Cosmic Geography***, 140; Bendt Alster, "On the Earliest Sumerian Literary Tradition," ***Journal of Cuneiform Studies*** 28 (1976): 122 [art.=109-126]. We now know that there is no contradiction in these views. Enki, in his primordial stage/state, is An.

397 See also G. Komoróczy, " 'The Separation of Sky and Earth': The Cycle of Kumarbi and the Myths of Cosmogony in Mesopotamia," ***Acta Antiqua Academiae Hungaricae*** 21 (1973): 21-45.

398 In one late Babylonian ritual text we read that "Anu had engendered heaven (And) Ea had founded earth." In another: "When Anu built the heavens; Nudimmud (Ea) built the

The second act of the cosmogonic process is a re-uniting of these elements: luminous heaven (*an*-An) reunites with the dark, aquatic 'earth' in a cosmic marriage, producing from this union the 'real world,' starting with the great gods.[399] The first great god produced from this union is (An-)Enki.

Enki's emergence is eloquently described: his luminous self (i.e. An) emerged from the seed (atom). He declares in the myth called *Enki and the World Order*: "I am the fecund seed, engendered by the great wild ox (An). I am the first born son of An."[400] This divine declaration is revealing. The seed or primordial atom engendered by that luminous numen (here explicitly identified with An) is itself identified with Enki. Again, An and Enki are the same divine being, God the Father and God the Son. The designation 'Enki' usually refers to An at his secondary stage, when the luminosity and the waters are joined in marriage. 'Marriage' is a positive metaphorical description of this stage. However, other texts use more negative metaphors, like 'descent' or, worse, 'captivity' and 'enslavement'. This is the case in the mythic fragment Thorkild Jacobsen called "The Descent of Enki."[401] In this mythic fragment Enki's descent to and enslavement within the aquatic underworld is recounted. The temporal setting of this 'descent' is explicitly stated to be after the separation of heaven and earth. An seems to have "shipped off" Enki (i.e. An himself) to this netherworld, where Enki is 'battered,' 'torn into,' and 'smote' by the raging waters. Jacobsen suggests that this divine descent in this mythic fragment concerns different "modes of being."[402] This seems right: a change in the *divine* 'mode of being'. That is to say, this 'descent' no doubt represents a change from the luminous An to the dual Enki who

---

Apsu, his home. Ea in the Apsu pinched off cla[y]." See Clifford, ***Creation Accounts***, 59, 60-1; Horowitz, ***Mesopotamian Cosmic Geography***, 150.

399 Clifford, ***Creation Accounts***, 18, 20, 24, 26.

400 Quoted from Clifford, ***Creation Accounts***, 34

401 Jacobsen, "Descent of Enki," 120-123.

402 Ibid., 123.

is a luminous god incarnated in a black, aquatic body. In other words, we have here to do with a *somatic* (*soma*=body) descent or transformation.[403]

We have a remarkable literary depiction of Enki's epiphany, i.e. An's emergence from the black waters *as Enki*:

> When Enki arose the fishes rose and adored him,
> He stood, a marvel unto the Apsu,
> Brought joy to Enqu,
> To the sea it seemed that An was upon him,
> To the Great River it seemed that terror hovered about him[404]

"That An was upon him" surely signifies the luminance of An radiating from Enki, even with his black body. Thus Enki's 'dark'

---

[403] That this 'descent of Enki' to the dark, aquatic underworld represents a *somatic* transformation is supported by current research indicating that these ancient Mesopotamian *descent* myths (e.g. *Descent of Ishtar to the Netherworld*) undergird later Gnostic *descent* myths, and as such both may be equally illuminating for the other. In particular, Mehmet-Ali Ataç has argued convincingly that these Mesopotamian myths are at the root of the later Manichaean cosmogonic myth of the luminous First Man to the Realm of Darkness ("Manichaeism and Ancient Mesopotamian 'Gnosticism'," ***JANER*** 5 [2006]: 1-39; see also Simo Parpola, "Mesopotamian Precursors of the Hymn of the Pearl," in R. M. Whiting [ed.] ***Mythology and Mythologies: Methodological Approaches to Intercultural Influences, Proceedings of the Second Annual Symposium of the Assyrian and Babylonian Intellectual Heritage Project Held in Paris, France, October 4-7, 1999*** [Melammu Symposia II; Helsinki: The Neo-Assyrian Text Corpus Project, 2001] 181-193). Manichaean cosmogonic myth begins with two coeval but antagonistic realms, the Real of Light (Good Realm) and the Real of Darkness (Evil Realm). The Lord of the Real of Light is the Father of Greatness, sends his first born son, the luminous First Man, who is a actually the Father at a secondary stage, down to the Realm of Darkness where he was 'devoured' and imprisoned by the darkness, becoming in the process "The Bright One in Darkness". As Ataç points out, "It is the Father of Greatness himself in his incarnation as the First Man who ultimately descends into the Realm of Darkness ("Manichaeism," 7). These two figures correspond well with An and Enki: An, the luminous Father, incarnates in his first born son, Enki, who is also luminous. When An 'ships off' Enki to the realm of darkness, it is actually he himself who descends. Like the Manichaean First Man, An-Enki becomes "the Bright One in Darkness." On the Manichaean First Man see Yuri Stoyanov, ***The Other God: Dualist Religions from Antiquity to the Cathar Heresy*** (New Haven and London: Yale University Press, 2000) 107-112; Hans Jonas, ***The Gnostic Religion: The Message of the Alien God & the Beginnings of Christianity*** (Boston: Beacon Press, 2001 [1958]).

[404] Translated in Rice, ***Archaeology of the Arabian Gulf***, 131.

temple is also said to "shine like the day," [405] a paradox which the 'Myth of the Black God' resolves beautifully.[406]

IV.1.3. *An-Enki* = *'Aḷah*

The 'resident god' of the Barbar Temple Complex in Eastern Arabia is thus the Black God of later Mesopotamian tradition. *En-ki*, "Lord of the Earth," is his Sumerian designation, though this is likely an epithet rather than a name. It is possible that he had an earlier, pre-Sumerian Semitic name. His Akkadian designation, *Ea*, is usually translated as 'House of Water.' But this is a Sumerian meaning, not Akkadian (in Sumerian *É-a* = House [*É*] of water [*a*]). Pointing this out Cyrus Gordon argues that Ea is actually a West Semitic name meaning "The Living One."[407] Samuel Noah Kramer suggests that Enki's Akkadian name *Ea* is actually pre-Sumerian, the name the Ubaidians gave this water-god. This too, however, seems to be an epithet rather than a name. The evidence indicates most clearly that his earliest Semitic name is the proto-Semitic *Aḷah*.

The cuneiform  is the Sumerian ideogram DINGIR indicating the god An and also the word 'god' in general and 'heaven/sky.' It has the phonetic value *an*. DINGIR often serves as a determinative for 'divinity' as well, affixed to a name to

---

405 Quoted in Langdon, "Two Sumerian Hymns," 163. It is also stated tat "The Temple of Eridu shines like the sun." Column III Line 21, Langdon translation page 171.

406 See True Islam, ***Truth of God***, Chapter V.

407 Cyrus Gordon, "Eblaitica," in Cyrus H. Gordon, Gary A. Rendsburg and Nathan H. Winter (edd.), ***Eblaitica: Essays on the Ebla Archives and Eblaite Language*** (Winona Lake, Indiana: Eisenbrauns, 1987) 19-20. Samuel Noah Kramer, ***In the World of Sumer: An Autobiography*** (Detroit: Wayne State University Press, 1986) 200-21. For an earlier attestation of Ea than previously thought see further Maria Vittoria Tonietti, "*É=Bītum* or = *'À*? About Ea in Early Dynastic Sources," in ***Semitic and Assyriological Studies Presented to Pelio Fronzaroli by Pupils an Colleagues*** (Wiesbaden: Harrassowitz Verlaq, 2003) 666-679. On the other hand Morris Jastrow Jr. saw the two as different deities, though this is unlikely: "Sumerian and Akkadian Views of Beginnings," ***JAOS*** 36 (1916) 294.

indicate that the name is that of a deity. As a determinative DINGIR is not pronounced and it appears in transliterations as a superscript 'd' (e.g. ^{d}ENKI).[408] DINGIR's Akkadian equivalent is . It has the same properties as the Sumerian: it indicates the god Anu, means as well 'god' in general, and serves as an unpronounced determinative for 'deity/divinity'. There is one critical difference, however: its phonetic value is **ʾḷ, i.e. the Proto**-Semitic *Aḷah*. In other words the Sumerian An is the same as the Akkadian **ʾḷ,**[409] **the Proto**-Semitic *Aḷah.* It has been demonstrated through theophorous names (names of individuals which include divine names in them) that **ʾḷ** is the predominant name of God in the Early Dynastic period amongst the Mesopotamian Semites, indicating that this Proto-Semitic deity was the chief deity.[410] There is therefore merit to Piotr Michalowski's suggestion that the divine pair that headed the early Mesopotamian pantheon, Enki and Ninhursag, are the same Il and Ashtar (read: *Aḷah and Aḷat*) of Early Dynastic Period.[411] Since  = the Sumerian An-Enki is identical with the Akkadian (thus Proto-Semitic) **ʾḷ** or *Aḷah.* In other words, AN-ENKI IS ALLAH. The resident deity of the Barbar Temple Complex in Eastern Arabia was therefore Allah, the Black God.

---

[408] Dietz Otto Edzard, ***Sumerian Grammar*** (Handbook of Oriental Studies 71; Atlanta: Society of Biblical Literature, 2003).
[409] Langdon, ***Semitic Mythology***, 65.
[410] I.J. Gelb, ***Old Akkadian Writing and Grammar*** (Materials for the Assyrian Dictionary [MAD] II; Chicago; University of Chicago Press, 1952) 6ff; idem, ***Glossary of Old Akkadian*** (MAD III, 1957) 26-36; J.J.M. Roberts, ***The Earliest Semitic Pantheon: A Study of Semitic Deities Attested in Mesopotamia before Ur III*** (Baltimore: John Hopkins University Pess, 1972) 31-35; ***TDOT*** 1:243 s.v.אל by F.M. Cross.
[411] Michalowski "Unbearable Lightness of Enlil," 245.

V. *From Afrabian* **'Aḷah** *to Egyptian* **Rah**

Yosef ben-Jochannan makes the following statement in his work, ***The Black Man's North and East Africa***:

> Should people of African origin have to continue compromising themselves to writings that profess a "SEMITIC JEHOVA" and/or "JESUS CHRIST," or even a "HAMITIC AL'LAH" as "…THE ONE AND ONLY TRUE GOD…"? No. Africans should be fully aware of the fact that "I AM" – the GOD RA…" of the Nile Valleys (Blue and White) and the Great Lakes regions of Alkebu-lan (Africa) predated all three of the other GODS mentioned before by thousands of years.[412]

In other words, because – according to ben-Jochannan – the Egyptian deity Rah predated the Islamic deity Allah (and Jehova and Jesus) by 'thousands' of years, African peoples have no business professing these Johnny-come-lately gods, profession that compromises us, presumably our 'African consciousness'. While strong in terms of cultural ideology, this claim is historically unreliable. Rah is mentioned in the Third Dynasty during the reign of Djoser (2635-2610 BCE) but doesn't come to prominence until the Pyramid Texts deriving from the Fifth Dynasty and dates to around 2400-2300 BCE.[413] We have

---

[412] Ben-Jochannan and Simmonds, ***Black Man's North and East Africa***, xiii.

[413] The earliest texts, those found in the tomb of Unis of the Fifth Dynasty, dates to ca. 2353-2323 BCE. See James P. Allen and Peter Der Manuelian, ***The Ancient Egyptian Pyramid Texts*** (Leiden: Brill, 2005) 1. Ben-Jochannan dates the *Book of the Dead*, which followed the Pyramid Texts, to 4100 BCE, but there is surely no evidence for such date. Hesy-Ra, the physician and scribe during the reign of Pharaoh Djoser (r. 2635-2610 BCE) has the phonetic spelling of Ra in his name. On the other hand, claims of a Second Dynasty date for the name Ra are unfounded. The Pharaoh called 'Raneb' (2852-2813 BC), i.e. 'The Lord is Ra', should actually be read as 'Lord of the Sun'. The inscription on his serekh features the sun-disk, not the phonetic 'Ra'. At that period the sun was identified with Atum and Ḥeru. As Rudolf Anthes notes: "The new concept of Re was the true successor of that of Horus…whatever we know of Re's mythological aspects and, mainly, his position as king was carried over from the earthly kingdom of Horus and from the concept of Atum." ("Egyptian Theology in the Third Millennium B.C.," ***JNES*** 18

demonstrated above that the Proto-Semitic language as reconstructed by linguists, which may have evolved anywhere from 9000 to 5000 BCE, included in its lexicon the name ***ʾḷh***, i.e. *ʾAḷah*, as the name of God.[414] Besides this Proto-Semitic evidence, the Semitic evidence is equally inconsistent with the above claim. The word ***ʾḷ*** appears at the top of a list of gods as the Ancient of Gods or the Father of all Gods in the ruins of the Royal Library of Ebla, in the archaeological site of Tell Mardikh in Syria dated to 2300 BCE.[415] The Akkadian evidence documents the name even earlier, to the Pre-Sargonic Period (2700-2600).[416] It cannot then be said that Rah predated Allah (as *ʾA****ḷah****)* "by thousands of years." Indeed, Rah is undoubtedly an Egyptianization of the Proto-Semitic *ʾA****ḷah.***

As described above, the Proto-Semites no doubt branched off in Western Asia (the Levant) – maybe around 9-8000 BCE – from an Afroasiatic stock that itself originated in Africa. Later, a group (or groups) of Afrabian (Kushite) Semites reentered North Africa – maybe around 6000 BCE – forming an important constituent part of the historic Egyptian population.[417] These Kushite Semites contributed to the language, art and religion of historic Egypt,[418] and may account for the obvious mythological and iconographic debt Egyptian civilization owes to Western

(1959): 181. We know that this pharaoh's name was not 'Raneb' because the Kings List list him as Kakau.

[414] William Sanford LaSor, "Proto-Semitic: Is the Concept No Longer Valid?" ***MAARAV*** 5-6 (Spring, 1990): 205 and above.

[415] Alfonso Archi, "*Il* in the Personal Names," ***Orientalistische Literaturzeitung*** 91 (1996): 138ff.

[416] Robert A. Di Vito, ***Studies in Third Millennium Sumerian and Akkadian Personal Names*** (Roma: Editrice Pontificio Istituto Biblico, 1993) 128; Archi, "*Il* in Personal Names"; Roberts, ***Earliest Semitic***, 31; ***TDOT*** 1:242-243 s.v. אל ʾēl.

[417] Steindorff and Seele, ***When Egypt Ruled the East***, 9-10.

[418] Elise J. Baumgartel, ***The Cultures of Prehistoric Egypt*** (London: Oxford University of Press, 1947) 119: "Interrelation between Egypt and certain centers of civilization in Western Asia must have existed at least since Naḳāda I times. Materials and with them spiritual possessions found their way from Asia to Egypt…"

Asia in many (though certainly not all or most) instances.[419] For example, aspects of the myth of Osiris clearly derive from West Asia. Already in 1922 Sidney Smith pointed out the parallels between the myths of Asar, Osiris's Egyptian name, and Assar, the Babylonian deity, parallels that "trade intercourse alone cannot be held to account for."[420] Not only are the names and aspects of their myth similar, but the hieroglyphs for their names too: both names are written with an eye and a throne.[421]

One particularly important mythological contribution these Afrabian Semites made to Egyptian religion is undoubtedly the introduction of the Sun God, *Rah*, to the Egyptian pantheon. He is explicitly documented only by the Fifth Dynasty when his priests became dominant and he ascended the top of the Heliopolitan pantheon.[422] The center of Rah's worship was called Annu, which the Greeks called 'Heliopolis,' meaning 'City of the Sun.' The city of Annu was founded by the Anu people, those Afrabians conquered by the Nubian 'Dynastic Race' which we encountered above. This fact alone should make the idea of Rah as an Afrabian introduction into Egypt unremarkable. E.A.

---

[419] Rice, ***Archaeology of the Arabian Gulf***, 324 suggests that the "Western Arabians were probably the carriers of many of the Asiatic influences which appear in late Predynastic Egypt". On this debt see H.S. Smith, "The Making of Egypt: A review of the influence of Susa and Sumer on Upper Egypt and Lower Nubia in the 4th millennium B.C" in Renée Friedman and Barbara Adams (edd.), ***The Followers of Horus: Studies dedicated to Michael Allen Hoffman 1944-1990*** (Oxbox Monograph 20. 1992) 235-246; Beatrice Teissier, "Glyptic Evidence for a Connection Between Iran, Syro-Palestine and Egypt in the Fourth and Third Millennia," ***Iran*** 25 (1987): 27-51; Helene J. Kantor, "Further Evidence for Early Mesopotamian Relations with Egypt," ***JNES*** 11 (1952) 239-250; Alexander H. Joffe, "Egypt and Syro-Mesopotamia in the 4th Millennium: Implications of the New Chronology," ***Current Anthropology*** 41 (2000): 113-123.

[420] Sidney Smith, "The Relation of Marduk, Ashur, and Osiris," ***Journal o Egyptian Archaeology*** 8 (1922): 41-44.

[421] Bojana Mojsov, ***Osiris: Death and Afterlife of a God*** (Malden, MA: Blackwell Publishing, 2005) 34.

[422] Stephen Quirke, ***The Cult of Ra: Sun-Worship in Ancient Egypt*** (New York: Thames & Hudson, 2001) 17, 82. See also George Hart, ***A Dictionary of Egyptian Gods and Goddess*** (London, Boston and Henley: Routledge & Kegan Paul, 1986) 180 s.v. Re.

Wallis Budge, in his study ***The Gods of the Egyptians***, informs us thus:

> In considering the struggle which went on between the followers of **Rā** and Osiris it is difficult not to think that there was some strong reason for the resistance which the priests of **Rā** met with from the Egyptians generally, and it seems as if the doctrine of **Rā** contained something which was entirely foreign to the ideas of the people. The city of Heliopolis appears always to have contained a mixed population, and its situation made it a very convenient halting-place for travelers passing from Arabia and Syria into Egypt and *vice versa*; it is, then, most probable that the doctrine of **Rā** as taught by the priests of Heliopolis was a mixture of Egyptian and Western Asiatic doctrines, and that it was the Asiatic element in it which the Egyptians resisted..It could not have bee sun-worship which they disliked, for they had been sun-worshippers from time immemorial.[423]

The myth and worship of Rah, like that of Osiris, seems indeed to have included elements derived from Afrabia. Budge is sure it is not sun-worship itself that is foreign, but his protégé and successor as Keeper of the Department of Egyptian and Assyrian Antiquities at the British Museum, Henry Reginald Hall, disagreed with his former teacher. In his great work, ***The Ancient History of the Near East***, Hall writes:

> while archaeology knows of no definite foreign invasion of the Nile Valley and (we) can with justification regard the whole of Egyptian culture as of (African) indigenous growth, a study of the religion does seem to shew a very early Semitic element.[424]

---

[423] E.A. Wallis Budge, ***The Gods of the Egyptians: Studies in Egyptian Mythology***, 2 vols. (New York: Dover Publications, Inc., 1969 [1904]) 334-335.
[424] Hall, ***Ancient History***, 86.

What are some of these 'Semitic elements' within Egyptian religion? The English Egyptologist and Assyriologist informs us, differing with his mentor:

> We find no trace of sun-worship in…the religious beliefs of the Neolithic Egyptians. It is the old veneration of the sacred animals…that are so characteristically Egyptian…the sun-god invaded from the East…He bore a Semitic name (Ra)…[425]

Nor did Egyptologist Elise J. Baumgartel, in her examination of Predynastic cultures, find any evidence of sun-worship. [426] Renowned American archaeologist, biblical scholar and linguist William Foxwell Albright made an important remark in his study, "Notes on Egypto-Semitic Etymology":

> The Egyptian Religion is the syncresis of African totemism and animism with Semitic nature worship…such divine names as…[Ra], Amun, Ptah, Min, ect. are almost certainly Semitic.[427]

While such terms as 'totemism' 'animisim,' and 'nature worship' are dated and inappropriate – not to say inaccurate – descriptions of African and Semitic religious traditions, the larger point appears sound: the sun-god of Egypt is an eastern deity with a Semitic name. American sociologist, historian and former chair of Stanford's African American Studies program, St. Clair Drake, in his landmark work, ***Black Folks Here and There***, suggests that Rah is "perhaps a solar god from Mesopotamia."[428] Rah's eastern origin seems confirmed by the Egyptian sources. In Papyrus Boulaq (17, II, 5) Amun-Re, the Sun-God, was called

---

[425] Hall, ***Ancient History***, 85.
[426] Elise J. Baumgartel, ***The Cultures of Prehistoric Egypt*** (London: Oxford University of Press, 1947) 47.
[427] ***American Journal of Semitic Linguistics and Literatures*** Volume 34, page 85
[428] ***Black Folk Here and There: An Essay in History and Anthropology***, 2 vols. (Los Angeles: University of California Center for Afro-American Studies, 1991 [1987]) I:177.

"the Beautiful-of-Face, who comes (from) Ta-Neter".[429] We have demonstrated that Ta-Neter is Afrabia. We have here what appears to be an acknowledgment of Rah's Afrabian derivation. But the Semitic solar deity was not named 'Rah,' it was ***Aḷah***.[430] We know that certain early hieroglyphics originally had Semitic values that were later Egyptianized.[431] Rah's hieroglyph no doubt conceals a Semitic original. The following is the hieroglyph for Rah:

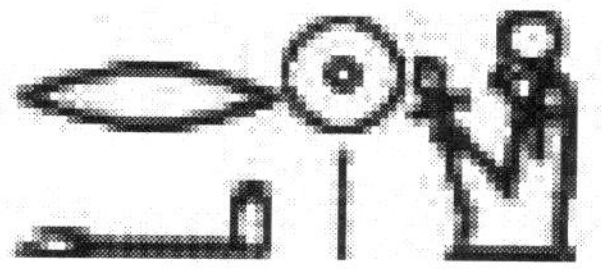

The disk, stroke and crouching figure are all determinatives. The only glyphs with phonetic value are thus[432]:

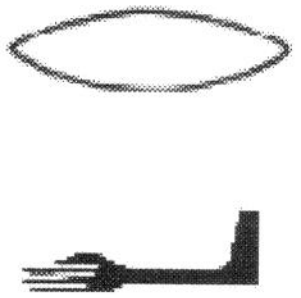

---

[429] Abdel-Aziz Saleh, "Notes on the Ancient Egyptian *T:-NṮR* 'God' Land'," ***Bulletin du centenaire. Supplement*** 1981, 107-117.
[430] See above and below.
[431] Ernst Zyhlarz, "Ursprung und. Sprachcharakter des Altägyptischen," ***Zeitschr für Eingeborenen Sprachen*** 23 (1932-3) 85ff; B.G. Trigger, "The Rise of Civilization in Egypt," in J. Desmond Clark (ed.), ***The Cambridge History of Africa, Volume I:From the Earliest Times to c. 500 BC*** (Cambridge: Cambridge University Press, 1982) 514; Roger D. Woodard, "Language in Ancient Syria-Palestine and Arabia: an introduction," in Roger D. Woodard (ed.), ***The Ancient Languages of Syria-Palestine and Arabia*** (Cambridge: Cambridge University Press, 2008) 3-4.
[432] Stéphane Rossini, ***Egyptian Hieroglyphics: How to Read and Write Them*** (New York: Dover Publications, 1989) 7.

The first glyph, the open mouth , is the Egyptian ‘r’, but it also doubles as ‘l’ *when translating or transliterating foreign words that include an ‘l’*.[433] Because Old Egyptian did not possess an ‘l’ phonetic value, when receiving foreign words that do, the foreign ‘l’ is converted to the Egyptian .[434] The second glyph, the forearm  transliterated as ‘, is a strong guttural sound like Arabic *‘ayn* or ‘ah’ sound,[435] equivalent to the Proto-Semitic ’, *ah*. Rah’s name thus possesses the same two phonemes as does the name of the Semitic solar deity, ***’ḷ*.** Underneath the hieroglyphic Rah is no doubt the Semitic *(a)lah.*

Rah had a female complement, Rat.[436] Like the Arabic al-Lah and al-Lat, the goddesses’ name is created simply by adding the feminine marker to the god’s name:

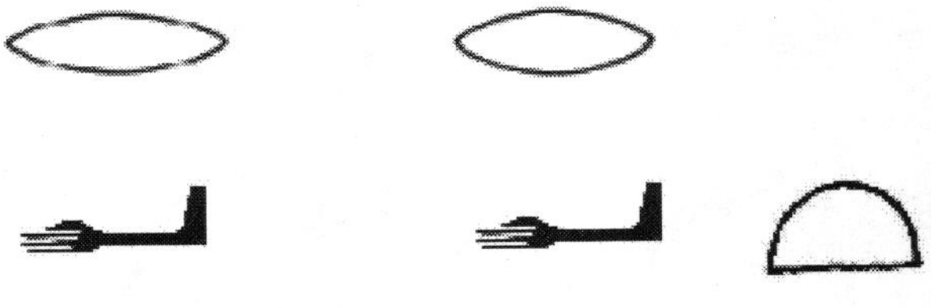

r’ (l’) *r’ t (l’t)*

Rah (Lah) ***Rat (Lat)***

---

[433] Sir Alan Gardiner, ***Egyptian Grammar, Being an Introduction to the Study of Hieroglyphics*** (Oxford: Griffith Institute, 1957 [1927]) 27; Sir E.A. Wallis Budge, ***Egyptian Language: Easy Lessons in Egyptian Hieroglyphics*** (New York: Dover Publications, 1966) 31

[434] Hilary Wilson, ***Understanding Hieroglyphics. A Complete Introductory Guide*** (New York: Barnes & Noble, 1993) 30, 32.

[435] Gardiner, ***Egyptian Grammar***, 27; Mark Collier and Bill Manley, ***How to Read Egyptian Hieroglyphics*** (Berkley and Los Angeles: University of California Press, 1998) 3.

[436] Budge, ***The Gods of the Egyptians*** ,287, 328; Françoise Dunand and Christiane Zivie-Coche, ***Gods and Men in Egypt: 3000 BCE to 395 CE*** (Ithaca and London: Cornell University Press, 2004) 25; Veronica Ions, ***Egyptian Mythology*** (Middlesex: Paul Hamlyn, 1968) 41.

Thus:

Alah (Al-Lah)	Alat (Al-Lat)
↓	↓
Rah	Rat

V.1. *Rah and the Myth of the Black God*

Further evidence of Rah's eastern origin is his myth, the main contours of which are clearly rooted in the 'new religion' of the Bull and Woman that developed in the Levant in the late Epipaleolithic/early Neolithic.[437] Rah's myth is based in the city of Annu (Heliopolis), where he was incorporated into the local divine triad: Khepri, Rah and Atum.[438] These were not viewed as separate deities but as 'transformations' (from the Egyptian word *kheper*, 'to come into being; to transform') of the singular solar deity.[439] Though Atum's name closes this triad, he actually opens the myth. Atum, whose name means 'the All,' was conceived both as "the *totality of being* before the creation set in motion,"[440] the "sum of all matter",[441] as well as that "internal,

[437] There is some evidence of the presence in Predynastic Egypt of the religion of the Bull and Woman: evidence of the worship of the mother goddess as cow and the male 'Bull of his mother'. See Rosalie David, ***Religion and Magic in Ancient Egypt*** (New York: Penguin Books. 2002) 54; Bojana Mojsov, ***Osiris: Death and Afterlife of a God*** (Malden, MA: Blackwell Publishing, 2005) 6-7.

[438] J. Gwyn Griffiths, "Triune Conceptions of God in Ancient Egypt," ***Zeitschrift für Ägyptische Sprache und Altertumskunde*** 100 (1973): 28-32; Pascal Vernus, ***The Gods of Ancient Egypt*** (London and New York: Tauris Parke Books, 1998) 45; David, ***Religion and Magic***, 58.

[439] Françoise Dunand and Christiane Zivie-Coche, ***Gods and Men in Egypt: 3000 BCE to 395 CE*** (Ithaca and London: Cornell University Press, 2004) 23: "Despite this tripartition…he was one."

[440] Dunand and Zivie-Coche, ***Gods and Men in Egypt***, 25.

[441] Quirke, ***Cult of Ra***, 25.

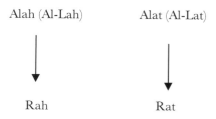

unconscious force, that became conscious of itself then manifested itself of its own will."[442] In other words, 'Atum' was the attribute given both to the dark, aquatic primordial matter – later to be called Nun – and the luminous force that resided hidden and unconscious within this matter.[443] At a certain point divine unconsciousness turned into divine consciousness and the divine luminosity concentrated itself into an atom, symbolized by the luminous egg within the dark ocean.[444] Compelled by his own will, the luminous aspect of Atum emerged – self propelled –

---

[442] Dunand and Zivie-Coche, ***Gods and Men in Egypt***, 47.

[443] On the dark primordial matter and divine luminosity within see Helmer Ringgren, "Light and Darkness in Ancient Egyptian Religion," in ***Liber amicorum. Studies in Honour of Professor Dr. C.J. Bleeker. Published on the Occasion of his Retirement from the Chair of the History of Religions and the phenomenology of Religion at the University of Amsterdam*** Leiden: E.J. Brill, 1969: 140-150; Dunand and Zivie-Coche, ***Gods and Men in Egypt***, 45-46; James P. Allen, "The Cosmology of the Pyramid Texts." In ***Religion and Philosophy in Ancient Egypt*** (New Haven: Yale Egyptological Series, 1989): 1-28.

[444] See E.A. Wallis Budge, ***The Egyptian Book of the Dead (The Papyrus of Ani). Egyptian Text Transliterated and Translated*** (New York: Dover Publications, Inc. 1967) xcviii, who quotes: "there was in the beginning neither heaven nor earth, and nothing existed except a boundless primeval mass of water which was shrouded in darkness and which contained within itself the germs or beginnings, male and female, of everything which was to be in the future world. The divine primeval spirit which formed an essential part of the primeval matter felt within itself the desire to begin the work of creation, and its word woke to life the world, the form and shape of which it had already depicted to itself. The first act of creation began with the formation of an egg out of the primeval water, from which broke forth Rā, the immediate cause of all life upon earth." On the cosmogonic egg in Egyptian tradition see further: Ringgren, "Light and Darkness," 141; Orly Goldwasser, " *'Itn* – the 'Golden Egg' (CT IV 292b-c [B9C[a]])," in ***Essays on Ancient Egypt in honour of Herman te Velde*** (Groningen: Styx, 1997): 79-84; Clifford, ***Creation Accounts***, 106, 112; R.T. Rundle Clark, ***Myth and Symbol in Ancient Egypt*** (London: Thames and Hudson, 1959) 56. On the cosmogonic egg see further Marie-Louise von Franz, ***Creation Myths*** revised edition (Boston and London: Shambhala, 1995), Chapter Eight ("Germs and Eggs"); ***ER*** 5:36-7 s.v. Egg by Venetia Newall; idem, ***An Egg at Easter: A Folklore Study*** (Bloomington: Indiana University Press, 1971) Chapter One; Anna-Britta Hellbom, "The Creation Egg," ***Ethnos*** 1 (1963): 63-105; H.J. Sheppard, "Egg Symbolism in Alchemy," ***Ambix*** 6 (August, 1958): 140-148; Philip Freund, ***Myths of Creation*** (New York: Washington Square Press, Inc, 1965), Chapter Five; Martti Haavio, ***Väinämöinen: Eternal Sage*** (Helsinki, 1952) 45-63; On the cosmic egg as *prima materia* see also C.G. Jung, ***Psychology and Alchemy*** (2nd ed.; Princeton: Princeton University Press, 1968) 202. On the golden cosmogonic egg and the primordial atom see Freund, ***Myths of Creation***, Chapter 15.

out of the dark, aquatic matter. This initial, luminous, self-emergent stage of the deity's evolution is personified in the god *Khepri*, represented symbolically/hieroglyphically as a scarab beetle. The scarab beetle's apparently spontaneous emergence out of a ball of dung symbolized the creator-god's self-creation out of the primordial matter – that is, the self-formation of his own luminous anthropomorphic body.[445] With this luminous human form in all its irradiant glory the creator-god is called Rah (Lah). The 'Rah stage' in this divine evolution is represented by the midday sun at its greatest strength.

Rah is then said to have 'entered back into' the primordial waters (which are now personified as the cow goddess Nut/Hathor/Meheturet[446]) and assumed from them a black body: he is now the black, anthropomorphic god Atum (again).[447] Atum of the triad is Rah (Lah) himself, incarnat in a black body made from the primordial waters.[448] In later myth this black aquatic body of Rah is personified in the black deity Osiris, whose black body itself is represented by the black bull Apis, the

---

445 Hart, ***Dictionary***, 108-110 s.v. Khepri. On Atum-Rah as self-created creator-god see e.g. the inscription from Thebean Tomb 157: "O Rēʿ who gave birth to righteousness, sovereign who created all this, who built his limbs, who modeled his body, who created himself, who gave birth to himself." See further J. Zandee, "The Birth-Giving Creator-God in Ancient Egypt," in Alan B. Lloyd (ed.), ***Studies in Pharaonic Religion and Society, in Honour of J. Gwyn Griffiths*** London: The Egypt Exploration Society, 1992: 168-185; Dunand and Zivie-Coche, ***Gods and Men in Egypt***, 47-49.

446 On Hathor/ Meheturet as 'universal cow-goddess' and primordial ocean see Hart, ***Dictionary***, 76 s.v. Hathor. Vernus, ***Gods of Ancient Egypt***, 79.

447 On Rah re-entering the primordial waters and becoming Atum (again) see Dunand and Zivie-Coche, ***Gods and Men in Egypt***, 27, 45-46; Vernus, ***Gods of Ancient Egypt***, 45. On Rah darkening and transforming into Atum see See Ringgren, "Light and Darkness," 150; Karl W.Luckert, ***Egyptian Light and Hebrew Fire. Theological and Philosophical Roots of Christendom in Evolutionary Perspective*** (Albany: State University of New York Press, 1991) 73. On Atum as a black god see Jules Taylor, "The Black Image in Egyptian Art," ***Journal of African Civilization*** 1 (April, 1979) 29-38.

448 When Rah enters the dark, aquatic Duat or Underworld, he is actually assuming the dark form of Atum, who is therefore called *Auf-Rah*, 'the flesh of Rah'. See Quirke, ***Cult of Ra***, 48; Ions, ***Egyptian Mythology***, 42-43; Alexandre Piankoff, and N. Rambova. ***The Tomb of Ramesses VI: Texts***. (Bollingen Series XL; New York: Pantheon Books, 1954) 36-37.

personification of the primordial waters.[449] The Egyptian Rah-Atum is thus equivalent to the Mesopotamian An-Enki. Atum, like Enki, is a duality, the *Coniunctio oppositorum*: in the Pyramid Texts he is both *Wbn-wrr*, "the Great One who shines forth," as well as "Father Atum who is in Darkness".[450] This duality is illustrated further by the hieroglyph for 'flood': it is a heron bird perched on a stick, an allusion to the common sight during the summer high Nile of birds clinging to wood. The heron is the sign of the Benu bird, the primeval bird of Rah-Atum.[451] The Benu embodies the radiance emanating from the sun.[452] This hieroglyph is consistent with other Egyptian sources which affirm that the Benu bird presides over the flood. We thus have symbolized in this hieroglyph the conjunction of the solar and the aquatic.[453] Atum, like Enki, *is* the conjunction between the solar (Rah) and the aquatic (primordial waters).

---

[449] The myth of Rah joining Osiris in the Duat or Underworld is actually a picturesque way of presenting Rah's incarnation in the black body, personified in Osiris, ruler of the Duat. The Duat represents the primordial waters and is explicitly identified with the black body of Osiris. See: Allen, "Cosmology," 21; Hans-Peter Hasenfratz, "Patterns of Creation in Ancient Egypt," in Henning Graf Reventlow and Yair Hoffman (edd.), ***Creation in Jewish and Christian Tradition*** (JSOTSup 319; Sheffield: Sheffield Academic Press, 2002) 176; Jan Assmann, ***The Search for God in Ancient Egypt***, translated from the German by David Lorton (Ithaca and New York: Cornell University Press, 2001) 41; idem, ***Death and Salvation in Ancient Egypt***, translated from the German by David Lorton (Ithaca and London: Cornell University Press, 2005) 188; Clark, ***Myth and Symbol***, 158; Martin Lev and Carol Ring, "Journey of the Night Sun," ***Parabola*** 8 (1983): 14-18; Terence DuQuesne, "Re' in the Darkness," ***Discussions in Egyptology*** 26 (1993): 96-105; Albert Churchward, ***Signs & Symbols of Primordial Man: The Evolution of Religious Doctrines from the Eschatology of the Ancient Egyptians*** (Brooklyn: A&B Publishers Group, 1994, reprint) 63-66, 274-6, 322. On Apis, the black bull (*k' km*) of Egypt, as the personified waters of the Nile which was regarded as a type of Nun, the dark, primeval watery mass out of which creation sprang see Émile Chassinat, "La Mise a Mort Rituelle D'Apis," ***Recueil de travaux relatifs a la philology et a l'archeologie egyptiennes et assyriennes*** 38 [1916] 33-60; Budge, ***Book of the Dead***, cxxiii. On the black-skinned Osiris and the black bull Apis see also Vos, "Varius Coloribus Apis," 716; idem, "Apis," ***DDD*** 70.

[450] Ringgren, "Light and Darkness," 142.

[451] George Hart, ***A Dictionary of Egyptian Gods and Goddesses*** (London, Boston and Henley: Routledge & Kegan Paul, 1986) 57-58 s.v. Benu.

[452] Quirke, ***Cult of Ra***, 28.

[453] Quirke, ***Cult of Ra***, 29-30.

As we would expect, Rah-Atum is the Black Bull. An inscription fragment from the Hatshepsut Temple at Deir el-Bahri records an invocation to Rah: "Rise, rise: shine, shine. Ascend, O he who emerges from his egg (atom), Lord of Appearances, Primeval God of the Two Lands, the Bull of Iunu (Annu)".[454] Rah-Atum is represented on earth in the Menwer or Mnevis Bull ("Meni the Great"), called the "Great Black," *Kemwer*, because his hide was totally black and there was a sun disk and Uraeus between his horns.[455] The Woman in this Egyptian articulation of the Levantine 'new religion' is Nut/Hathor, the primordial waters personified in the cow goddess.[456] Hathor's Egyptian name – Het-Heru – literally means 'House of Horus,' Horus being another manifestation of Rah the solar deity.[457] This motif of Hathor (primordial waters) as the 'house' of the deity parallels the Mesopotamian motif of Nammu (primordial waters), Enki's mother, as his temple-residence. The primordial cow-goddess (Nut/Hathor) is described as mother, wife and daughter of Rah,[458] just as Nammu is both Enki's mother and wife.[459] The Woman's other name in Egypt is Rat, the feminine complement to Rah.

It is therefore clear that the Egyptian solar deity Rah and his basic myth originated in Afrabia east of the Red Sea and is an *Egyptianization* of the Proto-Semtic/Semitic deity ('A)ḷah, just as Ilu is a *Babylonianization* and Eloah (Elohim) is a *Hebrewization* of

---

[454] Stephen Quirke, ***The Cult of Ra: Sun-Worship in Ancient Egypt*** (New York: Thames & Hudson, 2001) 55.
[455] Conrad, ***Horn and the Sword***, 76; Quirke, ***Cult of Ra***, 109; Hart, ***Dictionary***, 125-126 s.v. Mnevis; Ions, ***Egyptian Mythology***, 40, 123.
[456] On Hathor as universal mother, primordial cow and "female complement of the solar creator," see Ions, ***Egyptian Mythology***, 78; Quirke, ***Cult of Ra***, 31.
[457] Hart, ***Dictionary***, 76 s.v. Hathor; ibid., 94 s.v. Horus.
[458] Quirke, ***Cult of Ra***, 31; Hart, ***Dictionary***, 76 s.v. Hathor; ibid., 145 s.v. Nut; Alexander Piankoff, "The Sky-Goddess Nut and the Night Journey of the Sun," ***Journal of Egyptian Archaeology*** 20 (1934) 57-60.
[459] See above.

the same deity.[460] Local area linguistic innovations over time have obscured the fact that at the root of all of these divine names is the Proto-Semitic divine name that will be retained in the Arabic as: Aḷḷāh. Such claims that the Egyptian Rah predated the Semitic Aḷḷāh by "thousands of years" is therefore completely unwarranted.

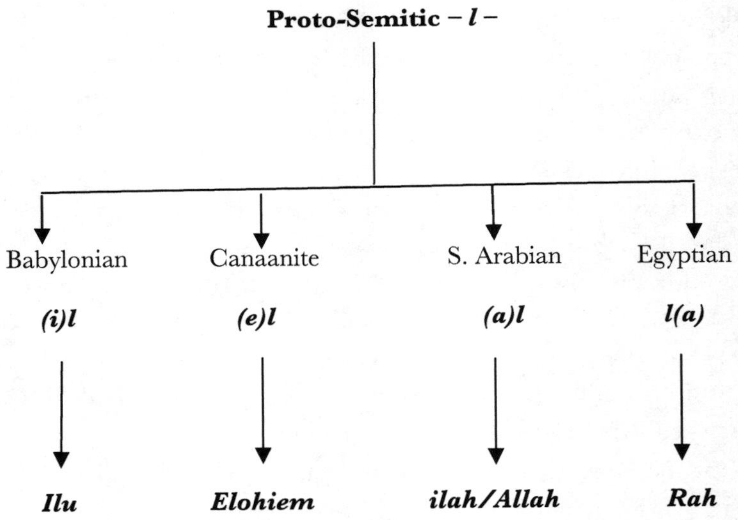

[460] D. Pardee remarks that "The Hebrew word ***ʾĕlōah*** is derived from a base ***ʾilāh,*** perhaps a secondary form of the common Semitic word ***ʾil-***, 'god'...The word ***ʾĕlōah...***shows the characteristic Canaanite shift of /ā/ to /ō/." ***DDD***, 285-86 s.v. Eloah אלה.

Chapter Four

Aḷḷāh: Black God of Pre-Qur'ānic Arabia

"The most disastrous of all colonizations of the oppressor is the colonization of the image of God."

Dr. John Henrik Clarke

I. *Aḷḷāh Derived From Allāt?*

According to ben-Jochannan the Islamic god Aḷḷāh was 'launched' in Arabia by the Arabian prophet Muḥammad b. 'Abd Allāh, who apparently (according to ben-Jochannan) converted the female goddess Allāt into the male god Aḷḷāh.[462] The implication is of course that before Muḥammad replaced the female deity Allāt with his own creation, the male god Aḷḷāh, no one worshipped the latter.[463] Hindu nationalist Purushottan Negesh Oak likewise suggests that the male Aḷḷāh derived from the early goddess.[464] This is a most unfortunate historical reconstruction in that, while it is completely disproven by linguistic, epigraphic and historical data, it nonetheless is frequently repeated in some Afrocentrist circles. But as pioneering Canadian scholar of Islam Arthur Jeffrey points out:

---

[462] Yosef A.A. ben-Jochannan and George Simmonds, ***The Black Man's North and East Africa*** (Baltimore: Black Classic Press, 2005 [1971]) 25; Yosef ben-Jochannan, ***African Origins of the Major "Western Religions"*** (The Black Man's Religion, Volume I; Baltimore: Black Classic Press, 1991 [1970]) 212, 213.

[463] Wayne B. Chandler makes the same unwarranted claim, quoting from the non-Arabist and non-Islamicist Amaury de Riencourt's critique of feminism, ***Sex and Power in History*** (New York: Dell Publishing, 1974). See Chadler's article "Ebony and Bronz: Race and Ethnicity in Early Arabia and the Islamic World," in Rashidi and Sertima, ***African Presence***, 272.

[464] P.N. Oak, ***World Vedic Heritage: A History of Histories***, 2 vols. (3rd Edition; New Delhi: Hindi Sahitya Sadan, 2003) I:696.

"The name Allah… was well known in *pre-Islamic* Arabia. Indeed, both it and its feminine form, Allat, are found not infrequently among the theophorous names in inscriptions from North Arabia."[465] The male and female pair **A̤l̤l̤āh**/Allāt coexisted in Arabia before Mu**ḥ**ammad's time, with Allah receiving recognition as supreme creator deity. Western Islamicist and historian from the University of Minnesota, Caesar E. Farah, affirms that "Allah, the paramount deity *of pagan Arabia*, was the target of worship in varying degrees of intensity from the southernmost tip of Arabia to the Mediterranean."[466] Samuel M. Zwemer notes as well: "But history establishes beyond a shadow of a doubt that even the pagan Arabs, *before Mu**ḥ**ammad's time*, knew their chief god by the name of **A̤l̤l̤āh**, and even, in a sense, proclaimed his unity."[467]

British Islamicist William Montgomery Watt has shown that **A̤l̤l̤āh**, before the time of Mu**ḥ**ammad, was what students of comparative religion know as a 'high god.' This means that while only one of several gods whose existence was acknowledged, **A̤l̤l̤āh** was the supreme deity over the others.[468] One of these subordinate gods was in fact the goddess Allat, who was considered both the feminine complement of the male **A̤l̤l̤āh** and his 'daughter', just as we would expect by now.[469] To suggest that

---

[465] ***Islam: Muhammad and His Religion*** (New York: The Liberal Arts Press, 1958) 85.

[466] Caesar E. Farah, ***Islam: Beliefs and Observances*** (Hauppauge, NY: Barron's, 2003 [1965]) 28.

[467] Samuel M. Zwemer, ***The Muslim Doctrine of God*** (1924) 24.

[468] Montgomery W. Watt, "The Qur'ân and Belief in a High God," ***Der Islam*** 56 (1979): 205-211; idem, "Pre-Islamic Arabian Religion in the Qur'an," 15 (1976): 73-79; idem, "Belief in a '***high god***' in pre-Islamic Mecca', ***Journal of Semitic Studies***, 16 (1971): 35-40.

[469] Thus Jacques Ryckmans, French historian of Pre-Islamic Arabia, writing on the gods of Pre-Islamic North Arabia notes: "Al-Ilāt or Allāt ("the Goddess"), was known to all pantheons. She is daughter or a consort, depending on the region, of al-Lāh or Allāh, Lord of the Kaʿbah in Mecca": ***Encyclopedia Britannica*** 2004 s.v. Arabian Religion

Muḥammad somehow 'converted' the female deity Allāt into the male Aḷḷāh is completely without warrant.

Prophet Muḥammad did not 'launch' Aḷḷāh or his worship in Arabia. Second century CE inscriptions from Sumatra Harabesi in the Tektek mountains, Edessa Syria, document this. At an Arab sanctuary the 'governor of the Arabs (*šalīṭā' a-'arab*)' left the following inscription dated to 165 CE:

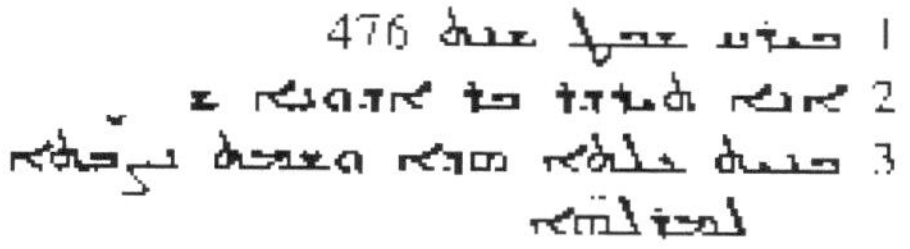

(2) I, Tiridates, son of Adona, governor of 'Arab, (3) built this altar and set up a pillar for *Mār 'Allāhā*, *'Lord Allah'*[470]

In another Sumatra inscription, dated to the mid-2nd century CE, we read what sounds like an ancient Qur'anic passage:

I, Allāh
See him
I see him
and behold

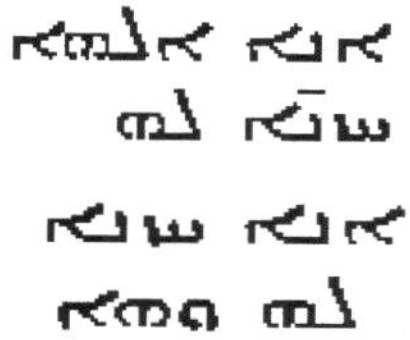

These inscriptions are 400 years prior to the beginning of Muḥammad's reform movement in Mecca. But there are more, earlier examples as well. Evidence of the worship of Allah in

by Jacques Ryckmans. See further: F. V. Winnett, "The Daughters of Allah," ***Moslem World*** 30 (1940): 113-130.

[470] Retsö, ***Arabs in Antiquity***, 441, 616 n. 5; Han J.W. Drijvers and John F. Healey, ***The Old Syriac Inscriptions of Edessa and Osrhoene: Texts, Translation and Commentary*** (Leiden: Brill, 1999) 104.

ancient Arabia has been found in both the Northern and Southern portions of the peninsula. It is most documented for the Liḥyan tribe in Northern Arabia. Four hundred Liḥyanite and Dedanite inscriptions dating back to the fifth century BCE were found in the Nejd (Central Arabia). In these inscriptions are invocations to Allah. For example:

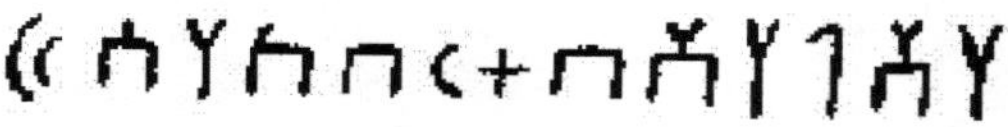

H'lh 'btr bk hsrr
'O Alah, (god) without offspring; in Thee be joy'[471]

F.V. Winnet, who has translated these inscriptions, lists others in his article, "Allah Before Islam."

> *O Allah, permit me to accomplish salvation…*
> *O Allah, God without offspring, greeting*
> *O Allah, guide me that I may attain prosperity…*
> *O Allah, God without offspring, knower of men…*[472]

Aḷḷāh is called in these inscriptions "The Exalted": *Give favor to this rock, O Exalted Allah.*[473]

This Lihyanite inscriptional material gives evidence of an early Aḷḷāh cult center 1100 years *before Muḥammad.* And who were the **Banū Liḥyān**? According to al-**Ṭabarī** the **Banū Liḥyān** were the survivors of Jurhum, one of the twelve original Kushite

---

[471] F.V. Winnett, ***A Study of the Lihyanite and Thamudic Inscriptions*** (Toronto: University of Toronto Press, 1937) Plate IV.
[472] F. Winnet, "Allah Before Islam," ***The Moslem World*** 28 (1938): 243.
[473] F. Winnet, ***A Study of The Lihyanite and Thamudic Inscriptions*** (Toronto: University of Toronto Press, 1937) 27.

tribes in Mecca.[474] They were a division of the ancient tribe Hudhayl in the northern vicinity of Mecca and al-**Ṭ**ā'if, of whom the ***Encyclopedia of Islam*** describes: "Their skins were black and shinning; their looks...were not hollow but round and teeming."[475] This was an ancient center of *Black* worshippers of A**ḻḻ**āh that preceded Mu**ḥ**ammad in Arabia by over a millennium. The evidence for the cult of A**ḻḻ**āh in Arabia, however, does not begin with the Li**ḥ**yanites, as we saw, but goes back to the Proto-Semites.

II. *Ancient Temples of the Black God Aḻḻāh*

In the 1950's American archaeologist Wendell Phillips and his team from the American Foundation for the Study of Man (AFSM) excavated the remains of a huge temple complex in Mārib (in today's Republic of Yemen), which was the capital of the ancient kingdom of Sa'ba. Called today the Awwām Temple, the Sun Temple, and Ma**ḥ**ram Bilqīs (Temple of the Queen of Sheba), this excavated complex is the largest temple complex so far discovered in South Arabia and is dedicated to the national god of the ancient Sabaeans, 'Almaqah. It includes an oval-shaped precinct around 30 feet high, 300 feet long and 250 feet broad. There had once been 32 pillars, each about 4.25 m tall, surrounding a precinct, and there were (are) eight massive columns standing outside of the oval wall (Figure 31). Parts of the complex originated in the 7th century BCE, while others seem to go back to the second millennium BCE (1500-1200 BCE). This huge temple complex shows remarkable architectural skill, as pointed out by international journalist Joël Donnet, who covered the most recent excavations:

---

[474] Ed. de Goeje, ***Annales***, 749.
[475] "Hudhayl," ***Encyclopedia of Islam***, 3:540.

The engineering required of the ancient builders to erect these eight monoliths – each of them much heavier than 10 tons – is as impressive as that needed to build the biggest monuments of the Ancient Times, such as the Great Pyramid of Giza or the Acropolis in Athens. This explains why Bill Glanzman[476] doesn't hesitate to call it the "eighth wonder of the world" and the Yemeni government wishes to have the site included on the UNESCO's World Heritage List…[477]

Figure 31
The eight massive columns or pillars of the Awwām Temple

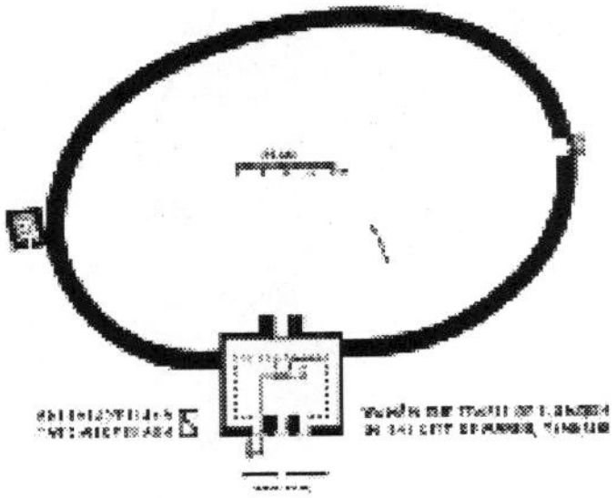

Figure 32
Ground plan showing oval wall

[476] Dr. Bill Glanzman is a professor at the University of Calgary, Canada, and AFSM field director during the last four years.
[477] Joël Donnet, "Looking for the Queen of Sheba," http://pagesperso-orange.fr/joel.donnet/News115.htm. Accessed August 15, 2009.

Between 1988 and 1997 the German Institute of Archaeology uncovered another temple complex dedicated to the Sabaean deity ʿAlmaqah. Called the Barʾān Temple or ʿArsh Bilqīs ("The Throne of the Queen of Sheba"), this complex is located in the ancient city of Ṣirwāh, which lies 40 kms to the west of the ancient city of Mārib. The Barʾān Temple is conspicuous by the five pillars, the tallest in southern Arabia, that rise from the temple altar (Figure 33). The excavated ruins give evidence of five different building phases, the second oldest of which is radiocarbon dated to the 9th century BCE, which means the temple actually originated some time before that, maybe in the second millennium BCE.[478]

Figure 33
Barʾān Temple ruins

[478] Jochen Görsdorf and Burkhardt Vogt, "Radio Carbon Datings from the Almaqah Temple of Bar'an, Ma'rib, Republic of Yemen: Approximately 800 CAL BC to 600 CAL AD," ***Radiocarbon*** 43 (2001): 1363-1369.

These two ʾAlmaqah temples are profoundly important, not just for the religious history of Pre-Qurʾānic Arabia, but also for the development of Islam. The Awwām Temple, for example, evinces "strong currents of continuity between ancient South Arabia and early Islam."[479] It was no ordinary temple but, like the Kaʿba in Mecca, a *ḥaram*, a sanctified 'protected zone' within which certain things were forbidden and where contending parties could peacefully settle disputes.[480] There was an annual pilgrimage to this ʾAlmaqah temple, similar to the Muslim Hajj.[481] As shown by William D. Glanzman, archaeologist from the University of Calgary who studied the temple ruins:

> The parallels to Islamic sacred places are so strong that we can assert that the origins of many Islamic practices within religious complexes of the Middle East can be found in pre-Islamic times within South Arabia. At the Maḥram Bilqīs that origin extends back in time at least to the late second millennium B.C.[482]

The continuity between these temples and Post-Qurʾānic Islam[483] is not restricted to concepts of sacred space. The name of the god to whom these temples were dedicated is in Epigraphic South Arabian written 𐩱𐩡𐩣𐩤𐩠 ʾLMQH. This name is traditionally vocalized as *ʾAlmaqah* or *Ilmuqah* but, as Julian Baldick reminds us, this is "a *purely conventional* vocalization (emphasis added),"[484] because the vowels were unsupplied. On

---

[479] William D. Glanzman, "Who Put the 'Ḥaram' in the Maḥram Bilqīs," in Elizabeth C. Robertson et al (edd.), ***Space and Spatial Analysis in Archaeology*** (Farmington Hills, Michigan: Gale Group, 2006) 97.

[480] Glanzman, "Who Put the 'Ḥaram'."

[481] Daniel McLaughlin, ***Yemen*** (Guillford, CT: The Globe Pequot Press, 2008) 144.

[482] Glanzman, "Who Put the 'Ḥaram'," 103.

[483] By Post-Qurʾānic Islam I mean Islam as it developed after the revelation of the Qurʾān to the Prophet Muḥammad during the 610-632. Pre-Qurʾānic Islam refers to Islam as it existed before this revaltion.

[484] Baldick, ***Black God***, 25.

the other hand Werner Daum and others, based on more recent data, have now made it clear that we are dealing with two words, the first of which is *'l*, the Proto- and Common Semitic name of 'God'.[485] In other words these were temples of the Proto-Semitic supreme god, *'Aḷah.*[486] According to Daum the second word of 'LMQH, *mqh*, is likely the participle form, *muqah*, of *taqahwa* ("to drink"), and thus means 'The intensively watering one.'[487] We thus have a name and an epithet: *'Aḷah Muqah* or *'Aḷah*, The Intensively Watering One. This South Arabian *'Aḷah Muqah* is a water-deity that was associated with a well,[488] similar to the resident god of the Barbar Temple in eastern Arabia and An-Enki (=Akkadian *'l*) of Mesopotamia.[489] In *'Aḷah Muqah*'s Bar'ān Temple ('Arsh Bilqīs) there was a ritual well, similar to that found in the Barbar Temple where it is believed to have represented the primordial waters.[490] The deity of the Barbar Temple, just as is the case with the Mesopotamian An-Enki (Akkadian *'l*), was represented by the Bull and ibex. *'Aḷah Muqah* likewise has as his primary attribute animal the Bull.[491] The Awwām Temple,

---

485 Daum, ***Ursemitische Religion***, 78-80; ***The Encyclopaedia Of Islam*** (New Edition), edd. C. E. Bosworth, E. van Donzel, W. P. Heinrichs & G. Lecomte, (Leiden: E. J. Brill, 1995) VIII: 664-665 s.v. Saba' by A. F. L. Beeston.

486 On 'A' as the opening vowel here rather than 'I' (i.e. *Ilmuqah*) see Daum, ***Ursemitische Religion***, 77, 78.

487 Daum, ***Ursemitische Religion***, 78-80. Beeston ("Saba'," 664) also connects this term with the root *k̲hw* meaning something like "fertility," related to the Arabic *kahā* "flourish".

488 Werner Daum, "A Pre-Islamic Rite in South Arabia," ***Journal of the Royal Asiatic Society*** (1987): 5-13.

489 On "'Almaqah" as a god of irrigation see ***Encyclopedia Britannica*** [2004] s.v. Arabian Religion by Jacques Ryckmans.

490 Rice, ***Archaeology of the Arabian Gulf***, 159; Ministry if Information, ***Barbar***, 7, 13.

491 Wendell Phillips, ***Qataban and Sheba: Exploring the Ancient Kingdoms on the Biblical Spice Routes of Arabia*** (New York: Harcourt Brace and Company, 1955) 299; J. Ryckmans, „Notes sur le rôle du taureau dans la religion sud-arabe," in ***Melanges D'Islamologie dédiés à la mémoire de A. Abel par ses collègue, ses élèves et ses amis***, Volume II (Brussels: Publication du Centre pour l'Etude des Problèmes du Monde Musulman Contemporain, 1977) 355-373; Jean François Breton,

according to an inscription there, was dedicated to *ʾAḷah Muqah Thahwān* or *ʾAḷah*, The Intensively Watering One, The Bull.[492] He is frequently depicted also as a black ibex with a human face and beard and called *shaība*, 'old man.'[493] This recalls the ibex-human deity on a fourth millennium BCE seal discussed by Franz Wiggerman and possibly associated by Piotre Michalowski with An-Enki.[494] *ʾAḷah Muqah Thahwān*, Daum has demonstrated, was a black god whose symbols – the black bull/ibex and black rain clouds – connoted his dark appearance.[495]

The Barbar Temple/South Arabia/Mesopotamia nexus suggested above is further strengthened by the architecture: both the Babar Temple of East Arabia and the Awwām Temple of South Arabia share the same peculiar oval-shaped wall, which is also found with the very early Sumerian temple complexes such as at al-Ubaid and Khafajah (Figure 34).[496] What is suggested here is that this peculiar sacred architecture and its peculiar resident deity – the supreme Black Bull/Water God – was indigenous to the same people who spread all over Arabia, north and south, then into Mesopotamian and further into India, where the Black Bull/Water God was also supreme,[497] and west

---

Arabia Felix from the Time of the Queen of Sheba: Eighth Century B. C. to First Century A. D. (Notre Dame, Indiana: University of Notre Dame Press, 2000) 120, 124.

492 St John Simpson, ***Queen of Sheba: Treasures from Ancient Yemen (London:*** British Museum Press, Jul 2002) 62-63; Breton, ***Arabia Felix***, 120.

493 Daum, ***Ursemitische Religion***, 64, 68-70.

494 Wggermann, "Discussion," 87-89; Michalowski, "Unbearable Lightness," 244.

495 Daum, ***Ursemitische Religion***, 99; Daum, "Pre-Islamic Rite," 9; Baldick, ***Black God***, 21.

496 See Rice, ***Archaeology of the Arabian Gulf***, 169; Ministry of Information, ***Barbar***, 9.

497 Conrad, ***Horn and the Sword***, Chapter Three; Asko Parpola, "Religion Reflected in the Iconic Signs of the Indus Script: Penetrating into Long-Forgotten Picto+Graphic Messags," ***Visible Religion*** 6 (1988): 114-127; Alt Hiltebeitel, "The Indus Valley 'Proto-Śiva', Reexamined through Reflections on the Goddess, the Buffalo, and the Symbolism of *vāhanas*," ***Anthropos*** 73 (1978): 767-797; Doris Srinivasan, "The So-Called Proto-Śiva Seal from Mohenjo Daro: An Iconological Assessment," ***Archives of Asian Art*** 29 (1975-76): 47-58; Wayne B. Chandler, "The Jewel in the Lotus: The Ethiopian Presence in the Indus Valley Civilization," in Runoko Rashidi and Ivan Van

into Egypt, bringing there the same deity and possibly architecture.[498]

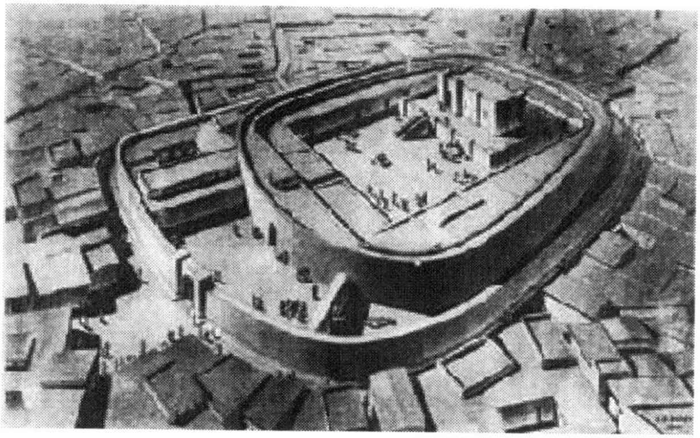

Figure 34
A reconstruction by Hamilton C. Darby of a Mesopotamian temple (Khafajah) from the early half of the third millennium B.C. excavated by the Iraq expedition of the Oriental Institute of the University of Chicago.

While the Bull/Water deity of the Barbar Temple remains for now unnamed, the cognate deity of the South Arabian temples is named *ʾAḷah* and he carries at least two epithets, *Muqah* and *Thahwān*, identifying him as the aquatic bull deity. The Mesopotamian Semites also identified the Bull/Water god with *ʾAḷah*, as did the Canaanites.[499] It is therefore not surprising that a number of scholars recognize the continuity between this deity and the Qurʾānic/Post- Qurʾānic Aḷḷāh. Egerton Sykes suggests

Sertima (edd.), ***African Presence in Early Presence*** (New Brunswick and London: Transaction Publishers, 1995) 97.

[498] On the very peculiar and "un-Egyptian" oval temple enclosure found in Hierakonpolis in Upper Egypt see Rice, ***Archaeology of the Arabian Gulf***, 169-170.

[499] See Julian Baldick regarding the Canaanite *ʾl*: "It appears that originally El was the real water-god of Canaanite religion, and that the Sea is to be perceived as an emanation from him…It is to be noted that in the myths of Ugarit El is called a bull - an animal who often represents the 'black god'. ***Black God***, 39.

that the Islamic Allah "seems to have been preceded by *Ilmaqah*,"[500] and highly influential German historian Ditlef Nielsen, in his 1922 study of the South Arabian pantheon, affirmed:

> …the divine father simply bears the name *Il* "God"…upon whom the entire life of the old Arabians completely depended…The ethical character of this Arabian high god can finally no longer be in dispute…this god still lives on as Allah in the Koran and Islam.[501]

The attributes of this South Arabian *ʾḷ* or *ʾAḷah* confirm continuity with the Islamic Aḷḷāh. The latter is often invoked as الله تعالى ***Aḷḷāh** taʿ**ālā*** ("God [**Aḷḷāh**] Most High"), which was already anticipated in the South Arabic description of *ʾḷ* as ***ʾl tʿly ʾAḷah*** Most High.[502] Similarly, the Pre-Qurʾānic motif of the 'Daughters of Aḷḷāh' – Allāt, al-ʿUzzā, and al-Manāt – is anticipated in the South Arabic 'Daughters of ***ʾḷ***,' Allāt, al-ʿUzzā and Manāt (?)[503]: "…the so-called 'Daughters of Il'…correspond to the 'Daughters of Allah' of pre-Islamic Mekka," Ryckmans informs us.[504] There is therefore no doubt that this ancient

---

500 Egerton Sykes, ***Dictionary of Non-Classical Mythology*** London: J.M. Dent & Sons, 1961) 7 s.v. Allah.

501 Ditlef Nielsen, ***Der Dreieinige Gott In Religionshistorischer Beleuchtung***, (Gyldendalske boghandel, Nordisk forlag, 1922) volume I: 86, 148. On the Qurʾānic Aḷḷāh as identical with the "old Ilāh" or Il of ancient South Arabia see also Langdon, ***Semitic Mythology***, 5. On *Allah*'s relation to *ʾl* and the Ugaritic "El" see also Finn O. Hvidberg-Hansen, "Fra El til Allah," in Frede Løkkegaard, Egon Keck, Svend Søndergaard, Ellen Wulff (edd.), ***Living waters: Scandinavian orientalistic studies presented to Frede Løkkegaard on his seventy-fifth birthday, January 27th 1990*** (Copenhagen: Museum Tusculanum Press, 1990) 113-127.

502 Oldenburg, "Above the Stars of El," 189-190; Arthur Jeffery, ***The Foreign Vocabulary of the Qur'an*** (Baroda: Oriental Institute, 1938) 60-67.

503 While it is not clear if Manāt was considered a 'daughter of *ʾḷ*', she is a part of the South Arabian pantheon. See Langdon, ***Semitic Mythology***, 20.

504 ***Encyclopedia Britannica*** [2004] s.v. Arabian Religion by Jacques Ryckmans.

Arabian *ʾḷ* **or** *ʾAḷah* is the same as the Israelite/Biblical ***ʾĔlōah/ʾĔlōhîm*** and the Islamic Aḷḷāh. All of these are descendent from the Proto-Semitic Black God uncovered by Werner Daum and who is, as Julian Baldick notes, "identical with the supreme or only god of the Semitic speakers: the God of Biblical and Islamic monotheism."[505]

Excursus A: ʾAḷah No Moon-God

It has become popular in Christian polemical literature to claim that the ʾAlmaqah of ancient South Arabia, and therefore the Allah of Islam, was a moon-deity and therefore an illegitimate 'pagan god.'[506] Such claims are based on a misrepresentation of the data, a fact that more sober Christian missionary writers have pointed out.[507] While it is true that it was the going scholarly opinion that ʾAlmaqah was a moon-god,[508] more recent scholarship has abandoned this view because it was based on an incorrect pretense. The trend, going back to Ditlef Nielsen in the early 20th century,[509] to reduce all of early Arabian religion to a triad of nature deities (Venus, moon, sun) has now been rightly rejected as oversimplifying and unsupported by current data.[510] Regarding ʾAlmaqah or *ʾAḷah*

---

505 ***Black God***, 21. On the Biblical ***ʾĔlōah/ʾĔlōhîm*** **and the Proto-Semitic Black God see esp. True Islam, *Truth of God*,** 163-171.
506 See esp. Robert Morey, ***The moon-god Allah in the archeology of the Middle East*** (Newport, PA : Research and Education Foundation, 1994); Yoel Natan, ***Moon-o-theism: Religion of a War and Moon God Prophet***, 2 volumes (Lulu.com, 2006)
507 See especially Rick Brown, "Who is 'Allah'?" ***International Journal of Frontier Missions*** 23 (2006): 79-82, 86.
508 Even Yusuf Abdullah, the president of the General Organization of Antiquities, Museums and Houses of Manuscripts, Yemen, labeled the Awwām Temple the 'Moon Temple' on account of this old but mistake belief.
509 ***Handbuch der altarbischen Altertumskunde I*** (Copenhagen, 1927) 177-250.
510 See e.g. Alfred F. L. Beeston "The Religions Of Pre-Islamic Yemen" in J. Chelhod (Ed.), ***L'Arabie Du Sud Histoire Et Civilisation Volume I: Le Peuple Yemenite Et Ses Racines*** (Paris, 1984) 260.

Muqah, Arabist and historian Alfred F. L. Beeston confirms that "there is nothing to indicate lunar qualities."[511] Daum agrees:

> According to popular opinion, 'Almaqah is a moon-god. For this opinion, derived from Mesopotamian parallels, there is no South Arabian proof.[512]

Bill Glanzman, a professor at the University of Calgary, Canada, and American Foundation for the Study of Man field director during the last four years of work at the Awwām or so-called 'Moon Temple' rightly rejects this designation. International journalist Joël Donnet reports:

> Almaqah was the main god of the Sabeans...Associated with fertility, agriculture and irrigation, it was first represented by a bull, and possibly by an ibex. It was also often associated with a moon crescent, which led numerous archaeologists - including Abdu Ghaleb and Dr. Yusuf Abdullah, the president of the General Organization of Antiquities, Museums and Houses of Manuscripts- to call it the Moon-God, and therefore to name Mahram Bilqis the Moon Temple. But Bill Glanzman disagrees with this vision, as he considers *the moon as only one symbol of Almaqah*, and certainly not the most important one, according to the numerous inscriptions from the site recovered during the 1950s and the last four years of the AFSM's fieldwork: "So far, the moon isn't even mentioned in the texts, and we have found only a few examples of Almaqah's crescent moon in artwork. We very commonly find the bull (thawran) associated with Almaqah in the inscriptions (emphasis mine-WM).[513]

---

[511] Beeston "The Religions Of Pre-Islamic Yemen," 263.
[512] Daum, ***Ursemitisch***, 30.
[513] Joël Donnet, "Looking for the Queen of Sheba," http://pagesperso-orange.fr/joel.donnet/News115.htm. Accessed August 15, 2009.

The nature of the Sabaean deity *'Alah Muqah* was studied in great detail by J. Pirenne[514] and G. Garbini[515] in the 1970s. They demonstrated that the motifs associated with this deity - the bull, the vine, and also the lion's skin on a human statue - are solar rather than lunar attributes. The Bull in fact was associated first with the sun-god, in Mesopotamia and Egypt,[516] only later being conscripted into the service of the moon-deities, in third millennium BCE Mesopotamia.[517] There is thus a growing consensus among scholars that this South Arabian deity was rather a sun-god: "Almaqah was a masculine sun-god," affirms Jean-François Breton, scholar with the Centre National de la Recherche Scientifique.[518] So too Jacques Ryckmans:

> Until recently Almaqah was considered to be a moon god, under the influence of a now generally rejected conception of a South Arabian pantheon consisting of an exclusive triad: Father

---

[514] "Notes D'Archéologie Sud-Arabe," ***Syria***, 49 (1972): 193-217.

[515] "Il Dio Sabeo Almaqah," ***Rivista Degli Studi Orientali***, 48 (1973-1974): 15-22.

[516] Conrad, ***Horn and Sword***, 39; Donald B. Redford (ed.), ***The Ancient Gods Speak: A Guide to Egyptian Religion*** (Oxford: Oxford University Press, 2002), 30 s,v. Bull Gods by Dieter Kessler. It was the sun-god – An, Utu, Ra, etc., – who incarnated in the bull.

[517] Dominique Collon, "The Near Eastern Moon God," in Diederik J.W. Meijer (ed.), ***Natural Phenomena: Their Meaning, Depiction and Description in the Ancient Near East*** (North-Holland, Amsterdam, 1992) 19; Gudrun Colbow, "More Insights into Representations of the Moon God in the Third and Second Millennium B.C.," in I.L. Finkel and M.J. Geller (edd.), ***Sumerian Gods and their Representations (Cuneiform Monographs 7)*** (Groningen: STYX Publications, 1997) 25-26; Tallay Ornan, "The Bull and its Two Masters: Moon and Storm Deities in Relation to the Bull in Ancient Near Eastern Art," ***Israel Exploration Journal*** 51 (2001): 3-4.

[518] Breton, ***Arabia Felix***, 120. On *Almaqah* as a sun-god see further Beeston, "Saba'," 664-665; idem, "The Religions Of Pre-Islamic Yemen" in J. Chelhod (Ed.), ***L'Arabie Du Sud Histoire Et Civilisation (Le Peuple Yemenite Et Ses Racines)***, 1984, Volume I:263.

Moon, Mother Sun…and Son Venus. Recent studies underline that the symbols of the bull's head and the vine motif that are associated with him are solar and Dionysiac attributes and are more consistent with a *sun god*, a male consort of the sun goddess.[519]

That the moon was only *one* of *'Aḷah Muqah*'s symbols is a fact Christian polemicists overlook. For example, Joël Nathan, in his tome ***Moon-o-theism: Religion of a War and Moon God Prophet***, quotes the following statement from Wendell Phillip regarding the Awwām Temple that he excavated: "Near the top of the delicate stone shaft is a beautifully covered circular sun with a crescent moon". When the crescent moon did appear on *'Aḷah Muqah*'s temples it was conjoined with the solar orb, connoting the dual nature of this deity (diurnal=luminous and nocturnal=dark). Yet, Nathan concludes from Phillip and others who point to this solar orb and crescent moon symbol that "this suggests that Almaqah and Syn were moon-gods, not sun-gods."[520] How does a symbol with the sun *and* moon conjoined indicate a moon-god? Clearly such a conclusion is dogmatic rather than academic, and born no doubt from a desperate desire to *make* 'Almaqah a moon-deity for polemical purposes.

III. *Nabataeans and the Cult of Aḷḷāh*

The Pre-Qur'ānic cult of **Aḷḷ**āh in northern Afrabia was also not restricted to the Li**ḥy**ān. The precursors in northern Afrabia to the Muslim Arabs – ethnically and religiously – were the Nabataeans,[521] an ancient group of Arabs of southern Jordan,

---

519 ***Encyclopedia Britannica*** 2004 s.v. Arabian Religion by Jacques Ryckmans.
520 ***Moon-o-Theism***, I:342-342.
521 John E. Healey, ***The Religion of the Nabataeans: A Conspectus*** (Leiden: Brill, 2001), 83.

Canaan, and northern Arabia. Their origin may have been in southern Arabia,[522] though in both biblical and Islamic tradition they are considered descendents of Ishmael of northern provenance.[523] In the same sources the Nabataeans are 'brothers' of the black Qedar Arabs, Nabīt and Qedār appearing as the eldest sons of Ishmael.[524] On the other hand, Ernst Axel Knauf argues that the Nabataean's actually emerged out of the Qedar tribe.[525] They first explicitly appear in history maybe in Assyrian records of the eighth century BCE in the area of Iraq and later in 312 BCE in Syria-Palestine. The Romans annexed the Nabataean kingdom in the second century CE.

Like the Qedar, the Nabataeans were a black tribe. The anonymous *Akhbār al-zamān* (11th cent) lists the Nabataeans among the descendents of Canaan (son of Ham) and claims "Nabīṭ signifies 'Black'."[526]Al-Dimashqī (13th century) too, **in his *Kītāb nukhbat al-dahr fi ʿajāʾib al-barr waʾl-baḥr*,** lists the Nabataeans along with the Copts, BrBr (Berbers) and S**ū**dān (Blacks from Africa) as descendants of Black Ham.[527] Anthropologist Dana Marniche explains:

> The word Nabataean…its meaning (had) originally nothing to do with blackness, however, due to the African appearance of the Nabataeans…the word came to signify black. Certain bedouin clans of the Nabataean regions like Petra, Wadi Rum

---

[522] Nelson Glueck, ***Deities and Dolphins: The story of the Nabataeans*** (New York: Farrar, Straus and Giroux, 1965) 4.
[523] Nabīt and Qedār are the two eldest sons of Isma'il: Gen. 25:13; Jaroslav Stetkevych, ***Muḥammad and the Golden Bough: Reconstructing Arabian Myth*** (Bloomington and Indianapolis: Indiana University Press, 1996) 69.
[524] Ibid.
[525] Ernst Axel Knauf, ***Ishmael*** 2nd edition (Wiesbaden, 1989) 109' idem, "Kedar (Person)," ***ABD*** 4:9-10.
[526] ***L'abrégé des Merveilles***, ed., Carra de Vaux (1984) 1057.
[527] Ed. A.F. Mehren (St. Petersburg, 1866; repr. 1923) 266. On the blackness of the Nabataeans see further Goldenberg, ***Curse of Ham***, 313, n. 82.

and other areas of Jordan such as the Huwat'at[528]...who claim descent from the Nabataeans, are still near black in color.[529]

In his study of Nabataean religion John Healy remarks: "features of Nabataean religion...seem to prefigure religious ideas which became much more prominent in Islam."[530] No doubt, the cult of Aḻḻāh in Mecca (Pre- and Post-Qur'ānic) is in many ways a continuation or at least a cognate of the cult of Petra, the Nabataean capital. The Nabataeans were not simple 'polytheists' but honored a 'dyotheistic pair,' a supreme male god and his female partner. All other deities were subordinate.[531] Inscriptional evidence makes it clear that the male god was the paramount deity of the Nabataeans.[532]

Who is this supreme deity? He is called in inscriptions *Dhu 'l-Sharā* (ذو الشرى), but this is no divine name, only a place name (toponym), an epithet meaning "He who is of the Sharā (mountains)," the mountain range around Petra and the ancient mountain homelands of the Biblical Edomites and the domain of Yahweh (Num 33:42-43).[533] Toponyms are common in ancient Semitic tradition, and these frequently replace and disguise the

---

528 When anthropologist Austin Henry Layard encountered in Hebron a Howeitat shaykh from Petra in the 19th century he noted that his complexion was "scarcely less dark than a negro." Austin Henry Layard, ***Early Adventures in Persia, Susiana, and Among the Bakhtiyari and Other Wild Tribes Before the Discovery of Nineveh*** 2 vols. (London: John Murray, 1887) 1:32.

529 Dana Marniche, "The Afro-Arabian Origins of the Israelites and the Ishmaelites: Part 1" at http://www.africaresource.com/rasta/sesostris-the-great-the-egyptian-hercules/the-black-and-comely-sons-and-daughters-of-ismail-ishmael-dana-marniche/ accessed August 21, 2009.

530 Healey, ***Religion of the Nabataeans***, 191.

531 Healey, ***Religion of the Nabataeans***, 84; Restö, ***Arabs in Antiquity***, 62.

532 Healey, ***Religion of the Nabataeans***, 82, 85; Teixidor, ***Pagan God***, 83. *Contra* Glueck, ***Deities and Dolphins***, 283, who claimed, based on slim evidence, that his consort Atargatis (Allāt) was the supreme deity.

533 W.J. Jobling, "Desert Deities :Some New Epigraphic Evidence for the Deities Dushares and Al-Lat from the Aqaba-Ma'an Area of Southern Jordan," ***Religious Traditions*** 7-9 (1986): 27, 37; Healey, ***Religion of the Nabataeans***, 86; Teixdor, ***Pagan God***, 83.

true name of the deity.[534] In this situation "scholars have been much concerned with trying to find the true name of this supreme god."[535] It has been suggested that the name of the god is Ruḍa,[536] or even A'ara,[537] but the arguments in support of these are weak.[538] Rather, "it is most likely that Dushara is referred to simply as *'lh'*, 'the god' *par excellence.*" [539] In other words, as F.V. Winnet pointed out, "the Nabataean word for 'God' is *Allāhā,*"[540] for "Allāh...enters into the composition of numerous personal names among the Nabataeans."[541] While theophorous names compounded with the name *Dhu 'l-Sharā* are rare, names compounded with **Aḷḷāh** predominate, such as *Yahballāhā*, "Allah has given" and *Itallāhā*, "Allah is".[542] The supreme god of these Black north Arabians was therefore **Aḷḷāh**,[543] and his female complement was Allāt, also called al-**'Uzzā**.[544]

---

[534] Teixidor, ***Pagan God***, 37, 91.***Encyclopedia Britannica*** [2004] s.v. Arabian Religion by Jacques Ryckmans.
[535] Healey, ***Religion of the Nabataeans***, 85.
[536] Teixdor, ***Pagan God***, 88.
[537] ***EI²*** 2:246 s.v. Dhu 'l-Sharā by G. Ryckmans.
[538] Healey, ***Religion of the Nabataeans***, 94-95, 97-100. Restö, ***Arabs in Antiquity***, 604, points out that "Ruḍa is never mentioned in the...Nabataean inscriptions."
[539] Healey, ***Religion of the Nabataeans***, 92.
[540] Winnett, "Allah Before Islam," 247.
[541] ***ERE*** 1:664 s.v. Arabs (Ancient).
[542] Winnett, "Allah Before Islam," 247; idem, "The Daughters of Allah," ***MW*** 30 (1940): 117; Healey, ***Religion of the Nabataeans***, 85; Teixdor, ***Pagan God***, 83; ***ER¹*** 10:287 s.v. Nabatean Religion.
[543] Healy's comment to the contrary is incoherent because self-contradictory: "it is most likely that Dushara is referred to simply as *'lh'*, "the god" *par excellence.* In addition...among the Nabataeans there is only one doubtful piece of evidence for the worship of Allāh, an inscription from Ruwāfa, probably of post-Nabataean date, in which the dedication is to *'lh' 'lh...*, "Ilāhā, god of..." Healey, ***Religion of the Nabataeans***, 92. Here, Healy rightly points out that the deity is called *'lh'*, which transliterates as Ilāhā and then identifies this transliteration with Allāh. In other words, all of the inscriptional references to the god as *'lh'* (Ilāhā) are references to the god as Allāh, because Healy appropriately confesses that Ilāhā = Allāh.
[544] As Healey notes (***Religion of the Nabataeans***, 114, and further108, 113) "it is probable that al-'Uzzā, 'the Mightiest', is treated in the Nabataean context as an epithet

What are the natures of these deities, the Nabataean Aḷḷāh (*Dhu 'l-Sharā*) and Allāt? They were clearly anthropomorphic,[545] worshipped in both aniconic and iconic (anthropomorphic) form.[546] While it is true that the iconic conventions were imported from the Hellenistic tradition and the anthropomorphic statues represent an *interpretatio graeca*, this amounted only to a Greek veneer on a Semitic anthropomorphic tradition.[547] The Nabataean's *iconic* Aḷḷāh (*Dhu 'l-Sharā*) was, as well said by Nelson Glueck, a "Hellenized, Oriental deity."

> The irresistible Hellenism of their era affected all forms of self-expression and was modified in turn by their own enduring Orientalism. Most of the gods and goddesses of their (the Nabataeans) maturity seem at first glance to have been modeled completely after those of Greece, but closer examination reveals fundamental characteristics that are unquestionably Semitic…They chose…to fashion their gods primarily in accord with *their traditional loyalties and religious convictions* and the dictates of their origins and environment, however much they responded to cultural factors and examples of non-Semitic sources. They

---

of Allāt…". See further Iain Browning, ***Petra*** (London: Chatto & Windus, 1973) 45; Nielsen, ***Dreieinigen Gott***, I: 321. Cf. Restö, ***Arabs in Antiquity***, 604, who disagrees, but his reasons are unconvincing.

545 *Contra* Healey, ***Religion of the Nabataeans***, 187.

546 G.W. Bowersock, "An Arabian Trinity," ***HTR*** 79 (1986): 20-21.

547 On ancient Near Eastern/Semitic anthropomorphism generally see J. Hamori, ***"When Gods Were Men": The Embodied God in Biblical and Near Eastern Literature*** (BZAW 384; Berlin and New York, 2008); Tallay Ornan, ***The Triumph of the Symbol: Pictorial Representations of Deities in Mesopotamia and the Biblical Image Ban*** (OBO 213; Fribourg, 2005); Mark S. Smith, ***The Origins of Biblical Monotheism: Israel's Polytheistic Background and the Ugaritic Texts*** (Oxford, 2001), 27-35; Maryo Christina Annette Korpel, ***A Rift in the Clouds: Ugaritic and Hebrew Descriptions of the Divine*** (Münster, 1990; but on Korpel's forced attempt to impute metaphoric intentions to the Canaanites see the review by Marvin H. Pope in ***UF*** 22 [1990]: 497-502); James B. Pritchard, "The Gods and their Symbols," in idem, ***The Ancient Near East in Pictures, Relating to the Old Testament*** (Princeton, 1954), 160-85; Stephen Herbert Langdon, *Semitic Mythology* (Boston, 1931).

preferred their familiar gods, altered as they may have been by Hellenistic influences…(emphasis mine-WM)[548]

In other words, even though the later *statues* reflected Hellenistic conventions, the anthropomorphic deity himself was authentically Semitic. The Nabataean **A**ḷḷāh (*Dhu ʾl-Sharā*) was, like his predecessors, both a solar and aquatic deity. He had two attribute animals: an eagle with outstretched wings indicating his solar character[549] and a bull signaling his chthonic/aquatic nature.[550]While his temples had a solar orientation,[551] they were also located by streams.[552] These dual attributes (eagle/bull) indicate that, like the *ʾAḷah Muqah* of South Arabia, An-Enki of Mesopotamia and Rah of Egypt, the Nabataean Aḷḷāh (*Dhu ʾl-Sharā*) is the *Coniunctio oppositorum.* Before the Nabataeans embraced the Hellenistic convention of depicting their deities in fully anthropomorphic statues, they represented Aḷḷāh (*Dhu ʾl-Sharā*) in a black, rectangular stone,[553] a *baetyl* (from ***bêt*** *ʾēl*, 'house-of-God') which was regarded as "the container of the god."[554] Allāt/al-ʿ**Uzzā** was "the deity of springs and of water as

[548] Glueck, ***Deities and Dolphins***, 10, 247.
[549] ***EI²*** 2:247 s.v. Dhu 'l-Sharā by G. Ryckmans; Healey, ***Religion of the Nabataeans***, 102-5; Langdon, ***Semitic Mythology***, 16. According to Strabo, *Geography*, xvi.4.26.
[550] "Appropriately, bulls were the beasts of Dusares, the leading male deity who was originally a fertility god; the brute strength and tremendous virility of this animal were at the command of this god." Browning, ***Petra***, 185; Glueck, ***Deities and Dolphins***, 205-206, 247.
[551] Glueck, ***Deities and Dolphins***, 57.
[552] Healey, ***Religion of the Nabataeans***, 89, 106; ***ER¹*** 10:287 s.v. Nabatean Religion.
[553] ***EI²*** 2:246 s.v. Dhu 'l-Sharā by G. Ryckmans; Langdon, ***Semitic Mythology***, 16; Teixidor, ***Pagan God***, 86.
[554] Healey, ***Religion of the Nabataeans***, 157.

befits a fertility goddess".[555] She was the "Mother of the gods,"[556] even the mother of Aḻḻāh (*Dhu 'l-Sharā*).[557]

Aspects of the Nabataean myth of Aḻḻāh and Allāt are revealed in the *actia dusaria* or the festivals held in his honor at Petra. According to the 4th century CE Christian writer Epiphanius (*Contra Haeres.*, LI, 22, 9-12), bishop of Salamis in Cyprus, the Nabataeans celebrated on the sixth of January a feast in honor of the birth of Aḻḻāh (*Dhu 'l-Sharā*) to the virgin Χααβου, *kaabu.*[558] The name Epiphanius gives to the virgin has been associated with the Arabic *ka'ba*, "cube," (from the Arabic *ku'ba, ka'***iba***).[559] He says these festivals took place in Petra, Elusa and Alexandria. Epiphanius gives details regarding the Alexandrian festival but indicates that the festival in Petra took place similarly.[560] There was a pilgrimage to his Petra temple to celebrate Aḻḻāh's (*Dhu 'l-Sharā's*) birth, which was believed to have occurred on December 25, the time of the winter solstice.[561] In this festival celebrating the virgin begetting the god, the image of a babe was brought out of the temple sanctuary and greeted by the worshippers with loud acclamations of 'the virgin has begotten'. The image of the god/babe is carried around the sanctuary *seven times*, and then returned to its place buried in the ground. Jan Restö summaries the myth no doubt associated with these two deities:

---

555 Browning, ***Petra***, 47. See also Glueck, ***Deities and Dolphins***, 381-392. She was thus identified with the Greek goddess Aphrodite, who was born form the sea. See Restö, ***Arabs in Antiquity***,

556 Langdon, ***Semitic Mythology***, 17.

557 Healey, ***Religion of the Nabataeans***, 105.

558 Correction from Χααμου; R. Eisler, ***ARW*** 1 (1912): 630; ***EI²*** 2:246 s.v. Dhu 'l-Sharā by G. Ryckmans; Langdon, ***Semitic Mythology***, 16.

559 ***EI²*** 2:247 s.v. Dhu 'l-Sharā by G. Ryckmans; ***EI¹*** 4:586 s.v. Ka'ba by A.J. Wensinck; Langdon, ***Semitic Mythology***, 16.

560 Langdon, ***Semitic Mythology***, 18; Healey, ***Religion of the Nabataeans***, 103. He says explicitly, after describing the Alexandrian festival, "This also takes place in the same idolatrous manner in Petra" (51:22).

561 Langdon, ***Semitic Mythology***, 16.

The cult of the young goddess giving birth to a divine child manifest as the morning star is part of a complex of religious ideas current in the eastern Mediterranean in antiquity. Isaac of Antioch describes how women belonging to the 'sons of Hagar' (i.e. Arabs) worship 'the star,' *kawkabtā*. We also hear how the Saracens in Elusa worship Lucifer, Venus' son. According to Hieronymus, in Hebrew he is called *Chocab* which means 'star.' His name is a Latin translation of the Greek *phōsphoros*, 'light-carrier'...A god manifest in the morning star is well documented in ancient epigraphic monuments, in Latin by the name *bonus puer phosphorus*, 'the good lad, the light-carrier'. This makes it likely that Isaac of Antioch also refers to a cult of a new-born child manifest in the morning star. The star, *kawkabtā*, would thus be the male god, Dusares/Dioysus/Phosphoros/Eōsphoros/Lucifer, not the female ('Uzzā)/Aphrodite. The feminine form of the word belongs to Syriac grammar, not to Arabian mythology. Contrary to what was assumed by earlier scholarship, it has become clear that there is no definite evidence for an identification between the morning star and the female god of Arabia.[562]

Aḻḻāh (*Dhu 'l-Sharā*) of the Nabataeans was a solar/astral deity born of the virgin 'night', a metaphor for the feminized, dark aquatic matter of the pre-cosmic world. According to Restö "This mythology and cult can be traced far back in Semitic religion.[563] This Petra cult remarkably parallels the later Meccan cult: Aḻḻāh and Allāt, the feminized *ka'ba*, black stone, and seven-fold circumambulation all prefigure these aspects of the Aḻḻāh cult in Mecca. There may be some relation between the Nabataeans of Petra and the Quraysh of Mecca.[564] Elements of

[562] Restö, ***Arabs in Antiquity***, 605.
[563] Restö, ***Arabs in Antiquity***, 606.
[564] **Alī b. Abī Ṭālib** reportedly claimed that the Quraysh were Nabataeans, and Ibn Manẓūr, ***Lisān*** s.v. نبط quotes Ibn '**Abbās** as saying "the Quraysh were Nabaṭ from

this cult – the bull/aquatic and eagle/solar symbolism, the feminine complement that has aquatic associations and is associated with the 'house' of the male deity, the black stone, a myth of the god born from his aquatic mother/spouse – can all now be understood in the context of the 'new religion' from Epipaleolithic/Neolithic Levant.

Kutha in Iraq." See also Al-**Ṭabarī**, ***Tārīkh***, 1:314 who reports: "And out of Nabīt and Qaydar God propagated the Arabs." Further D.S. Margoliouth, ***Mohammed and the Rise of Islam***, 2nd edition [New York and London: G.P. Pulnam's Sons, 1905] 10.

Chapter Five

Islam Before Muḥammad

> "Islam, as an organized religion, had its origin in the Arabian desert...Without begging the question by asserting that Islam is older than Muhammad, consider that such a posture has been taken by all religions when assailed for having a place and time of origin...Islam had such a beginning; in fact, as we know it, Islam began with Muhammad"
>
> Molefi Kete Asanti, ***Afrocentricity*** [1988]

I. *From Petra to Mecca: The Pre-Qur'ānic Cult of the Ka'ba*

Religion in Afrabia, particularly in Mecca prior to Muḥammad's seventh century CE movement, is frequently characterized as barbarous, idolatrous, and polytheistic, all connoted by the Arabic term *Jāhilī*, "ignorant," which Muslim writers use to describe the Arabs' pre-Qur'ānic spiritual state. More recent critical scholarship has demonstrated that this characterization is inadequate and, indeed, inaccurate. It is true that mention is made in seventh century BCE Assyrian inscriptions of idols of six "gods of the Arabs" that are captured by Sennacherib in Dumah (NW Arabia).[565] But neither the multiple deities nor their idols confirm the popular (Islamic) characterization. Javier Teixidor, studying hundreds of ancient Near Eastern Semitic inscriptions from the first millennium BCE, has documented a 'Pagan monotheism' in Afrabia.[566] According

---

[565] See Restö, ***Arabs***, 601.

[566] Javier Teixidor, ***The Pagan God: Popular Religion in the Greco-Roman Near East*** (Princeton: Princeton University Press , 1977).

to Teixidor, there was no indiscriminant polytheism. Rather there was the belief in one supreme god, *'l*, with whom other deities were *subordinately* associated. At least some of these lesser deities were apparently members of *'l*'s divine assembly.[567] Herodotus, writing in the fifth century BCE, knew the Arabs to venerate only two supreme deities, a male and a female (III, 8). Origen, the Christian apologist and church father of the 2nd – 3rd centuries BCE, in his *Contra Celsum* (5.37) likewise noted that Arabs worshipped this duo, "for in them the male and female are glorified."[568] From the inscriptions it is clear that these male and female deities of the ancient Arabs were Aḷḷāh and Allāt.

These male and female deities of the Arab cult during this period were worshipped through a sacred stone, called a baetyl (in Arabic *nuṣub*), a term derived from the West Semitic *bêt 'ēl*, "house-of-God". This designation indicates that the stone itself was not the object of veneration but was instead "the residence of the god-or, rather…the place in which the god was embodied."[569] Clement of Alexandria in the second century CE knew the Arabs to venerate their god through a stone (*Protreptika*, IV, 46, 1) as did his contemporary Maximus Tyrius (*Sermon* 38). It is during this same period (second century) that we get evidence of the existence of the cubic Meccan temple, the Ka'ba, in which the cubic stone was undoubtedly located. Ptolemy (*Geography* vi. 7) writes in place of Mecca 'Macoraba,' which is likely rooted in the South Semitic *mikrāb*, "temple." "From this," Semitic scholar Ardent J. Wensinck informs us, "one may

---

567 Oldenburg, "Above the Stars of El," 191.

568 Trans. H. Chadwick (Cambridge: University Press, 1965) 294. Strabo in the first century CE (*Geography*, XVI, 1, 11) and Arrian in the second century CE (*Anabasis*, VII, 20) report that the Arabs venerate two deities, but both male. This is clearly an error, no doubt based on linguistics.

569 Teixdor, ***Pagan God***, 87; Karel van der Toorn "Worshipping Stones: On the Deification of Cult Symbols," ***JNSL*** 23 (1997) 1-14.

conclude that the Ka'ba already existed in the second century A.D."[570] There is evidence that it existed centuries earlier. Greek historian of the first century BCE, Diodorus Siculus, alluded to the Ka'ba, noting that it was "exceedingly revered by all Arabians."[571] The stone and cubed temple were not peculiar to the Arabs, but were an authentic characteristic of Semitic worship.

> Abstract representations of deity in the form of a square or cube was common throughout the (Pre-Hellenic) Semitic Near East...This was the *baetyl*, or stone cult object, the focal point of so many temples not subject to Classicising influences...Indeed, the ancient Semitic idea of the sacred cube reaches culmination in the center of Semitic worship today: the Ka'ba...at Mecca.[572]

Wensink pointed out that the Meccan shrine "possessed in a high degree the usual qualities of a Semitic sanctuary."[573] The stone was frequently a black stone (Figure 35), and Hildegard Lewy's important study of the ancient cults of Jerusalem and Mecca enlightens us as to why this was so.[574] According to Lewy,

---

570 ***EI^1*** 4:586 s.v. Ka'ba by A.J. Wensinck. Walter Williams' comment is therefore nonsensical: "If Mecca is supposed to be the birthplace of the Prophet Muhammad (570 ACE), thereby, making Mecca a supposed Holy City, I ask the question again, why was Mecca called Macoraba during the Byzantine era and not called Mecca?" ***Historical Origin***, 94. In point of fact, Macoraba was not a general Bzyantinian designation, but that of Ptolemy and his use of this term actually supports the existence of the city and its shrine, not cast doubt on it.

571 His full quote is: "And a temple has been set-up there, which is very holy and exceedingly revered by all Arabians."*Bibliotheca historica*, trans. C H Oldfather in ***Diodorus Of Sicily*** (London: William Heinemann Ltd., & Cambridge, Massachusetts: Harvard University Press, 1935) II: 217. Tisdall appropriately suggests that "The Ka'bah is, in all probability, the spot referred to by Diodorus Siculus": ***Original Sources***, 34.

572 Warwick Ball, ***Rome in the East: the transformation of an empire*** (Routledge, 2000) 379-380.

573 ***EI^1*** 4:591 s.v. Ka'ba by A.J. Wensinck.

574 Hildegard Lewy, "Origin and Significance of the *Mâgên Dâwîd*: A Comparative Study in the Ancient Religions of Jerusalem and Mecca," ***Archiv Orientalni*** 18 (1950): 330-365.

an ancient Semitic tradition – out of which the cults of Jerusalem and Mecca evolved – centered on a black stone that was at the same time considered an embodiment of the nether waters and a piece of the body of a deity, the body being made from those waters. This stone, through which the deity was worshipped, was housed in a cubed temple or shrine covered in black curtains. The 'blackness' of this deity and his cult inspired associations with the astral deity Saturn, the 'Black Planet,"[575] whose temple was made of black stone, drapped with black curtains, and featured a black stone representing the deity or an anthropomorphic statue of the deity made from black stone.[576] Both al-Mas'**ū**di (d. 956)[577] and al-Dimasq**ī** (d. 1327)[578] report identifications of the Meccan Ka'ba with the cult of the black deity Saturn, as did the *Dabistān –i Mazāhib*.[579] But it is no doubt the black deity of ancient Afrabia to which the Meccan cult was dedicated. The shrine and stone confirm this.

Figure 35
The baetyl of Aphrodite
from Palaepaphos,
Cyrus

[575] The Babylonians called Saturn *Mi* "The Black". See Robert Brown, ***The Great Dionysiak Myth*** (London: Longmans, Green and Co., 1878) 329. According to the *Dabistān –i Mazāhib* or "Schools of Religions" Saturn's temple was constructed out of black stone as was his statue that stood there. In addition, Saturn's officiating ministers were all black complected persons, Ethiopians, etc. ***The Dabistán or School of Manners***, trans. David Shea and Anthony Troyer (New York and London: M. Walter Dunne, 1901) 22.

[576] Lewy, "Origin and Signigicance," 339; ***Dabistán***, 22.

[577] ***Murūj al-dhahab wa ma'ādin al-jawāhar*** 4:44.

[578] ***Kitāb Nukhbat al-Dahr fī 'Ajā'ib al-Barr wa-'l-Baḥr*** (ed. Mehren; St. Pétersbourg, 1886) 40.

[579] ***Dabistán***, 30.

The Shrine: The Kaʿba was originally enigmatically built in a wadi, the *baṭn Makka*. As such, "The story of the Kaʿba is a story of devastating floods."[580] Knowing the destructive impact of the flooding, why would the Afrabians choose a wadi for the site of their holiest shrine? Werner Daum's evidence suggests the answer: "The Kaʿba is one of the sanctuaries of the ancient Arabian water and fertility religion," i.e. the religion of the ancient Afrabian Black God.[581] Within the shrine was apparently a sacred well whose waters were associated with the primordial waters of the netherworld.[582]

The Kaʿba in Mecca has two peculiar, seemingly mutually exclusive characteristics: on the one hand it was known as *baytullah* or 'House of Allah," but on the other hand it was consistently – from pre- to post-Qurʾānic times – feminized.[583] The shrine is dressed as a 'bride' and even popularly addressed in Mecca as *al-bunayya*, "the little girl." Not understanding these two characteristics in their right context – the context of the ancient Afrabian religion of the Black God – has created much confusion and spawned much misinformation. It is not the case that the Kaʿba cult was centered on the worship of a goddess who was later replaced by pathetically patriarchal Muslims with a male god, Allah.[584] The masculine and feminine aspects of the cult were always there. As Robert Eisler explains in his

---

[580] Daum, "Pre-Islamic Rite," 13.
[581] Daum, "Pre-Islamic Rite," 14; idem, ***Ursemitisch***, 108-111.

[582] Arent J. Wensinck, ***The Ideas of the Western Semites concerning the Navel of the Earth*** (Amsterdam, J. Müller 1916) 30; Lewy, "Origin and Significance," 345.
[583] See esp. William C. Young, "The Kaʿba, Gender, and the Rites of Pilgrimage," ***International Journal of Middle East Studies*** 25 (1993) 285-300; T. Fahd, ***Le Panthéon de l'arabia central à veille de l'Hégire*** (Paris: P. Geuthner, 1968) 171-172.
[584] E.g. Oak, ***World Vedic Heritage***, I:696.

Weltenmantel und Himmelszelt ("Cosmic Cloak and Heavenly Canopy"):

> The house is a feminine deity, or…the feminine deity is called the habitation, dwelling (of a masculine god)…This explanation…can be applied to the Ka'aba. Because inside of her, the holy stone of the moon-god Hubal[585] was erected…As far as Arabia, Syria and the Euphrates countries are concerned, we do have a row of direct testimonies for the independent cult of the holy house, as explained above by Hommel in the sense of 'Astarte = Ašritu = 'house, temple, dwelling'… Thus, we read in a list of pagan-Arabic cults by Abu l'Farad: "The Himyarites worshipped Šams, the sun, the Beni Kinanah the moon, the tribes Tašm the star Al Debaran, the Lakhm and Dshorhom the planet Jupiter, the Tay the Canobos-, the Kays the Sirus star, the Asad the Mercury, and the Takiff a small temple in the upper part of Mahlak, which ones calls Allât." The expression is quite plain and says in clear words that the small tribal temple, the *baitan* itself was called *'l-Lât*, 'the goddess'…[586]

Figure 36
The Ka'ba in Mecca

[585] Hubal was the leading male idol of the Jāhilī Arabs of Mecca and was prominently placed in the Ka'ba.
[586] Robert Eisler, ***Weltenmantel und Himmelszelt*** ; ***religionsgeschichtliche untersuchungen zur urgeschichte des antiken weltbildes***, two volumes (München: C. H. Beck, 1909 -1910) I: 120-121, 162.

We have already discussed the significance of the feminization of the square temple of the male deity: the square temple or 'house' represents the imminent material body of the male god, a body composed of the black, aquatic primordial matter that is personified as a goddess. The temple, itself called All**ā**t the goddess, is *baytullah*, the house of Aḷḷāh, for in it/her he sits enthroned. In other words, the scene of the male god enthroned within a square or rectangular shrine is a symbolic picture of his *incarnation* within a black body. This is confirmed by the presence of the black stone and its central role in the cult.

Al-Hajar al-Aswad: The black stone of the Meccan Ka'ba, Lewy has well argued, must be understood against the backdrop of the broader Semitic cult of stones: "the Black Stone...was thought to be...a part of the body of a great god...(I)n the form of a black meteorite a piece of the deity's astral body was visible to the congregation at all times..."[587] This stone was associated with water, so we should think of an *aquatic* divine body. While the shrine is feminized and therefore identified with the goddess, the stone inside the shrine is identified with the male god, Aḷḷāh.[588] This point is explicitly made in a Muslim tradition according to which al-Zubayr was digging in al-**Ḥ**ijr while rebuilding the Ka'ba and found a stone on which was written: ***innānī*** *Aḷḷāh* ***Dhū Bakka***, "I am Aḷḷāh, Lord of Bekka."[589]

---

[587] Lewy, "Origin and Significance," 345. 348, 349.
[588] Contra Wayne Chandler, "Ebony and Bronz: Race and Ethnicity in Early Arabia and the Islamic World," in Rashidi and Sertima, ***African Presence***, 272, quoting Idris Shah, ***The Sufis*** (London: Octagon Press, 390.
[589] Al-Azraq**ī**, ***Kitāb Akhbār Makka,*** *apud* ***Die Chroniken der Stadt Mecca***, ed. Ferdinand Wüstenfeld (Leipzig, 1858-61) 42-3; **Ṭ**abar**ī**, ***Tafsīr*** **(Cairo ed.)** III:61.

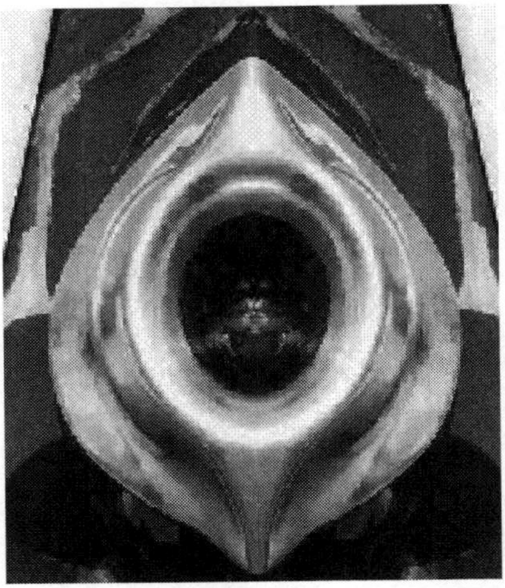

Figure 37
Al-Hajar al-Aswad (the Black Stone) of Mecca

The relation of the blackness of the stone and the blackness of the deity is suggested, if not confirmed, by the tradition of the warrior Khālid b. al-Walīd (d. 642), who was dispatched by Muḥammad to destroy the shrine of the goddess al-**'Uzzā**. Al-**'Uzzā,** "the Mighty One," whose cult was based in Nakhlah, east of Mecca towards al-**Ṭā**'if, was the greatest idol among the Quraysh, Muḥammad's tribe. She was joined with All**āt and** al-**Manāt**, and the three were considered by the Meccans to be the 'daughters of Aḷḷāh.' Al-**'Uzzā** was worshipped through a black cubic stone and three sacred trees. When Khālid arrived in Nakhlah at the goddess's shrine, one of her priests was outside. Suddenly a black woman with disheveled hair emerged from the shrine, and the priest yelled to her: "O al-**'Uzzā**, be courageous."[590] Khālid is said to have shook with terror, then

[590] Ibn al-Kalbī, ***Kitāb al-Aṣnām***, 25 (Eng.).

composed himself and severed the woman's head. After reporting his deed to Muḥammad the later said: "That (i.e. the Black woman) was al-'**Uzzā**. But she is no more." Al-'**Uzzā**, the 'daughter' and likely 'spouse' of Al̤l̤āh was thus viewed as a Black woman, represented by a black stone. When we consider that the three 'daughters' of a male deity reflect the nature of that deity himself,[591] this conception of a black al-'**Uzzā** shines some light on the popular conception of Al̤l̤āh.

II. *Pre- Qur'ānic Islam*

> "From the old Arabian religion, Islam has canonized a festival, a sanctuary, and a god. In the great annual pilgrimage to Mecca, the old pagan main festival of Mecca, with its holy stone, is still living on. Still today it is the holy place of all Muhammedans. And the old Arabic main-god is still existing as the Allah of Islam. In the Koran he is still mentioned as the old main-god. And this pre-Islamic Allah we do get to know now better through the inscriptions. He bears the same name as in the Koran."
>
> Ditlef Nielsen, ***Der Dreieinige Gott In Religionshistorischer Beleuchtung***

The worship of Al̤l̤āh, centered on a black stone and associated with a cubic shrine, Ka'ba, was a part of Afrabian religion long before the birth of Muḥammad b. 'Abd Al̤l̤āh in sixth century Arabia. We find it in Pertra and in Mecca. Joseph

[591] Cyrus H. Gorden, "The Daughters of Baal and Allah," ***MW*** 33 (1943): 50-51.

Henninger has described pre-Qur'ānic religion in Mecca on the eve of Muḥammad accordingly:

> Here then are the elements of this religion: Allah, creator of the world, supreme and undisputed lord, but relegated to the background in the cultic and practical life of the people; next, manifesting the rudiments of a polytheism, several *astral divinities*...and *atmospheric divinities*...finally, ancestors and *jinn*, these last having more importance in the belief system than in the cult (emphasis original).[592]

The 'pagan monotheism' that characterized Semitic religion in Arabia at least since the first millennium BCE grew increasing vague, particularly in Mecca on the eve of the Prophet. While Aḷḷāh was still recognized as the supreme creator god and the other deities considered his subordinates, the latter became increasing important in the life of the Meccans and Aḷḷāh increasing irrelevant. 'Associationism' rather than straight 'polytheism' was the theological scandal from the Qur'ān's perspective. Aḷḷāh's different attributes had been personified and exalted, and relied upon in the place of the god himself or 'associated' with him in prayers. This was the situation that Muḥammad found and eventually set out to correct (though he was not the first). As J. Waardenburg explains:

> It was deviant believers or *mushrikūn* ('associators') who had substituted for the cult of the supreme god particular cults of his names and attributes as independent entities, as 'daughters of Allah' or as other deities.[593]

---

592 Joseph Henninger, "Pre-Islamic Bedouin Religion," in Merlin L. Swartz (ed.), ***Studies on Islam*** (New York and Oxford: Oxford University Press, 1981) 15.

593 J. Waardenburg, "Changes of Belief in Spiritual Beings, Prophethood, and the Rise of Islam," in H.G. Kippenberg, H.J.W. Drijvers and Y. Kuiper (edd.), ***Stuggles of Gods.***

The nature of Arabian religion before Muḥammad's reform movement is demonstrated most admirably in two studies of the pre-Qur'**ānic** *talbiyāt* (sing. *talbiya*) or formulaic ritual invocations by S.M. Ḥusain and M.J. Kister.[594] The *talbiya* is the invocation/prayer made by Hajj pilgrims to the Ka'ba. The current Muslim *talbiya* is as follows:

> Here I am at Thy service O Aḷḷāh, here I am. Here I am at Thy service and Thou hast no partners. Thine alone is All Praise and All Bounty, and Thine alone is The Sovereignty. Thou hast no partners.

But the 'pagan' tribes before the time of Muḥammad who made the pilgrimage uttered a similar version of this *talbiya*:

> Here I am at Thy service O Aḷḷāh, here I am. Here I am at Thy service and Thou hast no partners *except such partner as thou hast; Thou possessesth him and all that is his*.

Muḥammad adapted his *talbiya* from that of the pagan's, particularly the *talbiya* of the Banu Ash'**ariyyūn,** monotheizing it.[595] These pre-Qur'**ānic** *talbiyāt* shine significant light on the religion of the tribes to whom the Prophet preached. While each tribe had its idol which it associated with Aḷḷāh, they still acknowledged Aḷḷāh's supremacy over their tribal idol. The Qays '**Aylān**, e.g., confessed in its *talbiya* to be with its idols in humble submission to *al-Rahmān*, the Merciful. The Ban**ū** Thaqīf aksed Aḷḷāh for forgiveness of sins and confessed that their goddesses,

Papers of the Groningen Work Group for the Study of the History of Religions (Berlin: Mouton Publishers, 1984) 276.

[594] S.M. Ḥusain, "Talbiyāt al-Jāhiliyya," in ***Proceedings and Transactions of the 9th All-India Oriental Conference*** (Lucknow, 1937) 361-69; M.J. Kister, "Labbayka, All**ā**humma, Labbayka...On a monotheistic aspect of a J**ā**hiliyya practice," ***Jerusalem Studies in Arabic and Islam*** 2 (1980):33-49.

[595] Ḥusain, "Talbiyāt," 362, 364; Kister, "Labbayka," 34.

Allāt and al-'**Uzzā**, were in Aḷḷāh's hands and yielded obediently to him.[596] Kister describes:

> The *talbiyāt* reflect the ideas of the tribes about the supreme God as well as their perception of the relation between the lesser gods and the supreme god…the tribes (of the Jāhiliyya) of course had their gods…They believed however in a supreme God, who had His House in Mecca. On their pilgrimage to Mecca they directed themselves to the God, who held supremacy over the tribal gods…The Jāhiliyya tribes cannot be said to be straightforward polytheists; they were *mushrikūn*, i.e. while accepting and admitting the existence and supreme authority of God, they associated other deities with Him."[597]

Particularly important is the *talbiya* of the Banū Ḥimyar, the Black tribe.[598] They stress therein that they address Aḷḷāh on behalf of their kings who are pious and stay away from sin *due to Islam* (*tanazzuhan wa-islām*)! Here the word *islām* likely means "exclusive devotion to one god (Aḷḷāh)." [599] In other words, the pre-Qur'ānic tribal worship of Aḷḷāh was even called Islam, at least by some of the tribes.

It is acknowledged by both Muslim and non-Muslim scholars that Muḥammad was no innovator: practically the whole religious system associated with him is a carry-over from the 'pagan' religion, or better 'Kushite' religion, of the pre-Qur'ānic period. Abū al-Fidā, in his *Tawarikh al-Qadimah* (p. 180), confirms for example:

---

[596] See sources in Ḥusain, "Talbiyāt," 363; Kister, "Labbayka," 38.
[597] Kister, "Labbayka," 38, 47-48.
[598] Wayne Chandler, "Ebony and Bronze: Race and Ethnicity in Early Arabia and the Islamic World," in Rashidi and Sertima, ***African Presence***, 271; Houston, ***Wonderful Ethiopians*** 121.
[599] Kister, "Labbayka," 39.

> The Arabs of the time of ignorance used to do things which the Sharia (Islamic revelation) has adopted ...they...used to make Pilgrimage (Hajj) to the House (the Ka'ba) and visit the consecrated places, and wear the Ihrām and perform the **Ṭ**awwāf (circumambulation around the Ka'ba), and run (between the hills Al-**Ṣ**afā and al-Marwah) and take their stand at all the Stations, and cast the stones...at the devil in the valley of Mina...

That the pre-Qur'ānic religion of Mecca included the Hajj (pilgrimage) is well documented, notwithstanding the ridiculous and undocumented (and undocumentable) claim of Walter Williams that "It was Ibn Al-'Arabi (in the 13th century CE) who first created the ritual of going on a Hajj to Mecca, an imaginary mental state."[600] As Jacques Ryckmans informs us, the details of the Islamic pilgrimage ritual were observed in the period before Mu**ḥ**ammad:

> Throughout pre-Islāmic Arabia, 'truces of God' allowed people to attend in security the yearly pilgrimages to important shrines. The rites included purifications and the wearing of ritual clothing, sexual abstinence, abstention from shedding blood, and circuits performed (***ṭawāf***, *dawār*) around the sacred object; they were concluded by the slaughter of animals, which were eaten in collective feasts. Today such practices still form the core of the Islāmic pilgrimage to Mecca. The classical, Nabataean, Li**ḥy**ānite, and Sabaean sources mention pilgrimages.[601]

Even the details of ritual purity, so characteristic of Islamic ritual practice, is a carry-over.

---

600 ***The Historical Origin of Islam*** (Chicago: Maathian Press, INC, 2001) 93.
601 ***Encyclopedia Britannica*** 2004 s.v. Arabian Religion by Jacques Ryckmans.

South Arabian texts confessing offenses against ritual cleanliness, along with data from classical sources and the Muslim tradition on pre-Islāmic customs, contribute to outline an ancient Arabian code of ritual cleanliness similar to that of the Leviticus and of Muslim jurisprudence, although some Islamologists, unaware of the pre-Islamic Arabian epigraphic material, have attributed the Muslim code on ritual cleanliness (***ṭahā****rah*) to a Jewish influence on early Islām in Medina.[602]

Thus W. St. Clair Tisdall rightly concluded:

> Not only in reference to Allah Ta'ala and to reverence for the Black Stone and the Ka'bah but in many other matters also Islam has borrowed from the Arabs of more ancient times. It is not too much to say that most of the religious rites and ceremonies which now prevail throughout the Muhammadad world are identical with those practiced in Arabia from immemorial antiquity.[603]

Muḥammad's therefore was a not a 'new religious movement' but a *reform* movement.[604] His intent was to rid the ancient cult of Aḷḷāh, already called 'Islam' in some instances,[605] of the

---

[602] Ibid.

[603] W. St. Clair Tisdall, ***The Original Sources of the Qur'an*** (London: Society for Promoting Chrsitian Knowledge, 1911) 43.

[604] Jacques Waardenburg, "Towards a Periodization of Earliest Islam According to its Relations with Other Religions,"in ***Proceedings of the ninth congress of the Union européenne des arabisants et islamisants, Amsterdam, 1st to 7th September 1978*** (Leiden: Brill, 1981) 304-326, esp. 308, 313 acknowledges Muḥammad's early movement as being originally a Meccan religious purification movement against idolatry and a reform movement with regard to the *ahl al-kitāb*, that is Jews and Christians.

[605] D.S. Margoliouth confirms regarding the name 'Muslim' that "it may be said with practicle certainty that (the name) existed with religious value before Mohammed's time" and that "the word (Islam) was known (already) to the Prophet…and some other persons…in the sense of monotheist." "On the Origins and Import of the names Muslim and Ḥanīf," ***JRAS*** 35 (1903): 470, 476.

innovations that foreigners had introduced into it. As Cheikh Anta Diop confirms, Muḥammad's movement was a reformed continuation of the ancient Afrabian (Kushite) religion:

> The religion (of ancient Arabia) was of Kushite origin...It would remain the same until the advent of Islam...all of the elements necessary for the blossoming of Islam were in place more than 1,000 years before the birth of Mohammed. Islam would appear as a purification of Sabaeanism by the 'Messenger of God'.[606]

It thus cannot be said that Muḥammad introduced a new religion, Islam, onto the Arabian scene. Philip Hitti said it best: "Islam...in its original form is the logical perfection of Semitic religion."[607] So too did Frederick Max Müller, founder of the discipline of comparative religions, correctly perceive the situation and report in his study of "Semitc Monotheism":

> Mohammedanism...is a Semitic religion, and its very core is monotheism. But did Mohammed invent monotheism? Did he invent even a new name of God? Not at all. His object was to destroy the idolatry of the Semitic tribes of Arabia, to dethrone the angels, the Jin, the sons and daughters who had been assigned to Allah, and to restore the faith...in one God.[608]

III. *Muḥammad, the Ka'ba and the Cult of the Black God*

We have every reason to believe that the cult of the Ka'ba had the same significance for the prophet Muḥammad that it did

---

[606] Diop, ***African Origin***, 126, 127.
[607] Philip K. Hitti (***The Arabs in History***, 10th Edition [London: MacMillan, 1970 (1937)] 8)
[608] Max Müller, "Semitic Monotheism," in idem, ***Chips from a German Workshop*** (New York: Scribner, Armstrong and CO., 1873) 366-67.

prior, minus the excessive idolatry: it was the cult center of the Black God, Aḷḷāh. As Lewy well argues in her study of the cult of the Black God in Mecca and Jerusalem:

> the Black Stone…was thought to be…a part of the body of a great god…(I)n the form of a black meteorite a piece of the deity's astral body was visible to the congregation at all times…It was…no break with the ancient religion of Mecca when Mohammed…set up the Hajar al-aswad in a place where it was accessible to the eyes and the lips of the worshipers…It is…pertinent to recall that, before designating…the Ka'ba as the qibla…Mohammed ordered his followers to turn their faces in prayer toward the sacred rock in Jerusalem. The significance of this command becomes apparent if it is kept in mind that the qibla is an outgrowth of the belief…that man can address his prayers only to a being visible to the eyes[609]…when praying…the worshipper turned his eyes either to the heavenly body itself or, in it absence, to the stone or statue representing it on earth. If, however, he was not present in the town where a sacred stone, assumed to be a part of the deity's astral body, was visible to the congregation, he still turned his eyes in the direction of this sanctuary, it being supposed that, having visited and inspected the deity's body on the occasion of the annual pilgrimage, he could visualize it and thus address his prayer to it even from a distant point or locality.[610]

Muḥammad's reported interaction with *Al-Hajar al-Aswad* or the Black Stone is equally suggestive. He is known to have circumambulated the Ka'ba on camelback while pointing to the Black Stone with a staff exclaiming, *Aḷḷāh Akbar* (Aḷḷāh is the

---

[609] We are here reminded of the famous "Ḥadīth of Jibrīl" in which Muḥammad defines ***iḥsān*** as "to worship God as though you see Him, and if you cannot see Him, then indeed He sees you."

[610] Lewy, "Origin and Significance," 348, 349, 351.

greatest).[611] He was observed touching the stone with a stick and then kissing the stick. According to ‘**Abd Allāh b.** ‘Umar, son of the second caliph, Muḥammad would touch the Black Stone, kiss it, and weep for a long time. He reportedly said to ‘Umar “O ‘Umar, this is the place where one should shed tears.” It is not made clear why interacting with the Black Stone was a source of such sadness,[612] but that the Prophet made some intimate, deeply emotional association between the stone and Aḷḷāh is quite evident from these reports. In this regard, a famous hadith of the Prophet is relevant: “The Ka‘ba (stone) is the Right Hand of Aḷḷāh and with it He shakes the hands of His servants as a man shakes the hand of His friend.”[613] “Right Hand” here seems to be synecdoche (a part of something standing for the whole). In the history of religious symbolism the Hand symbolized a transmitter of spiritual and physical energy.[614] This is an apt description of the secondary black body that the creator-god made for himself in order to be able to transmit his divine luminosity to earth without scorching it. That the Black Stone as Right Hand of Aḷḷāh actually represents Aḷḷāh himself is further suggested by some Nabatean remains. At the Qaṣr el-Bint temple at Petra dedicated to Aḷḷāh (*Dhu 'l-Sharā*) there has been found in the *adyton* (sanctuary) a representation of the god as a marble hand.[615]

The Black Stone is situated in the southeast corner of the Ka‘ba precisely facing the winter sunrise, where the sun is reborn. This brings to mind the Nabataean ritual in which the birth of the solar/aquatic deity Aḷḷāh (*Dhu 'l-Sharā*), represented

---

[611] Bukharī, ***Ṣaḥīḥ***, II, 697.
[612] Maybe the motif of the ‘death’ of the Black God is involved. See
[613] Ibn Qutayba, ***Ta' wil Mukhtalif al-Hadith*** (1972) 215 (=1995 ed; p. 198, 262); Al-Qurtubi, ***al-Asna fi Sharh Asma' Allah al-Husna***, II:90-91.
[614] Jack Tressidder, ***Symbols and Their Meanings*** (New York: Barnes and Noble, 2006) 22.
[615] Healey, ***Religion of the Nabataeans***, 97.

by a black stone, was celebrated at the Kaʿba in Petra with rituals similar to those associated with the Meccan (Islamic) Black Stone, such as the seven circumambulations. In the Petra ritual, Epiphanius suggests, **Aḷḷāh** (*Dhu 'l-Sharā*) is portrayed as a babe, the new born sun/son of the virgin. In the light of this we cannot help but notice that the silver casing enclosure of the Black Stone at the Meccan Kaʿba is in the shape of a woman's dilated vulva and the stone itself resembles the crown of the newborn Black God (Figure 37)! To be sure, this silver casing that strikes us so much like a dialated vulva was not in existence in Muḥammad's time. It was the anti-caliph **ʿAbd Allāh** b. al-Zubayr (d.692) who first encircled the stone with silver rings, subsequent caliphs providing the frame. Yet this visual recall of the ancient Semitic motif of the black mother giving birth to the black god is astonishing and highlights the words quoted above of Warwick Ball: "the ancient Semitic idea of the sacred cube reaches culmination in the center of Semitic worship today: the Kaʿba…at Mecca."[616]

IV. *Muḥammad and the Reformation of Islam*

The monotheistic revolt against Arabian idolatry and 'associationism' did not begin in the seventh century with Muḥammad.[617] A number of 4th-5th century CE inscriptions evidence a radical religious change in South Arabia: 'associationism' gives way to a monotheism focused on a deity called simply *Raḥmān-ān*, "the Merciful." This pre-Qur'**ānic** Arabian monotheism seems to be of neither Jewish nor Christian

---

616 Ball, ***Rome in the East*** 379-380.

617 On Arabian idolatry on the eve of Muḥammad's reform see Michael Lecker, "Was Arabian Idol Worship Declining on the Eve of Islam?" in idem, ***People, Tribes And Society In Arabia Around The Time Of Muhammad*** (Burlington, VT: Ashgate, 2005) 1-43.

origin.[618] The Orthodox Christian Sozomenos (wrt. ca. 443-450), who was aware of the fact that the Arabs first observed the same monotheistic customs as the pre-Mosaic ancient Hebrews but over time succumbed to the idolatry of their neighbors, reported that some northern Arabs at his time also rejected this idolatry and returned to the monotheistic way of life.[619] Patricia Crone recognized the implications of this report for Islamic tradition:

> What Sozomen's information adds up to is that by the fifth century the Arabs themselves had become familiar with the idea that they were Abrahamic monotheists by origin, at least in the Gaza area (a Qurashī *matjar*), and that some of them reacted by becoming what the Islamic tradition describes as ***ḥanīfs***.[620]

The ***ḥunafā***ʾ (sing. ***ḥanīf***) were individuals spread out in the urban areas - Mecca, Yahtrib (Medina), al-Ṭāʾif, etc. - who adhered to a non-idolatraous monotheism, called ***ḥanīfiyya***, long before Muḥammad emerged on the scene. As Tisdall noted:

> Muhammad was by no means the first of his nation who became convinced of the folly and worthlessness of the popular religion of the Arabs of the time, and desired to effect reform. Some years before his appearance as a prophet...a number of men arose in Medina, Ṭâif, and Mecca...who rejected the idol-worship and polytheism of the people at large...the men of whom we speak determined to restore the worship of God Most High (Allâh Taʿâla) to its proper place by abolishing, not only the

[618] Alfred F. L. Beeston "The Religions Of Pre-Islamic Yemen" in J. Chelhod (Ed.), ***L'Arabie Du Sud Histoire Et Civilisation Volume I: Le Peuple Yemenite Et Ses Racines*** (Paris, 1984) 268.
[619] *Ecclesiastical History*, 299.
[620] Patrician Crone, ***Meccan Trade and the Rise of Islam*** (Princeton: Princeton University Press, 1987) 191 n. 104.

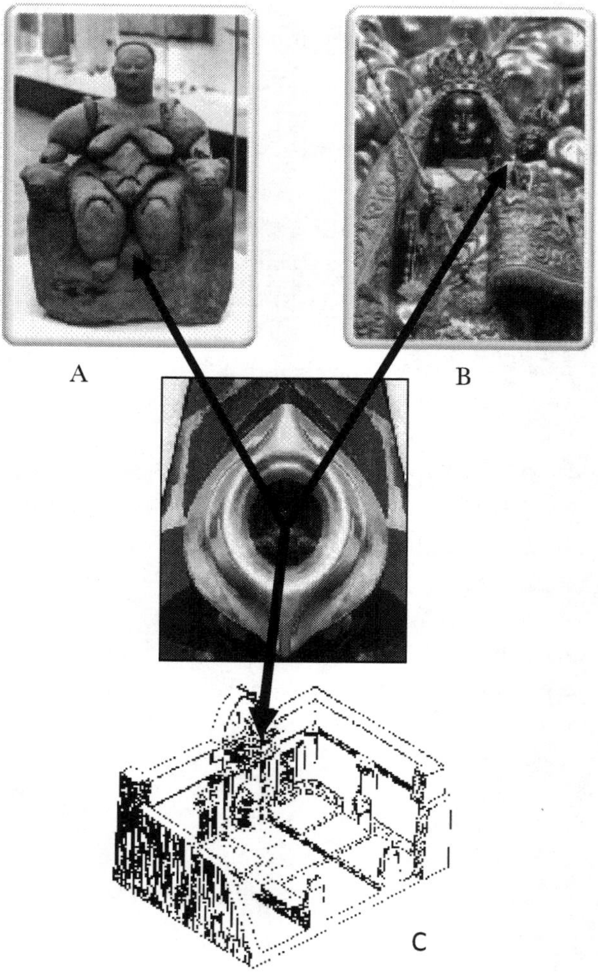

Figure 38
The Black Stone, representing Allah, as analogous to the divine cranium emerging from Central Anatolian Mother-Goddess (A); the divine Black Child who emerged from the divine Black Madonna (B); and the divine Bull that emerges from the womb of the Mother Goddess in her bear for (C)

cult of the inferior deities who had almost entirely supplanted Him, but also many of the most immoral of the practices then prevalent...[621]

The ***ḥunafā'*** rejected idolatry, abstained from wine and foods sacrificed to gods other than Allāh, made ablution (ritual purification), and avoided menstruating women.[622] The existence of these Arab monotheists before Muḥammad is certain.[623] **The *ḥunafā'*** were an expression of ancient Arabian monotheism and the precursor of Muḥammad's Islam.[624] Some of these 'Allāh-alone' worshippers, like the 'tall and black' Muḥammad b. Maslama of the Banū (tribe of) Aws in Medina and Abū **Ṣirma b. Abī Anas of the Banū 'Adiyy b. al**-Nijjā**r,** joined the prophet Muḥammad's movement once he stood up. Others, however, like Umayya b. Ab**ī l-Ṣalt of** al-Ṭā'if and Abū **Qays b. al**-Aslat of Medina, two prominent ***ḥunafā'***, became implacable ememies of the new prophet due to loyalties to the Quraysh.[625] Muḥammad even had a number of ***ḥunafā'*** in his own family. In fact, the four leading ***ḥunafā'*** in Mecca in his day – **Zayd b. 'Amr b. Nufayl,** Ubayd-Allāh **b. Jaḥsh, 'Uthmān b. Ḥuwayrith, and Waraqah b. Nawfal** – "were (all) related to Muhammad, being descended from a common

[621] W. St. Clair Tisdall, ***The Original Sources of the Qur'ân*** (London, 1911) 260.
[622] On the ***ḥunafā'*** and ***ḥanīfiyya*** see ***Encyclopaedia of the Qur'ān*** (6 vols.; ed. Jane Dammen McAuliffe; Leiden: Brill, 2001)II: 402-403 s.v. **Ḥanī**f by Uri Rubin.
[623] Hamilton A.R. Gibb, "Pre-Islamic Monotheism in Arabia," ***HTR*** 55 (1962): 271: "the existence of a group or groups representing a local monotheistic tradition can be regarded as historically certain"; Yehuda D. Nevo and Judith Koren, "The Origins of the Muslim Descriptions of the Jāhilī Meccan Sanctuary," ***JNES*** 49 (1990): 42: "The evidence amassed so far indicates that a basic form of (Arab) monotheism and emphasis on Abraham existed...in the Negev for several centuries before Islam". See further Charles J. Lyall, "The words '**Ḥanī**f' and 'Muslim'," ***JRAS*** 35 (1903): 774.
[624] Khalil Athamina, "Abraham in Islamic Perspective: Reflections on the Development of Monotheism in Pre-Islamic Arabia," ***Der Islam*** 81 (2004): 202.
[625] See especially Uri Rubin, ***"Ḥanīfiyya* and Ka'ba: An inquiry into the Arabian pre**-Islamic background of *dīn **Ibāhīm,"*** ***JSAI*** 13 (1990): 85-111.

ancestor Liwa'."[626] The first, **Zayd b. 'Amr b. Nufayl**, is particularly important because it was him, from the Black Quraysh tribe,[627] who introduced Muḥammad to 'Islam' when Muḥammad was still an idolator.

Zayd, a distant relative of the Prophet and cousin to Islam's second caliph, 'Umar b. al-Khaṭṭāb, was by far the most important ***ḥanīf*** for the development of Muḥammad's Islam. He was apparently an outspoken *public* critic of the Quraysh's idolatry and 'pagan' practices, in much the same way Muḥammad would be some years later.[628] He adhored idolatry, condemned the practice of burying baby girls alive, and refused to eat meat sacrified to gods other than Aḷḷāh. Some of his poetry is preserved in which his religious views are expressed:

Am I to worship one lord or a thousand?
If there are as many as you claim,
I renounce al-L**ā**t and al-'Uzz**ā** both of them
As any strong-minded person would would.
I will not worship al-'Uzz**ā** an her two daughters,
Nor will I visit the two images of the Ban**ū** 'Amr..
I serve my Lord the Compassionate (*al-Raḥmān*)
That the forgiving Lord may pardon my sin,
So keep to the fear of Aḷḷāh your Lord.

---

[626] Tisdall, ***Original Sources***, 273. Ubayd-Allāh b. Jaḥsh was son of maternal aunt of the Prophet, thus a cousin, and Waraqa and '**Uthmān** were cousins of his first wife Khadījah.
[627] See below.
[628] Ibn Is**ḥāq noted that:** "He publically rebuked the Quraysh." 98-99.

Most significantly, Zayd apparently described his ***ḥanīfiyya* as *islām*,** saying: "I have surrendered my face [*aslamtu wajhī*] to Him to Whom the earth…surrenders".[629] The verbal idiom, *aslama wajh*, found later in the Qur'**ā**n (3:20), is likely the root of the verbal noun ***islām*.** In other words, Zayd was a self-confessed *muslim* reformer before Mu**ḥ**ammad. We are even told that he prostrated in his worship of A**ḷḷ**āh, putting the palms of his hands to the ground as he bent his body down in worship.[630] This of course anticipates the Muslim *suj**ū**d*.

As an outspoken critic of the idolatry of the Quraysh, Zayd earn the latter's ire, as did Mu**ḥ**ammad later. Among his severest harassers was al-Kha**ṭṭ**ab, his uncle and the father of 'Umar, the second caliph. The harassment was so severe in fact, Zayd had to leave Mecca, retreating to the outskirts. He could reenter the city only secretly. After this exile, he spent considerable time in a cave in the mountain opposite the city, Mount **Ḥirā**'. When he died, five years before Mu**ḥ**ammad stood up, he was buried at the foot of the mount. Now this is the very mount to which Mu**ḥ**ammad would begin retreating to engage in certain religious practices before his Call. It was in one such cave, according to a number of reports, that the still 'pagan' Mu**ḥ**ammad encountered Zayd who introduced him to ***ḥanīfiyya/islām*.** [631] According to a tradition reported in Ibn Is**ḥā**q (d. 767),[632] A**ḥmad b. Ḥanbal (d.** 855),[633] al-Kharg**ūshī**

[629] On which see Charles J. Lyall, "The Words 'Ḥanīf' and 'Muslim,' ***JRAS*** 35 (1903): 783.

[630] Ibn Isḥāq, 99-100.

[631] Ibn al-Kalbī reports in his ***Kitāb aṣnān*** (Ed. A**ḥmad Zakī Pasha** [**Cairo,** 1914] 19.) **that** the Prophet "offered a white ewe to al-'**Uzzā following** the religious practices of his people." 19.

[632] Manuscript Qaraw**īyūn** 727 in Fez, translated and published by A. Guillaume, "New Light on the life of Muhammad,' ***Journal of Semitic Studies***, Monograph No. 1 (1960):27ff.

[633] ***Musnad***, III, 116-17, no. 1648.

(d. 1015),[634] Ibn Kath**īr**,[635] and others, Zayd b. 'Amr passed Mu**ḥ**ammad and Zayd b. **Ḥā**ritha, the Prophet's adopted son, while they were eating meat sacrificed to one of the idols in this cave. Mu**ḥ**ammad offered some to Zayd (b. 'Amr), who refused and admonished Mu**ḥ**ammad for this, declaring: "I don't eat meat offered to any god but ***Aḷḷāh*** *ta'**ālā***". Mu**ḥ**ammad was deeply affected by this. After the exchange he and Zayd b. **Ḥā**ritha are said to have went to the Ka'ba and circumambulated it, he forever forbidding Zayd b. **Ḥā**ritha from stroking the idols again. Mu**ḥ**ammad later claimed: "By A**ḷḷāh**, I did not draw near the idols at all (after this) until God granted me prophethood."[636] Uri Rubin perceives the significance of this encounter:

> the tradition…implies that [Zayd] was a monotheistic adherent of *d**īn Ibāhīm*** (the monotheistic religion of Abraham), while Mu**ḥ**ammad was still an idolater...From this tradition, which Muslim scholars indeed tried to reshape, one must…conclude that Zayd was indeed a ***ḥanīf*** who introduced to Muḥammad the monotheistic *d**īn Ibāhīm.***[637]

This inspiration from the ***ḥanīf*** **Zayd** might account for the fact that Mu**ḥ**ammad first called his reform movement ***ḥanīfiyya,*** only later adoting 'Islam' as the name of his brand of ***ḥanīfiyya.***[638] But this too, as we saw, is consistent with Zayd who seems to have used both descriptions. It was thus through these early 'A**ḷḷāh**–alone' advocates, the prominent ones in Mecca being members of his own [Black] family,

---

634 ***Sharaf al-Muṣṭafā.***

635 ***Al-Bidāya wa 'l-nihāya*** (Beirut and Riyadh, 1966) II:240.

636 On the various versions of this tradition see M.J. Kister, " 'A Bag of Meat': A Study of an Early '**Ḥadīth**'" ***BSOAS*** 33 (1970): 267-275.

637 Uri Rubin, ***"Ḥanīfiyya*** **and Ka'ba**: An inquiry into the Arabian pre-Islamic background of *d**īn Ibāhīm,"*** ***JSAI*** 13 (1990): 101 [art.=85-111].

638 Waardenburg, "Towards a Periodization," 311: "Significantly, the movement took the name of the **Ḥanīfiyya**…before becoming known as Isl**ā**m."

that Muḥammad is introduced to ***islām.*** It has elsewhere been demonstrated that the popular, orthodox tale of the Prophet's encounter in the cave with the angel Jibrīl, an encounter said to have initiated him into his prophethood, is a secondary pious fiction created by weaving multiple, independent (and at times contradictory) traditions together.[639] This is not at all to suggest that there was no divine or angelic involvement in Muḥammad's 20 year prophetic reform movement; it is to say that his *introduction* to ***islām*** was through his own (Black) kinsmen. His own [Black] father, we recall, was named ***'Abd Allāh,*** 'servant of **Aḷḷāh**'.[640]

---

[639] Wesley Williams, "Tajalli wa-Ru'ya: A Study of Anthropomorphic Theophany and Visio Dei in the Hebrew Bible, the Qur'an and Early Sunni Islam," unpublished PhD dissertation, University of Michigan, Ann Arbor, 2008, Chapter Five.
[640] On the significance of which see Tisdall, ***Original Sources***, 34.

Chapter Six

Beyond Bilāl: *The Black Muslims in Arabia*

I. *Islam's Black Tribes*

Historian St. Clair Drake, in an otherwise remarkably astute discussion of Blacks and race in Islam, certainly understates the case when he states that "There were a few blacks among the original circle of believers (around Muḥammad)."[641] The most famous of these 'few' Black followers of Muḥammad is unquestionably Bilāl **b. Rabāḥ** (d. 642), the Ethiopian-turned-Arabian slave, who would go on to become the first Muslim caller of the faithful to prayer (Muezzin). Bilāl is *the* face of the Black contribution to Islam, such that ben-Jochannan, in his book ***The African Origins of the Major "Western" Religions***, focuses almost exclusively on him when treating the 'African Influence on Islam.'[642] So too did Dr. John Henrik Clarke, when discussing 'The Rise of Islam in Africa,' focus on Bilāl and one other, Zayd b. **Ḥāritha** (d. 630), whom Clarke misidentifies as a fellow Ethiopian.[643] An alternative ethnohistory of Islam, more consistent with currently available ethnographic data, is reflected in a report attributed to the prophet

[641] Drake, ***Black Folks***, 2:86.

[642] See Chapter IV. See further J.A. Rogers, ***World's Great Men of Color*** (New York: Macmillian, 1946) 143-147; Mohammed Abu-Bakr, ***Islam's Black Legacy: Some Leading Figures*** (Denver: Purple Dawn Books, 1993) 24-26; Edward W. Blyden, ***Christianity, Islam and the Negro Race***, 2 vols. (Edinburgh: Edinburgh University Press, 1967) I:230-231.

[643] Dr. John Henrik Clarke, *The Rise of Islam in Africa* (audio). On Zayd see below.

Muḥammad himself. We are told that Muḥammad had a dream in which he saw black and white sheep following him and the white sheep were so numerous that the black ones were hardly noticeable. When he consulted Abū Bakr, a known dream interpreter, it was explained:

> the black ones are the Arabs and the white ones are the non-Arabs who were converted to Islam after them (the black Arabs); they will be converted in such large numbers that the black ones will not be noticed any more. [644]

From this report we learn that the original Muslim followers of Muḥammad were the black Arabs who were later engulfed by the white non-Arab converts (Persians, Byzantines, Turks, etc.) to Islam. The historical data bears this out. That is to say, the Black contribution to Islam was not restricted to "a few" Blacks, most of whom were former slaves. Rather, instead of speaking of a 'Black contribution' at all, we must speak of the 'Black origins' of Islam, and the Black Arabs who are the main actors in the drama that was nascent Islam – both the protagonists and antagonists – were the Black Arabian descendents of the original Arabians. We will discuss here some of the most important black Arab tribes for the history of post-Qur'ānic Islam.

I.1. *Banū Quraysh*

No question, the most important tribe in the history of early Islam is the Quraysh, the tribe of the Prophet Muḥammad himself and the caliphs, as well as the dominant tribe in Mecca during the pre-Qur'ānic period. The Quraysh tribe was the

---

[644] **Rāghib al-Iṣfahānī, *Muḥāḍarat al Udabā'*, I,** 219; Ignaz Goldziher, ***Muslim Studies***, 2 vols. (London: George Allen and Uneven Ltd) 1:112.

paramount *black* tribe, considered the most noble of the Arab tribes. As Robert F. Spencer remarks: "It is said that the Quraysh explained their short stature and dark skin by the fact that they always carefully adhered to endogamy."[645] Al-**Jāḥiẓ** (d. 869), the important Afro-Iraqi scholar of ninth century Baghdad, noted in his *Fakhr al-s**ūdān** **'alā al**-bidan*, "The Boast of the Blacks over the Whites":

> The ten lordly sons of '**Abd al-Muṭṭalib** were deep black (*dalham*) in color and big/tall **(*ḍukhm*).** When Amir b. al-**Ṭ**ufayl saw them circumambulating (the Ka'ba) like dark camels, he said, "With such men as these is the custody of the Ka'ba preserved." '**Abd Allah** b. 'Abbas was very black and tall. Those of Ab**ū** **Ṭā**lib's family, who are the most noble of men, are more or less black (*s**ū**d*)."[646]

This report is important for our discussion, not only because '**Abd al-Muṭṭalib** and his ten black sons were pure Arabs, but also because they are the family of the Prophet, '**Abd al-Muṭṭalib** being his paternal grandfather.[647] The Syrian scholar and historian al-Dhahabī (d. 1348) too reported that '**Abd Allāh** b. 'Abbās, Mu**ḥ**ammad's first cousin, and his son, 'Alī b. '**Abd Allāh**, were "very dark-skinned."[648] 'Alī b. Ab**ū** **Ṭā**lib, first cousin of the Prophet and future fourth caliph, is described by al-Suy**ūṭ**ī and others as "husky, bald…pot-bellied, large-bearded…and jet-black (*shadīd al-udma*)."[649] 'Alī's son, Ab**ū** **Ja'far** **Mu**ḥammad,

---

645 Robert F. Spencer, "The Arabian Matriarchate: An Old Controversy," ***Southwestern Journal of Anthropology*** 8 (Winter, 1952) 488.
646 Al-Ja**ḥiẓ,** *Fakhr al-s**ūdān** **'alā al**-bidan*, in ***Risā'il Al-Jaḥiẓ***, 4 vols. (1964/1384) I:209.
647 See below.
648 al-Dhahabī, ***Siyar***, V:253
649 Al-Suy**ūṭ**ī, ***Tārikh al-khulafā*** (Cairo: Dar al-Fikr al-Arabi, 1975) 186. On *shadīd al-udma* as 'jet-black' see Berry, ***Unknown***, 54.

according to Ibn Sa'd (d. 845), described 'Alī thusly: "He was a black-skinned man with big, heavy eyes, pot-bellied, bald, and kind of short."[650]

This convergence of blackness, nobility and Qurayshī ethnicity is further demonstrated in these lines attributed to the seventh century CE Qurayshī poet, **al**-Fa**ḍ**l b. al-'Abb**ā**s, called *al-Akh**ḍ**ar al-Lahab**ī*** "The Flaming Black". **al**-Fa**ḍ**l is the Prophet Mu**ḥ**ammad's first cousin and he said: "I am the black-skinned one (*al-Akh**ḍ**ar*). I am well-known. My complexion is black. I am from the noble house of the Arabs."[651] Ibn Man**ẓū**r (d. 1311) notes the opinion that *al-Akh**ḍ**ar* here means *aswad al-jilda*, 'Black-skinned', and signifies that **al**-Fa**ḍ**l is from *kh**ā**li**ṣ** **al**-'arab*, the pure Arabs, "because the color of most of the Arabs is dark (*al-udma*)."[652] Similarly Ibn Barr**ī** (d. 1193) said also: "He (**al**-Fa**ḍ**l) means by this that his genealogy is pure and that he is a pure Arab (*'arab**ī** ma**ḥḍ***) because Arabs describe their color as black (*al-aswad*)."[653] Thus, **al**-Fa**ḍ**l's blackness (*akh**ḍ**ar*) is the visual mark of his pure, Qurayshī background, being born of a pure Arab mother and father.

The Quraysh consisted of several sub-clans. **'Abd al-Muṭṭalib** and his descendents, including Mu**ḥ**ammad, belonged to the Ban**ū** **Hāshim**. Henry Lammens takes notice of "les H**ā**šimites, famille où dominait le sang nègre" ("the Hashimites,

---

[650] Ibn Sa'd, ***al-Ṭabaqāt al-kubrā*** (Beirut: Dar Sādir) 8:25. On Ali as short and dark brown see Henry Stubbe, ***An Account of the Rise and Progress of Muhammadanism*** (1911) XX; I.M.N. al-Jubouri, ***History of Islamic Philosophy – With View of Greek Philosophy and Early History of Islam*** (2004), 155; Philip K Hitti, ***History of the Arabs***, 10th edition (London: Macmillan Education Ltd, 1970) 183.

[651] Ibn Man**ẓū**r, *Lis**ā**n al-'arab*, s.v. اخضر IV:245f.

[652] Ibn Man**ẓū**r, *Lis**ā**n al-'arab*, s.v. اخضر IV:245; E.W. Lane, ***Arabic-English***, I: 756 s.v. خضر.

[653] Ibn Man**ẓū**r, *Lis**ā**n al-'arab*, s.v. اخضر IV:245.

the family where Black blood dominated").[654] Lammens remarks that they are "généralement qualifies de آدم = couleur foncée" ("generally described as **ā**dam = dark colored"). But the Ban**ū** **Hā**shim were not the only sub-clans noted for their blackness. The Ban**ū** Zuhra, the tribe from which the prophet's mother, Amīa bt. Wahb, hailed, was likewise noted for its blackness. See for example the famous Sa'd ibn Abī Waqqās (d.ca. 646), cousin of Amīa and uncle of Mu**ḥ**ammad. He is described as very dark, tall and flat-nosed.[655] Mu**ḥ**ammad, it should be noted, was quite proud of his uncle Sa'd whose military contributions we shall discuss below. We are told that once Mu**ḥ**ammad was sitting with some of his companions and Sa'd walked by. The prophet stopped and taunted: "That's *my* uncle. Let any man show me *his* uncle."[656]

Another important Qurayshī sub-clan is the Ban**ū** 'l-Mughīra of the larger Qurayshī sub-clan the Ban**ū** Makhz**ū**m. Al-Ja**ḥiẓ** noted: "The clan of Mughīra is the *Khuḍr* of the tribe of Makhz**ū**m."[657] By "the *Khuḍr*" al-Ja**ḥiẓ** means the exceptionally black-skinned.[658] Thus, the second caliph 'Umar's mother, **Ḥantama bt. Hāshim b. al**-Mughīra, from Ban**ū** 'l-Mughīra, is described as black.[659] This was an exceptionally powerful Qurayshī clan. Hish**ā**m b. **al**-Mughīra was head (*sayyid*) of the Quraysh in Mecca, such that "Hish**ā**m" and "Mecca" were interchangeable terms. When he died the people of Mecca were summoned to the funeral of their 'lord (*rabb*)'.[660] They were also a

---

[654] ***Études sur le siècle des Omayyades*** (Beirut: Imprimerie Calholique, 1930) 44.
[655] al-Dhahabī, ***Siyar***, 1:97.
[656] 'Abd al-**Raḥmān Rāfat al-Bāsh**ā, ***Ṣuwar min ḥayāt al-Ṣaḥābah*** (Beirut: **Mu'assasat al**-Ris**ā**lah, 1974-75) 287.
[657] Al-Jā**ḥiẓ,** *Fakhr al-s**ūdān** '**alā al**-bidan*,
[658] See also Berry, ***Unknown Arabs***, 78.
[659] Al-Mas'**ūdī, *Prairies***, IV, 192; ***EI2*** 6:139 s.v. Makhz**ū**m, Ban**ū** by M.
[660] D.S. Margoliouth, ***Mohammed and the Rise of Islam***, 2nd edition (New York and Enemy: G.P. Pulnam's Sons, 1905) 12; ***EI²*** 6:137 s.v. Makhz**ū**m by M. Hinds.

significant part of the Meccan opposition to Muḥammd. In fact, the infamous 'Amr b. Hishām, better known as Abū Jahl ("Father of Ignorance"), the implacable enemy of Muḥammd who brought about the fateful boycott against the Prophet in 616-18, was the leader of the exceptionally black Banū 'l-Mughīra.[661] He commanded the Meccan forces in the battle of Badr, a prominent portion of which were from the Banū 'l-Mughīra. However, when Muḥammd conquered Mecca in 630, this black tribe accepted Islam and was incorporated into the new order.

This blackness of the Quraysh tribe is not insignificant to the religious history of Islam. The Quraysh were the custodians of the cult of the Ka'ba in pre-Qur'ānic Mecca and at religious ceremonies they would declare *naḥnu ahlu ḷḷāhi* ("We are the People of **Aḷḷāh**") and throughout Arabia they were known as *ahlu ḷḷāh*, the People of **Aḷḷāh**.[662] In other words, the black tribe *par excellence* was also the **Aḷḷāh**-tribe *par excellence* and custodians of the cult of the Black God. Nevertheless, or rather as a consequence, Muḥammad's greatest struggle was with his own kinsmen, this black, **Aḷḷāh**-venerating Quraysh tribe. In the end, however, it would be the black Quraysh that became the rulers of Islam, at least in the short term. Not only were the Sunni caliphs drawn from them, but the Shiite Imams, descendents of the black 'Alī b. Abū Ṭālib, were likewise black Qurayshī Arabs.[663] To be sure, this 'black Islam' will eventually be eclipsed by a "white" (i.e. Persian and Turkish) Islam: those "white sheep" who followed the black sheep into Islam in such large

---

661 ***EI²*** 6:138 s.v. Makhzūm by M. Hinds.
662 Uri Rubin, "The Ilāf of Quraysh: A Study of sūra CVI," ***Arabica*** 31 (1984): 165-188; Margoliouth, ***Mohammed***, 19.
663 Berry, ***Unknown Arabs***, 62-65.

numbers that the "black sheep" are now unnoticeable and forgotten.

I.2. *Banū Khazraj and Banū al-Aws*

The two most historically important groups for the history of early (Muḥammd's) Islam are the *Muhājirūn*, the 'Emigrants' or original followers of Muḥammad in Mecca who immigrated with him to Yathrib (Medina) due to Qurayshī hostilities, and the *Anṣār*, the 'Helpers' in Yathrib that received and aided Muḥammad and the *Muhājirūn*. The *Anṣār* consisted primarily of two Medinese tribes, the Khazraj and al-Aws. At the time of the *Hijra* or Emigration these tribes were involved in a bitter rivalry. They are actually two sub-clans of a common tribe, the very dark-complexioned Banū Azd. Originally a southern tribe, Azd divided in the third century CE into four main branches: Azd al-Sarāt, in the area around the Sarawat mountain range in the western portion of the peninsula; Azd al-Shanu'a in the Tihama on the Red Sea; Azd 'Umān, in Oman and Eastern Arabia; and Ghassan, in Syria.[664] The Banū Azd were a black tribe, a trait retained in its many sub-clans. The Ghassan were called black-skinned (*akhḍar*)[665] as was the Shanu'a (*adam*).[666] The Dawāsir, a bedouin tribe of the central desserts of Yemen and Nejd and a branch of Azd, were described by Burckhadt when he encountered them in the nineteenth century as "very tall men, and almost black."[667]

---

[664] ***EI²*** 1:811-813 s.v. Azd by G. Strenziok. For a history of the eastern branches of the Azd see Naji Hasan, ***The Role of the Arab Tribes in the East During the Umayyads (40/660 – 132/749)*** (Baghdad University, 1975-1976)

[665] Ibn Manẓūr, ***Lisān al-'Arab***, 1:848.

[666] Muslim, ***Ṣaḥīḥ***, # 239.

[667] ***Travels in Arabia***, vol. II (1829) 385. Robert Gordon Latham, ***Descriptive Ethnology***, 2 vols. (London: J. van Voorst, 1859) 2:83 too noted that the Dawāsir were "blacker than their neighbors".

Well-known representatives of the Khazraj and al-Aws were noted for their blackness. Ubāda b. al-**Ṣā**mit (d. 34/654), called "a negro" by Phillip Hitti,[668] was "an eminent An**ṣārī**"[669] from the tribe Awf b. al-Khazraj, in particular the subgroup Ban**ū** **Ghanm b.** Awf b. al-Khazraj.[670] Ub**ā**da was a pure, very black-skinned Arab.[671] Of the Aws there is Mu**ḥ**ammad b. Maslama (d.666), who was a ***ḥ**anīf* in Yathrib before the Prophet's arrival there. He was "black-skinned, and tall"[672]. So too Nabtal b. al-**Ḥ**ārith of the Aws, of whom al-Baladharī said: "He was tall and jet-black, with nappy hair, a huge body and red eyes."[673]

The point cannot be stressed enough: the two historically most significant groups in terms of the genesis and early evolution of Mu**ḥ**ammad's movement, the *Muhājir**ū**n* and the *Anṣār*, were drawn primarily from black tribes, the descendents of the ancient Afrabians. As such, most of the important figures in early, post-Qur'**ā**nic Islam were from among these *Black Muslims.* Zayd b. Th**ā**bit (d. 665-6), from the black Ban**ū** Khazraj, is illustrative of this point. He was Mu**ḥ**ammad's personal secretary who collected from him the verses of the Qur'**ā**n. It was he, Zayd (not to be confused with Zayd b. **Ḥā**ritha; see below), who prepared the first *mushaf* or text of the Qur'**ā**n and delivered it to the first

---

[668] Hitti, ***History of the Arabs***, 163. See further Abu-Bakr, ***Islam's Black Legacy***, 53-54.

[669] Ibn Hibb**ā**n, ***Mashāhīr 'ulamā' al-amṣār*** **(Beirut: Dār al-**Kutub al-'**Ilmiyah,** 1995) 66.

[670] Khal**īl Ibn Aybak Ṣafadī,** ***Kitāb al-wafī bi-'l-wafayāt,*** **ed. Helmut Ritter (Istanbul: Maṭba'at al-**dawlah, 1931-) 16: 618-619; Al-**Ṭabarī,** ***The History of Al-Ṭabarī,*** **Vol. VI:** ***Muḥammad at Mecca*** **(trans. W. Montgomery Watt and M.V. McDonald** (Albany: SUNY Press, 1988) 126.

[671] Mu**ḥammad b. 'Abd Allāh al-**Himyar**ī,** ***al-Rawḍ al-mu'aṭṭar fī khabar al-aqṭār*** **(Beirut: Maktabat Lubnān,** 1975) 553. See further Berry, ***Unknown Arabs***, 68-69.

[672] Ibn **Ṣa**'d, ***al-Ṭabaqat al-kubrā,*** 3:444; Al-Dhahabī, ***Siyar***, 2:371.

[673] Al-Balādhurī, ***Ansāb al-Ashrāf*** (Cairo: Dar al-Ma'rif, 1959) 275; Ibn Is**ḥā**q, ***Sīra***, 243 (Eng.).

caliph Abū Bakr.[674] Thus, the Muslim world is indebted to this early *Black Muslim* for its most holy text.

I.3. *When Black Was Still Beautiful: The Banū Sulaym*

The Banū Sulaym were a powerful tribe who commanded the road to Medina and access to Nejd and the Persian Gulf. Both al-Jāḥiẓ and **Ibn Athīr** (11th cent. CE) noted the Banū Sulaym's deep blackness and that they were 'pure Arabs'.[675] As Tariq Berry points out, a number of the so-called 'Arab Crows,' Arabian poets that were so black-skinned that they recalled the blackness of a crow, were Sulaymī's.[676] They played an important role in the struggle between Muḥammad and the Quraysh,[677] participating in the treacherous Biʾr Maʿūna ambush in 625 that killed 69 of 70 Muslims. They were also a part of the confederate of tribes that fought the Muslims at the Battle of Khandaq (Battle of the Trench) in 627. On the other hand, the Banū Sulaym adopted Islam in 630 and became very significant politically in the new order, as we will see below.

The Banū Sulaym were noted not only for their blackness, but for their beauty as well. Naṣr **b. Hajjāj b. ʿIlāt al**-Sulaymī's beauty caused such a commotion in Medina that the Caliph ʿUmar b. al-Khaṭṭāb had to exile him to Basra where the governor was a fellow Sulaymī, Mujāshiʿ **b. Masʿūd.** Naṣr's cousin, Abū Dhi'b, was also expelled on the grounds of his beauty.[678] This 'black beauty' no doubt played a role in the Banū

674 On Zayd b. Thābit see ***EI²*** s.v.

675 Al-Jaḥiẓ, *Fakhr al-sūdān ʿalā al-bidan,* translated by T. Khalidi in ***Islamic Quarterly*** 25 (1981): 23. On the blackness of the Sulaym see further Michael Lecker, ***The Banū Sulaym: A Contribution to the Study of Early Islam*** (Jerusalem: Hebrew University, 1989) 242-245; Berry, ***Unknown Arabs***, 76-77.

676 Berry, ***Unknown Arabs***, 77.

677 ***EI²*** 9:817 s.v. Sulaym by M. Lecker.

678 Lecker, ***Banū Sulaym,*** 79.

Sulaym's popularity. When 'Umar asked that prominent persons from the provinces be sent to him, all of those sent were reportedly Sulaymīs.[679] The prophet Muḥammad himself married a Sulaymī, Sanā' **bt. Asmā' bt. al-Ṣalt al-Ḥarāmiyya**, because of her beauty and intelligence.[680] On the other hand, he was also scandalized by their beauty. It is a Sulaymī**, Ṣafwān b. al**-Mu'**aṭṭ**al (d.638), whose beauty can be said to be at the center of the infamous *ifk* (lie) affair. While traveling '**Ā**'isha - reputedly the favorite wife of the prophet - got left behind accidentally by her caravan back to Medina. One of Muḥammad's companions, **Ṣafwān**, who was the caravan's rear guard, pulled up after several hours and brought '**Ā**'isha back to Medina on his camel. Immediately upon entering the city rumors spread that '**Ā**'isha and this young, handsome man (many reports stress his good looks!) had an affair on the way. '**Ā**'isha's honor was vindicated, according to Islamic tradition, by the revelation of surat Al-Nūr [24].[681]

I.4. *Banū **Muḥārib and** Banū Sakūn*

The Banū **Muḥārib** were a typical Bedouin tribe from the mountainous region of southern Nejd, between Medina and al-Yamāma. According to the renowned Islamic linguist of the 14th century CE Ibn Manẓūr the **Muḥārib** were *akhḍar*, black.[682] They were hostile to Muḥammad early in his campaign and he sent a number of expeditions against them. In 630, however, the Banū **Muḥārib** gave formal allegiance to the prophet of Islam.[683]

---

679 Lecker, ***Banū Sulaym***, 80.
680 Lecker, ***Banū Sulaym***, 85.
681 On him see ***EI²*** 8:819-820 s.v. **Ṣafwān b. al**-Mu'**aṭṭ**al by G.H.A. Juynboll.
682 Ibn Manẓūr, ***Lisān al- 'Arab***, 1:848.
683 ***EI²*** vol. 7 s.v. **Muḥārib** by G. Levi Della Vida. On the black Muḥārib see also Berry, ***Unknown Arabs***, 77.

The Banū Sakūn played a much more critical role in the early history of Islam. They were a branch of the Kinda tribe, which was an Arab tribe from Southern Arabia (Hadramawt).[684] According to a report in al-**Ṭabarī** (d.923) the Banū Sakūn were an Arab tribe distinguished by their "black complexion and straight hair".[685] These black Sakūnīs were involved in the more infamous episodes of early Islam. From the Sakūn came the sub-clan Banū Tujīb who were among the earliest settlers in Egypt and principally concerned in "the turning point in the history of Islam," the revolt against the third caliph **'Uthmān b. 'Affān**.[686] They were part of the Egyptian rebels that marched on Medina.[687] It was in fact a Sak**ūnī,** either **Sūdān b. Ḥumrān** or **Kināna b. Bishr**, who wielded the weapon and killed the caliph. And it was another Sak**ūnī, Khālid b. Muljam** who assassinated the fourth caliph **'Alī b. Abī Ṭalib.**[688] A memorable event in the Second Civil War also involved the Sakūn. The stone catapults that rained in 683 on the ***Ḥaram*** controlled by the anti-caliph **'Abd Allāh b. al**-Zubayr, catching the Ka'ba on fire, were those of **Ḥuṣayn b. Numayr** al-Sakūnī who conducted the siege of Mecca for the Umayyad Caliph Yazīd b. Mu'āwiya (d. 683).[689] **Ḥuṣayn** was governor of the important district of **Ḥimṣ** under Yazīd.[690]

---

684 ***EI*¹** 4:1019 s.v. Kinda by F. Krenkow.

685 Al-**Ṭabarī,** ***The History of Al-Ṭabarī*, Vol. XII: *The Battle of al-Qādisiyyah and the Conquest of Syria and Palestine*** (trans. Yohanan Friedmann; Albany: SUNY Press) 12.

686 ***EI*¹** 4:1019 s.v. Kinda by F. Krenkow.

687 Martin Hinds, "The Murder of the Caliph 'Uthmân," ***IJMES*** 3 (1972): 450-469.

688 Al-**Ṭabarī,** ***The History***, XII: 12-13; ***EI*²** 3:887-890 s.v. Ibn Muldjam by L. Veccia Vaglieri.

689 G.R. Hawting, ***The Fist Dynasty of Islam: The Umayyad Caliphate AD 661-750*** , Second Edition (London and New York: Routledge, 2000) 48.

690 ***EI*²** 5:119 s.v. Kinda by I. Shahîd; ***EI*²** 3:620 s.v. al-**Ḥuṣayn b. Numayr** by H. Lammens-[V. Cremonesi].

II. *Zayd b. Ḥāritha: Muḥammad's Black Son and Successor*

In 578 CE in the Dūmat al-Jabal area of Arabia Zayd b. **Ḥāritha** was born to an Arab father, **Ḥāritha b. Sharāḥīl** from the Southern Arabian tribe Banū Kalb, and an Arab mother, Su'**dā**, from the Banū Ma'n.[691] While a young boy, his village was attacked by a rival Arab tribe while his father was away. The young Zayd was among those taken as captives and eventually sold as a slave at the Ukāẓ market. His purchaser, **Ḥakīm b. Ḥuzām**, was a nephew of Khādija, Muḥammad's wife. She presented Zayd to Muḥammad as a gift. We are told that Muḥammad took an immediate liking to Zayd and freed him. Zayd will eventually grow so dear to Muḥammad that the latter adopted him as his son, such that the young man became known as Zayb ibn Muḥammad (Zayd the son of Muḥammad) as well as ***Ḥibb Rasūl Aḷḷāh,*** "the Beloved of the Messenger of God."

Zayd was very dark-skinned, short and rather flat-nosed.[692] On this basis many wrongly assume he was an enslaved Ethiopian. When he is described as a "negro slave"[693] the implication is that he, like the Abyssinian Bilāl, was an African enslaved in Arabia.[694] Dr. John Henrik Clarke even goes so far as to declare that Zayd and Bilāl were together two Ethiopian slaves.[695] This is surely incorrect. Zayd was actually a Black Arab

---

691 Khalid Muhammad Khalid, ***Men Around the Messenger*** (New Revised Edition; Kuala Lumpur, 2005) 232ff; ***EI²*** 4:492 s.v. Kalb b. Wabara by J.W. Fück; ***EI¹*** 8:1194 s.v. Zayd b. Ḥāritha by V. Vacca; Sir William Muir, ***The Life of Moḥammad from Original Sources*** (Edinburgh: John Grant, 1923) 35 n. 2; Abu-Bakr, ***Islam's Black Legacy***, 36.

692 Khalid, ***Men Around the Messenger***, 232.

693 Vasudeo B. Mehto, "If Europe had been Muslimised," ***Islamic Review*** 2 (1932): 220.

694 E.g. J.A. Rogers, ***Sex and Race: Negro-Caucasian Mixing in All Ages and All Lands*** (St. Petersburg, Fl: Helga M. Rogers, 1967; 9th edition) 96; idem, ***World's Great Men of Color*** 2 vols. (New York: Collier Books, 1996 [1973]) II: 539-40.

695 *The Rise of Islam in Africa* (audio).

from tribes descendent from the original Afrabians. His slave status resulted from inter-Arab conflict.

Some years after being with Muḥammad Zayd was spotted in Mecca by a relative who promptly gave the good news to his father **Ḥāritha** who was torn up by his son's disappearance and had searched far and wide for him. Receiving the good news, we are told, **Ḥāritha** and his brother rushed to Mecca and identified themselves to the now-prophet, requesting that he allow their son and nephew to return with them. Heart-broken, but knowing it to be the just thing to do, Muḥammad is said to have put the matter to Zayd himself, all parties agreeing to honor the young man's wishes. Zayd replied that Muḥammad was the best father and uncle he had known, and thus opted to stay. Upon hearing this, according to a report on the authority of the prophet's wife 'Ā'isha, Muḥammad took the hand of Zayd and went to the Ka'ba, declaring to the Quraysh that were gathered there: "Bear witness, all ye that are present, Zayd is my son: I will be his heir, and he shall be mine."[696] This implies that black Zayd is selected as the prophet's successor, except that he died before Muḥammad. What is implied here is explicitly stated in another report attributed to 'Ā'isha who says: "The Prophet never sent Zayd on an expedition except as commander, and if his life wasn't so short, he would have made him his successor."[697] Confirmation of Muḥammad's intent to make Zayd his successor is no doubt found in the fact that whenever the prophet was away on an expedition, he left Zayd as governor and commander in Medina. [698] In other words, Muḥammad always put Zayd in command in his absence, both on military

---

[696] Khalid, ***Men Around the Messenger***, 235; Muir, ***Life of Moḥammad***, 35.
[697] Khalid, ***Men Around the Messenger***, 236; Muir, ***Life of Moḥammad***, 322.
[698] ***EI¹*** 8:1194 s.v. Zayd b. Hāritha by V. Vacca.

expeditions and as governor of the nascent Muslim state in Medina.

After two failed marriages, Zayd married the prophet's Ethiopian foster mother, Baraka, and they bear a son, Usāma b. Zayd, who inherited from his parents black skin and a flat nose.[699] He also inherited from them Muḥammad's affection, being called ***Ḥibb Ibn Ḥibb Rasūl Aḷḷāh,*** "The Beloved, son of the Beloved of the Messenger of God." In accordance with the prophet's practice, the first caliph Abū Bakr would leave Usāma in charge in Medina while out on expeditions.[700]

III. *Muḥammad: Black or White?*

In his work, ***Islam's Black Legacy: Some Leading Figures*** (1993), Mohammed Abu-Bakr includes among 62 leading Black figures of Islam the prophet Muḥammad himself.[701] Abu-Bakr rightly notes:

> According to Muslim tradition, Muhammad descended in a straight line from Ishmael's second son Kedar (Arabic: Qaidar), whose name in Hebrew signifies 'black'...From the sons of Kedar inhabiting the northern Arabian desert, sprang the noblest tribe in Arabia, the Koreish (Quraysh), the tribe from which Muhammad descended.[702]

As we have also discussed above, the Arabian Qedar were a black tribe akin to the equally black Nabataeans, and these two

---

699 ***EI¹*** 8:1048 s.v. Usāma b. Zaid by V. Vacca; ***EI¹*** 8:1194 s.v. Zayd b. Hāritha by V. Vacca; Abu-Bakr, ***Islam's Black Legacy***, 36-40.

700 ***EI¹*** 8:1048 s.v. Usāma b. Zaid by V. Vacca.

701 Abu-Bakr, ***Islam's Black Legacy***, Chapter 1. See also Rogers, ***Sex and Race***, I: 95 who states that "Mohamet, himself, was to all accounts a Negro." Ben-Jochannon too accepted that Muḥammad was "in the family of the Black Race". ***African Origins***, 237.

702 Abu-Bakr, ***Islam's Black Legacy***, 1.

were in someway related to the Quraysh, the black tribe *par excellence* of Mecca. One would thus expect the Qurayshī prophet to be black too, especially since he reportedly claimed to be a pure Arab for the house of H**ā**shim[703]: this would make him very black-skinned like the pure Arabs from that tribe. Mu**ḥ**ammad's pedigree actually demands this as his whole immediate family tree were pure, black-skinned Qurayshī Arabs. I quote again Al-Jā**ḥ**i**ẓ**'s important note in his *Fakhr al-s**ūdān** 'alā al-bidan*:

> The ten lordly sons of '**Abd al Muṭṭalib** were deep black (*dalham*) in color and big/tall (***ḍukhm***). When Amir b. al-**Ṭ**ufayl saw them circumambulating (the Ka'ba) like dark camels, he said, "With such men as these is the custody of the Ka'ba preserved." '**Abd Allah** b. 'Abbas was very black and tall. Those of Ab**ū** **Ṭā**lib's family, who are the most noble of men, are more or less black (*s**ū**d*)."[704]

'**Abd al Muṭṭalib** (d. 578) was the prophet's grandfather and '**Abd Allāh**, one of his ten 'deep black' sons, was Mu**ḥ**ammad's father. Another deep black son, al-'Abbās, was father to the above mentioned '**Abd Allah** b. 'Abbās, described as black, and **al**-Fa**ḍ**l b. al-'Abb**ā**s, whose blackness was legendary. These were the uncle and first cousins of Mu**ḥ**ammad. Ab**ū** **Ṭā**lib, another deep black uncle, was father to 'Alī b. '**Abd Allāh**, another first cousin of the prophet who was described as jet-black. All of these father-son pairs shared this deep blackness, what about the '**Abd Allāh** - Mu**ḥ**ammad pair? We would expect the same, unless Mu**ḥ**ammad's mother made a mitigating contribution. But this is not likely. Amina, the prophet's mother, was an Arab from the

---

703 He is supposed to have described himself as "Arab of the Arabs, of the purest blood of your land, of the family of the Hashim and of the tribe of Quraysh."Quoted in Chandler, "Ebony and Bronze," 285.

704 Al-Ja**ḥiẓ,** *Fakhr al-s**ūdān** 'alā al-bidan*, in ***Risā'il Al-Jaḥiẓ***, 4 vols. (1964/1384) I:209.

Qurayshī sub-clan Banū Zuhra, which was a black clan. Amina's cousin and Muḥammad's maternal uncle, Sa'd ibn Abī Waqqās, also from Banū Zuhra, was very dark, tall and flat-nosed.[705]

But Muḥammad had more than just *Qurayshī* blackness running through his veins. His great, great grandfather was **'Abd Manāf** who bore with **Ātika bt. Murra *al-Sulaymī*** the prophet's great grandfather **Ḥāshim.** That is to say that the prophet's great, great grandmother was from the jet-black Banū Sulaym. **Ḥāshim**, the great grandfather, bore with **Salmā bt. 'Amrū** *'l-Khazrajī* the prophet's grandfather, **'Abd al Muṭṭalib.** This means that his paternal great grandmother was from the black Medinese tribe Banū **Khazraj. 'Abd al Muṭṭalib** stayed within the Quraysh, but he bore the prophet's father **'Abd Allāh** with **Fāṭima bt. 'Amrū *al-Makhzūmī,*** from the exceptionally black **Makhzūm** clan.[706] Muḥammad's maternal lineage is also mixed with non-Qurayshī black Arab blood. His mother, **Amina,** is the daughter of **Wahb b. 'Abd Manāf b. Zuhra** whose mother (**Amina**'s grandmother) is said to be a Sulaymī, another **'Ātika bt. Al**-Awqaṣ.[707] The black Sulaym are thus considered the maternal uncles of the prophet and he is therefore reported to have said: "I am the son of the many **'Ātika**s of Sulaym."[708] This all indicates that Muḥammad's lineage is a mix of Qurayshī, Sulaymī, and **Khazrajī** blackness.

---

[705] al-Dhahabī, ***Siyar***, 1:97.

[706] On the significance of these matrilateral listings in Muhammad's genealogy see Daniel Martin Varisco, "Metaphors and Sacred History: The Genealogy of Muhammad and the Arab 'Tribe'," ***Anthropological Quarterly*** 68 (1995): 139-156, esp. 148-150.

[707] Ibn Athīr, ***al-Nihāya fī gharīb al-ḥadīth*** (Cairo, 1385/1965) III:180 s.v. '-t-k; Lecker, ***Banū sulaym***, 114.

[708] **Muḥammad b. Yūsuf al-Ṣāliḥī al-**Shāmī, ***Subul al-hudā wa-'l-rashād fī sīrat khayr al-'bād*** (Cairo, 1392/1972) I:384-85; Lecker, ***Banū sulaym***, 114-115.

ʿAbd Manāf + Ātika bt. Murra AL-SULAYMĪ

↓

Ḥāshim

Ḥāshim b. ʿAbd Manāf + Salmā bt. ʿAmrū 'L-KHAZRĀJĪ

↓

ʿAbd al Muṭṭalib

ʿAbd al Muṭṭalib b. Ḥāshim + Fāṭima bt. ʿAmrū AL MAKHZŪMĪ

↓

Abd Allāh

ʿAbd Allāh + Amina bt [Wahb b. ʿAbd Manāf AL-ZUHR**Ī and ʿĀtika bt. Al-**Awqaṣ **AL-**SULAYM**Ī**]

↓

Mu**ḥammad**

We thus have every reason to expect Mu**ḥ**ammad to be black-skinned, and no reason to believe anything else was possible. We in fact find him described as such in Tirmidh**ī**'s ***Shamā'il al-Muḥammadiyyah***. The following is reported on the authority of the famous Companion of the prophet, An**ā**s b. M**ā**lik:

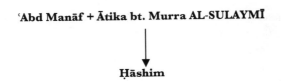

> The Messenger of Allah... was of medium stature, neither tall nor short, of a goodly build. His hair was neither curly nor

> completely straight. He had a dark brown (*asmar*) complexion and when he walked he leant forward [walking briskly].[709]

أسمر *asmar* is a dark brown as evidenced from other formations from the same root[710]: *samar* "darkness, night"; *al-ğ**ārra** al-samr**ā***ʾ "the black continent (Africa)".[711] With the pedigree that he had, any other complexion for Mu**ḥ**ammad would be incomprehensible. Yet, the same An**ā**s b. M**ā**lik who informed us of the dark brown complexion of the prophet, also informs us thusly:

> While we were sitting with the Prophet in the mosque, a man came riding on a camel. He made his camel kneel down in the mosque, tied its foreleg and then said: "Who amongst you is Mu**ḥ**ammad?" At that time the Prophet was sitting amongst us (his companions) leaning on his arm. We replied, "This white man reclining on his arm."[712]

There are several other reports that describe Mu**ḥammad** as أبيض *abya**ḍ*** white. How can the same man (An**ā**s b. M**ā**lik) describe another (Mu**ḥammad**) as both of dark brown complexion and as white? The problem, it turns out, is not in these texts but in our modern, Western inability to appreciate the pre-modern Arabic color classification system. We assume that terms such as white, green, blue, and red meant the same to the early Arabs that they do to us today. But as Moroccan scholar Tariq Berry explains in his book, ***The Unknown Arabs***, this is simply not the case:

---

[709] Al-Tirmidh**ī**, ***Shamā'il al-Muḥammadiyyah,*** # 2.
[710] J M. Cowan (ed.), ***Hans Wehr Arabic-English Dictionary*** 4th edition (Ithica: Spoken Language Services, Inc., 1994) 500 s.v. سمر.
[711] Berry, ***Unknown Arabs***, 49 notes: "When the Arabs of the past said that a person was brown, they meant that he was dark-skinned; close to black, which is actually a dark shade of brown."
[712] *Sahih al-Bukhari* vol. 1 no. 63:

> The term *white* can be very confusing to those reading about the description of people of the past because, in the past, when Arabs described someone as white, they meant something entirely different from what is meant today. In the past, when the Arabs described someone as white, they meant either that he had a pure, noble, essence or that he had a nice, smooth complexion without any blemishes. They meant he had a black complexion with a light-brownish undertone.[713]

Berry's point is confirmed by the appropriate Classical Arabic/Islamic sources. Ibn Manẓ**ūr** affirmed that "When the Arabs say that a person is white, they mean that he has a pure, clean, fautless integrity…They don't mean that he has white skin…"[714] Similarly, al-Dhahabī informs us that "When the Arabs say a person is white, they mean he is black with a light-brownish undertone."[715] Particularly important was the observation of the 9th century CE Arabic scholar Thalab, who tells us that : "The Arabs don't say that a man is white because of a white complexion. White to the Arabs means that a person is pure, without any faults. If they meant his complexion was white, they said 'red' (*aḥmar*)."[716] Indeed, as David Goldenberg notes, 'white أبيض' in pre-modern Arabic was about "luminosity, not chromaticity."[717] That is to say, أبيض connoted brilliance, not paleness of skin. The latter was described as 'red' □□□أ *aḥmar*, which is how non-Arab whites such as Persians and Byzantines were described.[718] In other words, what we call white today the early Arabs called red, and what they called white often was what we would today call black!

---

[713] Berry, ***Unknown Arabs***, 49.
[714] Ibn Manẓ**ūr, *Lisān al-ʿArab*** 7:124.
[715] Al-Dhahabī, ***Siyar aʿlām al-nubalā*** (Beirut: Risāla Establishment, 1992) 2:168.
[716] Ibn Manẓ**ūr, *Lisān al-ʿArab***. 4:210.
[717] Goldenberg, ***Curse of Ham***, 93.
[718] Goldziher, ***Muslim Studies***, 1:268.

It is certain that Mu**ḥ**ammad could not have been what we consider white today; he could not have been fair or pale-skinned at all, for a pale-skinned Arab was such an oddity that the prophet could not have claimed be a pure Quraysh**ī** Arab. The seventh century Arab from the tribe of Nakhā'ī, Shurayk al-Qā**ḍ**ī, could claim that, because it was such a rare occurrence "a fair-skinned Arab is something inconceivable and unthinkable."[719] So too did al-Dhahabī report that: "Red, in the language of the people from the Hij**ā**z, means fair-complexioned and this color is rare amongst the Arabs."[720] On the other hand, the Arabs prided themselves on being black, is conscious contrast to the pale-skinned non-Arabs. Al-Ja**ḥiẓ** could still claim in the 9th century:

العرب تفخر بسواد اللون

*al-ʿarab tafkhar bi-saw**ā**d al-lawn*

"The Arabs pride themselves in (their) black color"[721]

These noble Black Arabs even detested pale skin. Al-Mubarrad (d. 898), the leading figure in the Basran grammatical tradition, is quoted as saying: "The Arabs used to take pride in their darkness and blackness and they had a distaste for a light complexion and they used to say that a light complexion was the complexion of the non-Arabs".[722] Part of the reason for this distaste is that the slaves at the time were largely from pale-skinned peoples, such

---

[719] Ibn ʿAbd Rabbih, ***al-ʿIqd al-farīd*** (Beirut: Dar al-Kutub al-ʿIlmiya, 1983) 8:140.
[720] Al-Dhahabi, ***Siyar***, 2:168.
[721] Al-Ja**ḥiẓ,** *Fakhr al-s**ūdān** ʿ**alā al**-bidan*, 207. See also Goldziher, ***Muslim Studies***, 1:268 who notes that in contrast to the Persians who are described as red or light-skinned (*aḥmar*) the Arabs call themselves black.
[722] Quoted from Tariq Berry.

that *aḥmar* "red" came to mean "slave" back then, just as *'abid* "servant/slave" means black today in the now white Muslim world. As Dana Marniche observes:

> Anyone familiar with the Arabic writings of the Syrian, Iraqi and Iranian historians up until the 14th century knows that this is also their description of the early 'pure' Arab clans of the Arabian peninsula... [i.e. "blacker than the blackest ink – no shred of white on them except their teeth."]...The irony of history is that early Arabic-speaking historians and linguists made a distinction between the Arabs in Arabia and the fair-skinned peoples to the north; and contrary to what may be fact in our day, in the days of early Islam, those called 'Arabs' looked down condescendingly on fair-skinned populations and commonly used the phrase 'fair-skinned as a slave' when describing individuals in tribes in the peninsula that were pale in complexion...Of course, today due mainly to slavery and conversion of peoples to the 'Arab' nationality, the opposite is thought to be true by many in the West.

A red or pale-skinned Muḥammad would thus have been a profound oddity in 7th century Arabia and would have had little chance of success amongst the proud, *black* Meccans and Medinese. The Meccan objectors to his message accused him of some of everything, but *never of being a non-Arab!* There is absolutely no reason to believe he was pale-skinned other than much later representations that coincide with a major demographic change it the Muslim world, a change that brought with it a strong anti-black ideology.[723] We thus have every reason to accept the truth of Anās b. Mālik's description of the prophet as dark brown (*asmar*) and to conclude that, as his black cousins 'Alī and **al**-Faḍl resembled their black fathers (his black uncles),

[723] See below.

he resembled his black father, especially since his mother's side was black as well.[724]

[724] Chandler, "Ebony and Bronze," 280: "All of the chronicles that survive intact agree that Ismael and Muhammad were of the Black Race…A careful examination of history reveals that the Prophet Muhammad…was of the Black Race and was black in complexion."

Chapter Seven

Islam and Black Power: The Eras of the Rāshidūn and the Umayyads

I. *The Muslim Conquests and Black Power*

In 638 the Persian ruler Yazdgird III pleaded to the *T'ang* emperor of China, T'ai-tsung, for assistance against the Arabs who had invaded his realm. This assistance was refused. In 651 an embassy led by Sa'd b. Abī Waqqās, that tall, dark and flat-nosed uncle of Muḥammad who led the Persian campaign, arrived in China bearing gifts. There are two extant notices of this embassy in Chinese literature: in the ninth-century administrative text, *T'ung tien*, which was presented to the throne in 801 by Tu Yu. It covers the history of the world up to the reign of Hsüan-tsung (712-56); and in the *T'ang History*, the official dynastic history of the *T'ang* completed in 945. In these texts are notices regarding the Arabs (called there *Ta-shih*) encountered during the Yung-hui period (650-656). The notices read: "The Arab country was originally part of Persia. The men have high noses, are black and bearded."[725] These Black Arabs here described are those Muslim conquerors of Persia and the East. The conquerors of the West are similarly described, as demonstrated by the *Song of Roland* (wr. ca. 1100). Sir Roland was

[725] Robert G. Hoyland, ***Seeing Islam As Others Saw It: A Survey and Evaluation of Christian, Jewish and Zoroastrian Writings on Early Islam*** (Princeton, NJ: The Darwin Press, INC., 1997): 245, 250.

champion of Charlemagne's Frankish army who fought the Saracens, the invading Muslim armies in the eighth century. Roland is quoted describing his Muslim foes as "hordes blacker than the blackest ink – no shred of white on them except their teeth."[726] He further describes the Saracen commander:

> at their head rides the Saracen...no worse criminal rides in their company, stained with the marks of his crimes and great treasons, lacking faith in God, Saint Mary's son. *And he is black, black as melted pitch...*

Fourteenth century miniatures depicting Roland's battle with the Saracens, the Battle of Roncevaux, clearly depict the Black Muslims. In one from Charles V's *Grandes cronique de France*, Roland and his white-skinned forces charge the black-skinned Muslims led by their equally black King Marsile (Figure 39).[727]

We thus have testimony of the conquered peoples from the far east to the extreme west that the Muslim conquerors were Black. Ivan van Sertima's note that "Africans were pivotal...in the spread of Islam" is therefore an understatement.[728] So too is Drake's remark that "The jihad armies that erupted out of Arabia had black warriors in their ranks."[729] The ranks were predominantly Black.[730] The Muslim conquests were a true *Black Operation*, indeed a *Black Power* operation, one might say.

---

[726] On the Black Saracens of the *Song of Roland* see Van Sertima, ***Golden Age***, 43; Debra Higgs Strickland, ***Saracens, demons, & Jews: making monsters in medieval art*** (Princeton: Princeton University Press, 2003) 179-180.
[727] Image from Strickland, ***Saracens, demons, & Jews***, 180, Fig. 87.
[728] Ivan van Sertima, ***Golden Age of the Moor***, 19.
[729] Drake, ***Black Folks***, 103.
[730] Even Daniel Pipes observation that "numerous blacks fought for the early Muslims" is understated, in that he only considers the presence of Ethiopians (*Habashi*) and sub-Saharan Africans (*Zanj*) in the Muslim armies. He does not consider the Black Arabs or Afrabians. See Daniel Pipes, "Black Soldiers in Early Muslim Armies," ***International Journal of African Historical Studies*** 13 (1980): 87-94.

Figure 39
Battle of Roncevaux. *Grandes Chroniques de France*. Paris, 1370's.

These Black Arabs or Afrabians (African-Arabians) were not unruly hordes; rather, as Hugh Kennedy remarks, "the campaigns were directed by a small group of able and determined men," men who weren't Bedouins but members of an urban elite.[731] Their targets were clear and precise: between 630-730 CE, the Black Muslim armies swept through the southern portion of the Byzantine and the western portion of the Sassanian (Persian) empires. These two had been the pillars of White Power for several centuries before the Muslim conquests. The Persians, like the Byzantines, were Aryans, not Semites.[732] The Persian was considered "the whitest and most hook-nosed"

[731] Hugh Kennedy, ***The Great Arab Conquests: How the Spread of Islam Changed the World We Live In*** (Philadelphia: Da Capo Press, 2007) 52-53.
[732] Hitti, ***Arabs***, 158.

of all whies.[733] By the time of the conquests the Byzantine and Sassanian empires had been the dominant powers in Western Asia, North Africa and Europe for over 400 years. It was the Black Muslims of Arabia, led by "a Pleiad of brilliant generals of Meccan origin," who toppled these 'white powers'.[734]

These brilliant generals were as Black as their troops. The conquest of Syria and, initially, Iraq was led by "the greatest general of the Muslim army,"[735] the famous Khālid b. al-Walīd (d. 642), known also as *Sayfu l-Lāhi l-Maslūl*, the "Drawn Sword of God".[736] Khālid was not only from the paramount Black tribe Quraysh, but from the exceptionally black sub-clan the Ban**ū** l-Mugh**ī**ra.[737] Black and tall (over 6 ft we are told), Khālid engineered the decimation of the Byzantine troops in Syria and the Persian troops along the Iraqi frontier. In fact, he received the epithet "Sword of Allah" after putting Byzantines to the sword at Mu'ta.[738] In his first sweep of the border of lower Iraq and Yamama, Khālid and his forces are said to have killed upwards of 70, 000 Persians at Amgh**ī**shay**ā.**[739] At al-'**Udhayb** and Najaf Khālid reportedly massacred the Persian garrisons and took their wives and children captive, and he killed the Persian defenders at 'Ayn al-Tamr.[740]

---

[733] See e.g. Sextus Empiricus (ca. 200 CE), *Against Ethicists*, 43. ***Curse of Ham***, 95.

[734] Quoted description from M. El Fasi, "The Coming of Islam and the Muslim Empire," in I Hrbek (ed.), ***UNESCO General History of Africa***, ***III: Africa from the Seventh to the Eleventh Century*** (Abridged Edition; Paris, UNESCO, 1992) 25.

[735] Kennedy, ***Great Arab Conquests***, 81.

[736] On him see ***EI***[2] 4:928-929 s.v. Kh**ā**lid b. al-Wal**ī**d by. P.Crone.

[737] ***EI***[2] 6:138 s.v. Makhz**ū**m by M. Hinds.

[738] ***EI***[2] 4:928 s.v. Kh**ā**lid b. al-Wal**ī**d by. P.Crone.

[739] **Ṭabarī,** ***Ta'rikh al-Rusul wal-Mulūk*** **(Leiden,** 1879) I: 2036-7; Michael G. Morony, "The Effects of the Muslim Conquest on the Persian Population of Iraq," ***Iran*** 14 (1976): 47.

[740] Ab**ū** **Yūsuf,** ***Kitāb al-Kharāj*** (***Livre de l'impot foncier***) (Paris, 1921) 219-220, 226; **Ṭabarī,** ***Ta'rikh***, I:2063-4.

Of these brilliant generals from Mecca was also **Abū l**-A'**war b. Sufyān** from the exceptionally Black Ban**ū Sulaym. Abū l**-A'**war** was a prominent Sulaym**ī** during the Umayyad period, having fought with Mu'awiyya at **Ṣiffīn**. At the Battle of Yarmūk commanded by Khālid he was in command of a cavalry squadron, which included fellow Sulaym**īs**. However, after Khālid's death, **Abū l**-A'**war** commanded the Syrian army in the expedition of Ammuriya in 644 and raided Cyprus in 647.[741] The Syrian conquest was a true *Black Ops*. It is thus fitting that it was black Bil**ā**l who negotiated with the Byzantines the surrender of Damascus, causing Prince Constantine to exclaim: "I will have nothing to do with this black slave."[742]

After taking the Iraqi frontier cities al-**Ḥī**ra, Anb**ā**r, D**ū**mat al-Janbal, and Ayn Tamr, Kh**ā**lid was redirected by the caliph Ab**ū** Bakr back to Syria. Command of the Iraqi troops was given by the second caliph 'Umar to Ab**ū** Ubayd from the Ban**ū** Thaq**ī**f of **Ṭā**'if. Ab**ū** Ubayd led the Muslim troops at the disastrous Battle of the Bridge, the worst defeat suffered by the Muslims in the early conquests.[743] In the reorganization of the Muslim army 'Umar put in command the tall and black Sa'd b. Abī Waqqās. It was through Sa'd that redemption came to the Muslim troops and mission in Iraq. It was he who won the iconic Battle of Q**ā**disiyya in 636, which opened up all of Iraq to the Muslims. Sa'd led a small, improvised and ill-equipped army over the might of imperial Persia. The Persians were led by a new commander-in-chief, the legendary Rostam Farrokhz**ā**d who is today the touchstone of Iranian nationalists. Persians/Iranians thus loath the black Sa'd, who reportedly killed Rostam at Q**ā**disiyya and brought down the Sassanid empire. He is held

---

[741] Lecker, ***Banū Sulaym***, 140.
[742] Drake, ***Black Folks***, 2: 91.
[743] Kennedy, ***Great Arab Conquests***, 106.

responsible for the destruction of Persian civilization in the captial Ctesiphon, where he abolished the famous Sassanid library and great palaces. It was a routing for the Persians, whose fugitives were pursued by flank commanders Zuhra b. al-Hawiyya and Qa'qā b. Amr who "killed them in every village, reed thicket, and river bank".[744]

The Muslim conquests of Syria and Iraq therefore *were Black Muslim conquests.* The troops were predominantly Black Arabians, like the Mahra and Sulaym,[745] and the commanders were the famous Khālid b. al-Walīd, **Abū l-A'war b. Sufyān** and Sa'd b. Abī Waqqās, three Black generals. By bringing an end to the Byzantine and Sassanian empires, the Black Muslims from Arabia brought down the centuries-old 'white power' edifice in those areas. The same is true with the conquests of Egypt and North Africa.

I.1. *The Conquest of Egypt*

The conquest of Egypt by the Muslims in 641 was a *Black Op* from top to bottom. It was the second caliph, 'Umar b. al-Khaṭṭāb (d. 644), who was the chief architect of the Islamic state. It was his troops who "broke the power of the Persian Sassanid empire and proceeded to annex Iran and Iraq to Arabia."[746] He further brought Syria, Phoenicia, Persia, Jerusalem, and Egypt into the *Dār al-Islām.* With the destruction of Carthage in the third Punic War (150-146 BCE) Rome became the supreme power in North Africa. It was 'Umar and the Muslim troops that broke up this White power block in Africa.

---

[744] Morony, "Effects," 48.

[745] On the Mahra's participation in the Iraq and Egypt expeditions see ***EI²*** 6:82 s.v. Mahra. On the Sulaym's role in the Syrian and Iraqi expeditions see ***EI²*** 9:818 s.v. Sulaym by M. Lecker.

[746] Drake, ***Black Folks***, 2:90.

'Umar was a Black Qurayshī Arab. His mother **Ḥantama bt. Hāshim b. al**-Mughīra, was from the exceptionally black Banū **al**-Mughīra. Al-Mas'ūdī (***Prairies***, IV, 192) says she was Black.[747] His paternal grandmother was an enslaved Ethiopian.[748] He was certainly no "fair, pale man, with a touch of redness."[749] His famous son, '**Abd Allāh,** was himself "very dark-skinned and huge"[750] and said regarding their blackness: "We inherited our black complexion from our maternal uncles."[751]

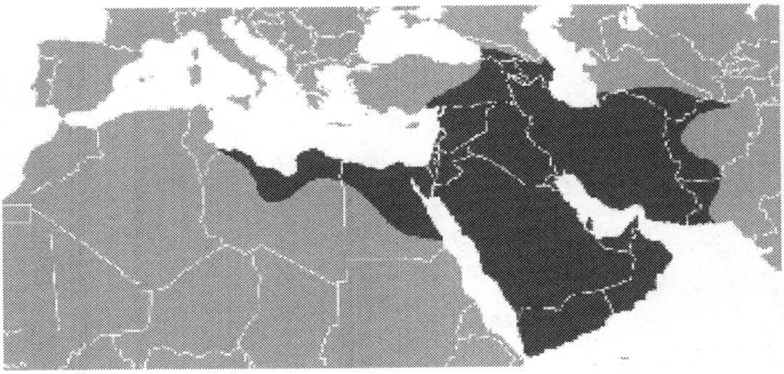

Figure 40
The Islamic Empire under 'Umar

Leading the troops into Egypt was the Arab general 'Amr b. al-'**Aṣ** who previously commanded the Muslim forces in southern Palestine. He too had an Ethiopian mother.[752] The troops he commanded in the Egypt expedition were mainly black Yemini

[747] ***EI2*** 6:139 s.v. Makhzūm, Banū by M Hinds.
[748] Muḥammad b. Habīb, ***Kitāb al-Muhabbar*** (Hyderabad, 1361/1992) 306.
[749] Contra Abu-Bakr, ***Islam's Black Legacy***, 32.
[750] Al-Dhahabi, ***Siyar a'lam al-nubala***, 3:158.
[751] Ibn Sa'd, ***al-Tabaqat al-kubra***, 3:325; Berry, ***Unknown Arabs***, 67.
[752] Ibn Habib, ***Kitāb al-Muhabbar***, ed. E. Lichtenstädler (Hyderabad, 1361/1942) 306; Bernard Lewis, "The Crows of the Arabs," ***Critical Inquiry*** 12 (1985): 89 [art.=88-97].

Arabs, such as the Mahra and the Akk.[753] When ʻAmr b. al-ʻ**Aṣ** requested reinforcements from ʻ**Umar**, the caliph sent 4 detachments of 1000 apiece. One detachment was headed by al-Miqd**ā**d b. al-Aswad ("son of the Black [man]"), who was black[754]; one by the "black-skinned and tall" Mu**ḥ**ammad b. Maslama[755]; one by the black ʻUb**ā**da b. al-**Ṣā**mit; and one by al-Zubayr b. al-Awwan, one of the very few pale-skinned Muslims involved in the expedition.[756]

A famous incident nicely illustrates the nature of the Muslim conquest of Egypt. When Cyrus, the Byzantine governor of Egypt, sought negotiations with ʻAmr b. al-ʻ**Aṣ** in October 640, the latter deputed ten of his officers to negotiate. Apparently not all ten were Black Arabs, but they were led by ʻUb**ā**da b. al-**Ṣā**mit. When the tall and black Ub**ā**da was ushered into Cyrus' presence, the governor was shocked and exclaimed: "Take away that black man: I can have no discussion with him!" The party insisted that Ub**ā**da was the wisest, best, and noblest among them and their appointed leader, declaring that "though he is black he is the foremost among us in position, in precedence, in intelligence and in wisdom, for blackness is not despised among us."[757] ʻUb**ā**da himself then replied to Cyrus: "There are a thousand blacks, as black as myself, among our companions. I

---

753 Almut Nebel et al, "Genetic evidence for the Expansion of Arabian Tribes into the Southern Levant and North Africa," ***American Journal of Human Genetics*** 70 (2002): 1595 [art.=1594-1596]: "tribes of Yemeni origin formed the bulk of the those Muslim contingents that conquered Egypt in the middle of the 7th century CE"; Diop, ***African Origin***, 52: "As for the Moors, they descended directly from post-Islamic invaders who, starting from Yemen, conquered Egypt, North Africa, and Spain between the seventh and fifteenth centuries"; Kennedy, ***Great Arab Conquests***, 147.

754 Y.A. Talib, "The African Diaspora in Asia," in Hrbek, ***General History***, 338.

755 Ibn **Ṣa**ʻd, ***al-Ṭabaqat al-kubrā***, 3:444; Berry, ***Unknown Arabs***, 72.

756 See Kennedy, ***Great Arab Conquests***, 151.

757 Ibn ʻAbd al-**Ḥ**akam, ***Futūḥ Miṣr***, ed. Charles C. Torrey (New Haven: Yale University Press, 1922) 66; Bernard Lewis, ***Race and Color in Islam*** (New York: Harper & Row, 1979)10; Alfred Butler, ***The Arab Invasion of Egypt and the Last Years of Roman Domination*** (New York: A&B Publishers, 1992 [1902])257.

and they would be ready each to meet and fight a hundred enimies together. We live only to fight for Allah, and to follow his will. We care nought for wealth, so long as we have wherewithal to stay our hunger and to clothe bodies. This world is nought to us, the next world is all." Benard Lewis makes an important observation here: "'Ubāda is not African nor even of African descent but (as the chroniclers are careful to point out) a pure and noble Arab on both sides."[758] The thousand fellow blacks, probably the detachment of which he was commander, are no doubt Black Arabs like him.[759]

II. *The Umayyads: Islam's Black Dynasty*

Arnold J. Toynbee, in his groundbreaking ***A Study of History***, notes that:

> the Primitive Arabs who were the ruling element in the Umayyad Caliphate called themselves 'the swarthy people,' with a connotation of superiority, and their Persian and Turkish subjects 'the ruddy people,' with a connotation of racial inferiority.[760]

This perceptive observation of early Umayyad ethnicity and racialist views is certainly to be understood in the context of the above quoted remark by Al-Mubarrad (d. 898): "The Arabs used to take pride in their darkness and blackness and they had distaste for a light complexion and they used to say that a light complexion was the complexion of the non-Arabs". Just how

---

[758] Lewis, ***Race and Color***, 10.
[759] Contra Pipes, "Black Soldiers," 87 who had to assume that, even though 'Ubāda was a Black Arab, the others must be African because he felt it unlikely that Black Arabs "would band together". There is absolutely nothing to commend this argument.
[760] Arnold J. Toynbee, ***A Study of History***, 2 vols. (London: Oxford University Press, 1956) I:226.

great this Umayyad distaste was is possibly indicated by a report regarding the first of the dynasty's caliphs, Mu'āwīya b. 'Abī Sufyān (d. 680). Mu'āwīya's ethnicity is indicated by the description al-Dhahabi gives of the caliph's son, Yāzid b. Mu'āwīya: "He was black-skinned, hairy and huge."[761] Ibn 'Abd Rabbih reports in his ***al-'Iqd al-farīd*** that Mu'āwīya said to two of his advisors:

> I see that these white folks (*humr*, pl. of *ahmar*) have become very numerous and are saying bad things about those who have passed. I can envision a daring enterprise from them against the authority of the Arabs. I am thinking of killing half of them and leaving half of them to set up markets and to build roads.[762]

Mu'āwīya the Umayyad caliph wanted to make slaves out of those 'white folks'. It was during Islam's first dynasty, which lasted from 661-749, that Islam was truly 'a Black thing'. Ira M. Lapidus very poignantly points out regarding the Umayyad Arabs:

> Muḥammad's implicit dream and the dream of his closest or religiously most sensitive followers might have been to convert the world to Islam, but for the Arab leaders (Umayyads) the world had been conquered in the name of Islam, not for the sake of converting it to Islam. For them, being Arab and being Muslim distinguished the conquerors from the masses of vanquished Middle Eastern peoples. Islam was to be the unifying emblem of the victorious Arab elite, the mark of the ruling class.[763]

---

761 ***al-'Ibar fī khabar man ghabar*** (Kuwait)_IV:198.
762 Ibn 'Abd Rabbih, ***al-'Iqd al-farīd,*** 3:361.
763 Ira M. Lapidus, "The conversion of Egypt to Islam," ***Israel Oriental Studies*** 2 (1972): 249.

This explains why conversion of the conquered peoples to Islam was such a slow, centuries-long process[764]: there was no interest on the part of the Muslims to convert them. G.R. Hawting says again:

> Although it can be debated whether the Koran was addressed to all men or to the Arabs only, the Umayyads and the Arab tribesmen who first conquered the Middle East regarded their religion as largely exclusive of the conquered peoples. There was no sustained attempt to force or even persuade the conquered peoples to accept Islam.[765]

Umayyad 'blackness' was not restricted to the Quraysh, of which the Umayyad's constituted a sub-clan. The Banū Sulaym were very important during this period. Not only were they generally supporters of the dynasty,[766] but "Sulaym's contribution to Mu'āwiya's success was fundamental."[767] This is seen in his selection of provincial governors. Because the *amīr* or governor represented the caliph himself in very important ways in the province, picking these officials was a serious task of the highest priority for the caliphs.[768] A great many of the Umayyad governors were Sulaymīs, such as **Abū l-A'war b. Sufyān** who was Mu'āwiya's governor in Urdunn and 'Abd Allāh b. Khāzim (d. 73/692) who governed Khurasan and also Marw.[769]

---

764 See especially Richard W. Bulliet, ***Conversion to Islam in the Medieval Period: An Essay in Quantitative History*** (Cambridge: Harvard University Press, 1979).
765 G.R. Hawting, ***The First Dynasty of Islam: The Umayyad Caliphate AD 661-750*** , Second Edition (London and New York: Routledge, 2000) 4.
766 Lecker, ***Banū Sulaym***, 245 n. 112.
767 ***EI²*** 9:818 s.v. Sulaym by M. Lecker.
768 Hawting, ***First Dynasty***, 35.
769 ***EI¹*** 1:47-48 s.v. 'Abd Allāh b. Khāzim by H.A.R. Gibb. On the many Sulaymī governors see ***EI²*** 9:818 s.v. Sulaym by M. Lecker.

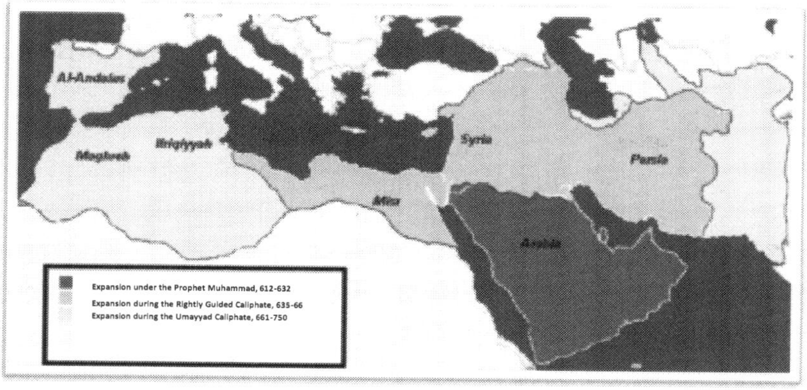

Figure 40. The Islamic Empire Under the Black Umayyads

II.1. *The Abbasid Revolution and the Aryanization of Islam*

Wayne Chandler, in his essay "Ebony and Bronze: Race and Ethnicity in Early Arabia and the Islamic World," advances (though he does not originate) a peculiar ethnohistory of Islam's political dynasties.[770] Following the ideas of early 20th century political activist and writer George Wells Parker,[771] Chandler argues that the Umayyads were Islam's white Semitic dynasty, while the Abbasids were "a Black nationalist movement". This ethnic division is based on an assumption operative throughout Chandler's essay: that there is a difference between 'Blacks' on the one hand and 'Semites' on the other, and that the latter were whites or the peoples described as 'Reds' in Arabic literature. These particular claims, based as they are on the lack of a purview of the relevant Arabic source materials, unfortunately diminish the value of an otherwise quite valuable discussion of

[770] In Rashidi and Sertima, ***African Presence***, 270-311.
[771] George Wells Parker, ***The Children of the Sun*** (Baltimore: Black Classic Press, 1978 [1918]), 20-22.

race and Islam. The historic and ethnographic evidence indicates quite clearly that the *opposite* situation played out on the ground: that is to say, the Umayyads were the 'Black nationalist movement', while the Abbasid revolution formally initiated the process of the *Aryanizing* of Islam.

The contrast between Blacks and Semites is a false one: the Semites of Arabia were Black, as we demonstrated above. 'Red' was the classical Arabic designation for the non-Semitic whites, the Aryans (Persians, Romans, Turks, etc.). Thus, the polarization "Non-Semitic Blacks vs. Red (White) Semites" contradicts the situation as we are able to picture it based on the primary source materials. The Umayyads were most definitely Black Semites, and the engine of the Abbassid Revolution was the 'Red' Persians. While it is true that the revolution was precipitated by the feud between two Black tribes, Azd (Yemen) and Tamīm (Mudar), the main figure of the uprising, the enigmatic Abu Muslim, was a Persian freedman at the head of an Azd tribal unit. And further, the "majority of supporters (of the revolution) were Iranian peasants and clients rather than Arabs".[772] As Jan Restö points out:

> the Abbasid revolution in 750 was, to a large extent, the final revolt of the non-'arab Muslims against the 'arab and their taking power. This revolt was dominated by the Iranian 'ağam (non-Semitic foreigners), and the outcome was the establishment of at least formal equality between the two groups.[773]

Thus, according to al-**Jāḥiẓ** (***Bayān*** III, 366) the Abbasid empire was ***'ajamiyya*** (of non-Arab foreigners) and Khurasanian (Persian), while the Umayyads were ***'arabiyya*** (Arab). The Abbasid Revolution was thus much more than a

---

772 Hitti, ***Arabs***, 284.
773 Restö, ***Arabs***, 24.

political revolution, but a cultural one as well. As Richard W. Bulliet aptly pointed out:

> Nothing influenced the emerging shape of Muslim society and culture so much as the massive influx of new Muslims who had no prior experience of life in Arabia or the culture of the Arabs.[774]

Ronald Segal notes the consequences of this influx:

> increasing intermarriage served to submerge the original distinctions, and increasing numbers of the conquered, having adopted the religion and language of the conquerors, *took to assuming the identity of Arabs themselves* (emphasis mine-WM).

In other words, Persians and others who were inexperienced in and ignorant of (Black) Arabic culture converted to Islam, adopted the Arabic language and began identifying themselves as Arabs. Yet they introduced into Islam and Arab culture what was non-existent before, in particular anti-Black sentiments. This is demonstrated most convincingly in a famous poem by the ninth century poet Ab**ū** al-**Ḥ**asan Al**ī** b. al-Abb**ā**s b Jurayj, also known as Ibn al-R**ū**m**ī** (d. 896), in which he blames the *Aryanized* Abbasids for…racism against the Prophet's family:

> You insulted them (the family of the Prophet Mu**ḥ**ammad) because of their blackness, while there are still pure-blooded black-skinned Arabs. However, you are blue (eyed) - the

[774] Richard W. Bulliet, ***Islam: The View From the Edge*** (New York: Columbia University Press, 1994) 44.

Romans (Byzantines) have embellished your faces with their color.[775]

The end of the Umayyad Dynasty in 750 CE signaled the effective end to Black Islam. The *Aryanized* Abbasid Dynasty will be followed by the rise of the Seljuks (Turks) and eventually the Ottoman Empire (Turks again). The white sheep have become so numerous and have dominated Islam for so long now, most people cannot conceive that Islam started among the black sheep.

III. *Black Islam: The Threat to White Supremacy*

According to Diop, "Except for the Islamic breakthrough, Europe has ruled Africa down to the present day."[776] This is an important observation, especially when we keep in mind that the breakthrough was a *Black* Islamic breakthrough. The establishment of the (Black) Islamic empire followed on the heals of the demolishing of the Byzantine and Sasanian empires in West Asia and Africa. In other words 'Black Power' replaced 'White Power' on the world stage and the agents of this transition were Black Muslims from Arabia. After overthrowing the Byzantines in North Africa the Muslims (Black Arab and African) headed to Europe and, after defeating the Visigoth army and killing the last Visigoth king, Roderick, in 711 added the Iberian Peninsula to the Islamic empire. For 800 years Black Muslims, called Moors, ruled southwest Europe.[777] As a consequence, in the psyche of White Christian Europe the Black Muslim

---

775 Quoted from Tariq Berry, "A True Description of the Prophet Mohamed's Family (SAWS)," http://savethetruearabs.blogspot.com/2009/08/true-description-of-prophet-mohameds_26.html. Accessed October 22, 2009.

776 Diop, ***African Origin***, p. 119.

777 On these Black Moors see especially Sertima, ***Golden Age***.

incarnated evil itself. As James Brunson and Runoko Rashidi note: 'because of his dark complexion and Islamic faith, the Moor became in Europe a symbol of guile, evil, and hate."[778]

The material coming out of Europe during this period leaves no room to doubt that the Black Muslim was perceived as the greatest threat to White Christendom. This fact is probably illustrated by the 11th century coat of arms commemorating Peter III of Aragon's victory over the Moors in 1096. During the battle four Moorish princes fell. On the coat of arms their black heads surround a Christian cross (Figure 41). This was updated on a gold coin after 1700 by King Charles of Hapsburg.[779] These Black Muslim heads on this European Christian coat of arms undoubtedly symbolized victory over the perceived chief threat.

It is more than likely that we should read all of this history into the admission by Lothrop Stoddard, American historian and political scientist, that *Black Islam* is a singular threat to 'white world supremacy.' In his, ***The Rising Tide of Color Against White World-Supremacy***, Stoddard confesses:

[778] "Moors in Antiquity," 28. See also Miriam De Costa, "The Portrayal of Blacks in a Spanish Medieval Manuscript," ***Negro History Bulletin*** 37 (1974): 193-196.
[779] Brunson and Rashidi, "Moors in Antiquity," 36.

Figure 41
Hapsburg gold coin of Aragon coat of arms. From Sertima, ***Golden Age***.

Concerning Islam's steady progress in black Africa there can be no shadow of a doubt. Every candid European observer tells the same story. 'Mohammedanism,' says Sir Charles Elliot, 'can still give the natives a motive for animosity against Europeans...' Twenty years ago another English observer, T.R. Threlfall, wrote: '...The rapid spread of militant Mohammedanism among the...tribes to the north of the equator is a serious factor in the fight for racial supremacy in Africa...' Islam is as yet unknown south of the Zambezi, but *white men universally dread the possibility of its appearance...*[780]

[780] Lothrop Stoddard, ***The Rising Tide of Color Against White World-Supremacy*** (New York: Charles Scribner's Sons, 1920) 94-96.

Chapter Eight

Islam and Africa

I. *Islam's Peaceful Penetration*

It is the case that the *empire* of (Black) Islam entered Africa with the sword. Black imperialism from all eras, including ancient Kemetic imperialism,[781] relies on military advancement. It is *not* the case, however, that the religion spread at the same time and by the same means. As we saw above, the Umayyads saw Islam as exclusive to themselves and refused to proselytize at all. The religion did not begin spreading in Africa until centuries later,[782] and when it did it was carried by merchants and religious specialists, not soldiers.[783] Too many scholars, black and white, have debunked the myth of Arabs violently imposing Islam on Africans for it to still have circulation, though in some circles it

---

[781] George Steindof and Keith C. Seele, ***When Egypt Ruled the East*** (Chicago: University of Chicago Press, 1957),

[782] See for example Michael Brett, who notes: "The stereotype of a religion preached initially by the sword has long given way to recognition of the fact that the Arab conquerors were more concerned with tribute, and to the conclusion that proselytism was against the interests of the new rulers, since conversion would diminish the number of tax-paying subjects." "The Spread of Islam in Egypt and North Africa," in Michael Brett (ed.) ***Northern Africa: Islam and Modernization*** (London: Frank Cass, 1973) 2.

[783] Nehemia Levtzion and Randall L. Pouwels, "Patterns of Islamization and Varieties of Religious Experience Among Muslims of Africa," in Nehemia Levtzion and Randall L. Pouwels (edd.), ***The History of Islam in Africa*** (Athens: Ohio University Press, 2000) 3: "conversion to Islam was the work of men of religion who communicated primarily with local rulers"; Randall Q. Pouwels, "The East African Coast, c.780 to 1900 CE," in ibid, 251: "Islam made its first impression [in East Africa] through commercial exchanges between Africans and Muslims…jihad never became the important instrument of conversion of enforcement in East Africa that it did in other places…the tenth through the fifteenth centuries was a time of steady and peaceful expansion (of Islam) southward in the wake of developing trade."

still does. Cheikh Anta Diop, in his *Pre-Colonial Black Africa*, affirms:

> Much has been made of Arab invasions of Africa: they occurred in the North, but in Black Africa they are figments of the imagination. While the Arabs did conquer North Africa by force of Arms, they quite peaceably entered Black Africa…From the time of the Umayyad setbacks in the eighth century, no Arab army ever crossed the Sahara in an attempt to conquer Africa, except for the Moroccan War of the sixteenth century…Nor was there ever any Arab conquest of Mozambique or any other East African territory. The Arabs in these areas, who became great religious leaders, arrived as everywhere else individually and settled in peacefully…The Arab conquests dear to sociologists are necessary to their theories but did not exist in reality.
>
> Only during the Almoravide movement of the first half of the eleventh century did some white people, Berbers,[784] attempt to impose Islam on Black Africa by force of arms…The primary reason for the success of Islam in Black Africa, with one exception, consequently stems from the fact that it was propagated peacefully at first by solitary Arabo-Berber travelers to certain Black kings and notables, who then spread it about them to those under their jurisdiction."[785]

Joseph E. Harris in his ***Africans and Their History*** says as well: "it is noteworthy that except for the northern coast, Islam spread rather peacefully until the eighteenth century, with one significant

---

[784] However, now we know that the Almoravids were a Black African movement: see James E. Brunson and Runoko Rashidi, "The Moors in Antiquity," in Sertima, ***Golden Age***, 61.

[785] Cheikh Anta Diop, ***Precolonial Black Africa: A Comparative Study of the Political and Social Systems of Europe and Black Africa, From Antiquity to the Formation of Modern States*** (Chicago: Lawrence Hill Books, 1987), 101-102, 162, 163.

interruption-the Almoravid conquests."[786] J. Spencer Trimingham, in ***A History of Islam in West Africa***, agrees:

> The role of the Murabitun (Almoravids) in the Islamization of the Sudan has been exaggerated. *The peaceful penetration of Islam along trade routes into borderland towns had begun before this movement* was born…The Murabitun simply accelerated a process that had already begun, and their conquest was ephemeral because the attraction of Morocco was stronger than that of the Sudan (emphasis mine-WM).[787]

I. Hrbek and M. El Fasi:

> During the great Arab conquests, there was certainly no attempt to convert the *ahl al-kitāb* (Jews and Christians) by force…generations of scholars have…clearly demonstrated that the image of the Muslim Arab warrior with sword in one hand and the Qoran in the other, belongs to the realm of mythology.[788]

And finally Z. Dramani-Issifou: "Prior to the twelfth century, Islam advanced on African soil without wars, without violent proselytism."[789]

---

[786] Joseph E. Harris, ***Africans and Their History***, Revised Edition (New York: New American Library, 1987)74.

[787] J. Spencer Trimingham, ***A History of Islam in West Africa*** (London: Oxford University, 1970) 29-31.

[788] I. Hrbek and M. El Fasi, "Stages in the Development of Islam and its Dissemination in Africa," in Hrbek, ***General History***, 31.

[789] Z. Damani-Issifou, "Islam as a social system in Africa since the seventh century," in Hrbek, ***General History***, 54.

II. *Relations of Black Muslims in Egypt and Black Christians in Egypt and Nubia*

The main weaknesses of Chancellor Williams classic discussion of the Muslim invasion of Egypt in 641 and attempted invasions of Nubia in 643 and again in 651-52 is his inaccurate *ethnographic assignments*. Williams saw the Muslim/Nubian conflict as one between White Arabs and Black Nubians: the Arab conquerors were "Caucasians," he informs us.[790] As we have demonstrated above, the Muslims who conquered Egypt were mainly Black Arabs from Southern Arabia led by Black Arabs from Mecca in North Central Arabia. We thus have to do with a *Black-on-Black* conflict, not a White on Black one. The fact is particularly important to keep in mind when considering the Egyptian Coptic response to the Muslim invaders who targeted and overthrew the oppressive Byzantine regime there. The great W.E.B. Dubois correctly noted: "the Arabs invaded African Egypt, taking it from Eastern Roman Emperors *and securing as allies the native Negroid Egyptians*".[791] As Mamadou Chinyelu put it as well: "These African Copts no doubt saw the African Muslims from Arabia as liberators; after all *they were kith and kin*."[792]

The Byzantine emperor Heraclius supported the minority Chalcedean church led by the Patriarch from the Caucasus, Cyrus, against the majority Coptic (Monophysite) church. Coptic sources tell of ruthless and systematic persecution.[793] As St. Clair Drake observes: "The Coptic Christians of Egypt welcomed the Arab Muslims as 'liberators' from what they considered the tyranny of their fellow Christians in

---

[790] Williams, ***Destruction***, 142-148.
[791] Du Bois, ***The World and Africa***, 185-186.
[792] Mamadou Chinyelu, "Africans in the Birth and Spread of Islam," in van Sertima, ***Golden Age***, 367.
[793] Kennedy, ***Great Conquests***, 144-145.

Constantinople."[794] According to Hugh Kennedy's research, the conquerors distinguished between the Egyptian Copts and what they called the 'Rūm' (Romans): the latter were considered the enemy and the former actually *assisted* the Muslim 'liberators' who were as Black as they.[795] Copts at Farāma for instance aided the Muslims, and at the little town of Bahnasā the Black Muslims slaughtered all the 'Rūmī' men, women and children they came across.[796]

There was no attempt to convert the Copts to Islam.[797] As Ira Lapidus explains:

> The necessary arrangements between the conqueror(s) and conquered were implemented in the reign of the second Caliph, 'Umar (634-644)…(A) principle of 'Umar's settlement was that the conquered populations should be disturbed as little as possible. This meant that the Arab Muslims did not, contrary to reputation, attempt to convert people to Islam…At the time of the conquests, Islam was meant to be a religion of the Arabs, a mark of caste unity and superiority. When conversions did occur, they were an embarrassment because they created status problems…Just as the Arabs had no interest in changing the religious situation, they had no desire to disturb the social and administrative order…local situations were left in local hands…(In the conquered lands) the whole of the former social and religious order was left intact.[798]

---

[794] Drake, ***Black Folks***, 90; Lewis, *Arabs in History*, 54.
[795] Kennedy, ***Great Conquests***, 149-150. Alfred Butler rejected the idea that the Copts assisted the Muslims (***Arab Invasion***, 211), but Kennedy (***Great Conquests***, 149) rightly points out that Butler wrote before valuable primary sources were made available and allowed his personal feelings towards the Copts and the Muslims to cloud his judgment on the matter.
[796] Kennedy, ***Great Conquests***, 150.
[797] See especially Ira M. Lapidus, "The Conversion of Egypt to Islam," ***Israel Oriental Studies*** 2 (1972): 248-261. See also Drake, ***Black Folk***, 2:106: "The Arab empire builders made no serious attempt to convert Egypt's Christian Copts to Islam."
[798] Ira M. Lapidus, ***A History of Islamic Societies***, 2nd Edition (Cambridge: Cambridge University Press, 2002)36.

In terms of the local Christian community, Lapidus points out that "Arab policy attached no liability to the church or to membership in it. Nor…did the Arabs encourage conversion to Islam."[799] the Black Muslims had a 'pro-Black' policy: in direct contrast to the Byzantines who empowered the minority, Roman church, the Muslims empowered the Coptic church.[800] In fact, the Muslims gave all of the Chalcedonian churches over to the Copts and refused to appoint any Chalcedonian Patriarchs. "Thus the [Copts] gained in Egypt and gained in Nubia as well."[801] The Umayyad caliphs Mu'āwīya and '**Abd** al-M**ā**lik (d. 705) built several churches in Alexandria and Fus**ṭāṭ**, as did the Egyptian governor '**Abd** al-'**Azīz b. Marwān** (d. 705). The Church of St. George and the monastery of Ab**ū Qarqar at Ḥawān** are but two examples.[802]

This policy lasted for most the Umayyad period, when Islam was 'a Black thing'. However, toward the end of this period, attitudes and then policy changed. The reign of 'Umar II (717-720) signaled this changed attitude. He was less protective of the Coptic church and more encouraging of conversion, though Egyptian policy did not change in that regard except that he decreed any converts exempt from the poll-tax that non-Muslims paid. By the Abbasid period, however, things are radically different. Chalcedian Patriarchs were being appointed again and their churches returned to them from the Copts. In other words, the transition from 'Pro-Black Isam' under the Black Umayyads to *Aryanized* Islam under the Abbasids signaled a change in the status for the Coptic church. From 767-868 numerous Coptic revolts occurred in Egypt. In the ninth century Egypt was mainly

799 Lapidus, "Conversion of Egypt," 250.
800 Lapidus, "Conversion of Egypt," 249.
801 Lapidus, "Conversion of Egypt," 249.
802 Lapidus, "Conversion of Egypt," 249.

governed by Turks. From 832 onward, Arabs and Copts together revolted against the government.

In terms of Nubia, ‘Amr b. al-‘**Aṣ**, the conqueror-turned-governor of Egypt, had a non-aggression policy. As Williams admits: “despite the continued raids by the Blacks [of the South] he (‘Amr) chose not to extend his operations into their land.”[803] This policy, however, will be revoked in 643 by then governor ‘Abd All**āh b. Abī Ṣarḥ**, who launched an invasion of the northern Nubian kingdom of Makuria. This invasion was a failure, to say the least: the Nubians dealt the Muslims a devastating defeat, and again in 651-652. Williams, aptly describing this conflict as ‘one of the decisive battles of history’, perceptively remarks: “The psychological effects of being defeated by the Blacks twice on national fronts caused the Arabs to adopt a peaceful relationship with these countries that lasted 600 years.”[804] This six-hundred year peace was the result of the *baqṭ* agreement, signed by both parties at the conclusion of the 651-652 battle. The *baqṭ* was both a non-aggression pact and a trade agreement between Muslim Egypt and Nubia, terms which were determined by the victors: Nubia.

1. The citizens of each country were allowed free passage to the other, with security guaranteed by the host country.
2. A mosque was to be built in Nubia and a church in Egypt.
3. 360 slaves annually sent by Nubia to Egypt, in exchange for 1300 ardeb of wheat and 1300 kan**ī**r of wine, linen and cloth.

---

[803] Williams, ***Destruction***, 145.
[804] Williams, ***Destruction***, 145.

The last stipulation has been the focus of some criticism and misrepresentation in some Christian and Africentrist circles, with support even from Muslim misrepresentation. This part of the agreement is often described as *tribute* imposed on the hapless Nubians by the lustful Muslim slavers, a covert plan to eventually conquer the Sudan.[805] But this interpretation completely fails to take proper notice of a simple fact: the Nubians were the victors and therefore had the leverage. As Jay Spauling explains:

> The Nubians won decisively. 'The Muslims...had never suffered a loss like the one they had in Nubia.' *For the next six centuries thereafter the Nubian authorities were able to impose their own terms upon relations with the Islamic world, an arrangement commonly known...as the baqt.* The *baqt* exemplified the institution of administered diplomatic trade through which eastern Sudanic kings normally preferred to conduct their foreign relations...With the passage of centuries, various Islamic intellectuals, eager to forget the initial Nubian victory, devised increasingly elaborate and fanciful accounts that undertook to construe *baqt* shipments as payment of tribute (emphasis mine-WM).[806]

The *baqṭ* was thus a Nubian arrangement made with the defeated Muslims, not the other way around, and it had precedent in common Sudanic diplomacy: trading with Nubian slaves goes back to ancient Kemet.[807] The arrangement

---

[805] Williams, ***Destruction***, 146.

[806] Jay Spaulding, "Precolonial Islam in the Eastern Sudan," in Levtzion and Pouwels, ***History of Islam in Africa***, 117.

[807] See especially Donald B. Redford, ***From Slave to Pharaoh: The Black Experience of Ancient Egypt*** (Baltimore and London: The Johns Hopkins Press, 2004).

guaranteed Nubia's independence and facilitated Nubian national/cultural progress for six centuries.

> The [*baqṭ*]...secured the independence of the Christian Nubian state for many centuries to come. Although there were occasional attempts to convert the rulers...the general policy of the Muslim Egyptian government was to leave the Christian kingdom undisturbed. The friendly relationship between the Egyptian rulers and Nubian monarchs opened the door for (Muslim traders).[808]

The resulting trade opportunities contributed to a Nubian florescence. As S. Jakobielski notes in his study of Christian Nubia:

> The truce was upheld throughout the next five centuries of Christian civilization in Nubia and in its initial phase was crucial for maintaining peace and the possibilities for national development. The lack of any real threat on the part of the Arabs and the possibilities of carrying on trade with Egypt and maintaining contacts with Byzantium led to the development of a distinctive Nubian culture...Thus the end of eighth century saw Nubia moving into its period of prosperity, which lasted up to and including over a half of the twelfth century and was also conditioned by a favorable economic situation.[809]

Hostilities between Muslim Egypt and Christian Nubia began in the 13th century. Egypt was ruled by the Turkish oligarchy, the Mamluks. In 1269 the Mamluk sultan Baybars rejected a

---

[808] Hrbek and Fasi, "Stages," 44.

[809] S. Jakobielski, "Christian Nubia at the Height of its Civilization," in Hrbek, ***General History***, 103. Williams makes the same point: "The 600-year *détente* with the Arabs in Egypt was a period of...reconciliation and progress...Even church and cathedral building expanded from this center of Black culture over the Western regions of Chad and adjoining states." ***Destruction***, 147.

Makuria *baqṭ* initiative, a rejection for which the Nubian king retaliated by sacking the Egyptian Red Sea port of Aydhab in 1272. Four years later Mamluk forces invade and conquer Makuria and by 1324 the land became a rich slaving ground for Muslim merchants. It is to be emphasized here that while Islam was 'still black', if you will, relations with the Copts and Nubians were peaceful and mutually beneficial. As John Henrik Clark admits: "The peaceful Arab and African partnership in the city-states of Africa went on for more than a century before the Arabs turned their normal trading apparatus into a human slave trading enterprise."[810] That century was the period of the Black Umayyad Dynasty. In post-Umayyad Islam which went through a process of *Persianization* and *Turkifization* (sic) or, in short, *Aryanization*, racism became rampant such that Islam went from Pro-Black to Anti-Black. This process impacted the literature, the theologies, and the policies of the Islamic world. The most horrendous legacy of this process is the East African Slave Trade.

III. *A Slave Religion?*

Chancellor Williams and Yusef Ben Jochannan, among other Africentrist scholars, have insisted in the past that Islam is, viz-a-viz African Peoples, a slave religion.[811] The claim is generally that African peoples are Muslims today primarily because Arab Muslims were deeply involved in the African slave-trade. While the latter point is certainly true and of great significance, it is not the case that Islam was first encountered by African peoples through the Arab slave-trade. First, as was demonstrated, *African peoples originated Islam* in Arabia and brought it back to Africa in

---

810 John Henry Clark, "Introduction," in Alfred Butler, ***The Arab Invasion of Egypt***, iv.

811 Williams, ***Destruction***, 193, 335, ect; Ben-Jochannan, ***African Origins***, 195-196.

the 7th century. Secondly, there was minimal forced conversion to Islam of Africans on the mainland before the 19th century.[812] Before then the religion – apart from the empire – spread throughout Africa rather peacefully, as we demonstrated above.

The institution of slavery is found throughout the ancient world and existed in traditional African society from antiquity to the modern world.[813] It thus comes as no surprise that it is found in North East Africa, i.e. Arabia, at the time of Muḥammad. The Qur'ān assumes its existence and does not ban it outright. Apparently like Ma'at of ancient Egypt, Islam was not deemed incompatible with the institution. Instead, like the Egyptian Negative Confessions which stipulated proper 'Maatic' behavior with regard to (among other things) slaves,[814] the Qur'ān does "enunciate precepts and injunctions aimed at mitigating the condition and encouraging manumission."[815] The early Muslims therefore did participate in the institution, though in its more 'humane' form (at least in the beginning).[816] But there is

---

[812] I. Hrbek and M. El Fasi, "Stages in the Development of Islam and its Dissemination in Africa," in Hrbek, ***General History***, 31. On the significance of the 19th century see Ronald Segal, ***Islam's Black Slaves: The Other Black Diaspora*** (New York: Farrar, Straus and Giroux, 2001) Chapter Ten.

[813] Mariam F. Ayad, "Slaves and Slavery in Ancient Egypt," in Peter Bogucki (ed.), ***Encyclopedia of Society and Culture in the Ancient World*** (New York: Facts On File, Inc., 2008); Rosalie David, "Slaves in Ancient Egypt," ***Handbook to Life in Ancient Egypt*** Revised Edition (New York: Facts On File, Inc., 2003); Paul E. Lovejoy, ***Transformations in Slavery: A History of Slavery in Africa***, Second Edition (Cambridge: Cambridge University Press, 2000); Babatunde Agiri, "Slavery in Yoruba Society in the 19th Century," in Paul E. Lovejoy (ed.), ***The Ideology of slavery in Africa*** (Beverly Hills : Sage Publications, 1981) 123-148; J.D. Fage, "Slaves and Society in Western Africa, *c.* 1445-*c.* 1700," ***Journal of African History*** 21 (1980): 289-310.

[814] In the *Papyrus of Nu*, one who enters the Hall of Ma'at must declare his innocence of a number of sins, including confessing: "I have not domineered over slaves (Confession 8)." Here the legitimate existence of the institution I assumed, and only improper treatment of slaves is deemed a sin.

[815] J.O. Hunwick, "Black Slaves in the Mediterranean World: Introduction to a Neglected Aspect of the African Diaspora" in Elizabeth Savage (ed.), ***The Human Commodity: Perspectives on the Trans-Atlantic Slave Trade*** (London: Frank Cass, 1992) 6.

[816] Segal, ***Islam's Slaves***, 4-6; Bernard Lewis, ***Race and Slavery in the Middle East: An Historical Enquiry*** (New York: Oxford University Press, 1990) 6. This is not

something very important regarding this early Muslim practice of slavery which often goes unnoticed: the preferred slaves for these Black Muslims were whites.[817] As Dana Marniche explains:

> ...people that were fair-skinned were recognized by Arabs as descendants of subject peoples and slaves... the idea of blacks in Africa being the predominant slaves of the Arabs comes from not knowing the history of the peninsula or in fact not being able to read Arabic, otherwise it would have been recognized that the Arabs were usually designated as "black" and "dark brown"... We know the Arabs were so predominantly black in color that even the term "white" in earlier days, according to Arabic linguistic specialists ... meant a black man with a clear skin... On the other hand many black Africans have been brought into Arabia as slaves more recently in the last several centuries. Many of the people that were taking black slaves from Africa were in fact not Arabs in the strict sense of the word but rather Muslim Iranians, Iraqis, [Turks], "white" Syrians and other "Arabized" settlers or inhabitants in the Near East, Arabia and North Africa...Most slaves...before the fall of Constantinople (Istanbul) in the 15th century were "whites" coming from the north and mixing with the very dark-skinned black and near black groups of people known as "Arabs" in Spain, North Africa and the Near East. ...thus, many Arabic speaking historians asserted up until the 14th century that the Arabs equated slave origins with fair skin or vice versa.[818]

---

to apologize for slavery in Islam. As a descendant of Africans enslaved in America, I cant as of now move past my abhorrence for the institution, regardless to how 'benign' it allegedly is: this goes for Islam, Christian, and Traditional African forms of enslavement.

[817] Segal, ***Islam's Black Slaves***, 49; Mark Perry, "Perceptions of Race in the Arab World," (Unpublished Paper, 2004) 5. Available at http://www.odidia.com/uploads/File/perceptionsofrace.pdf.

[818]Dana Marniche, "Afro-Arabian Origins of the Early Yemenites and their Conquest and Settlement of Spain" @ http://www.africaresource.com/rasta/sesostris-the-great-the-egyptian-hercules/afro-arabian-origins-of-the-early-yemenites-and-their-conquest-and-settlement-of-spain-dana-marniche/ accessed October 23, 2009.

The Muslim slave trade from Africa, to the extent that it happened in the early period, "involved a steady but relatively small flow over a millennium."[819] The more the Islamic world was *Aryanized*, however, the more the newly introduced anti-black sentiments shaped the institution of slavery in the Muslim world, until eventually (by the seventeenth century) the term 'slave', '*abid*, comes to mean 'Black person'.[820] The horrible 'East African Holocaust,' as the East African Slave Trade in the hands of Muslims has been called, was dominated by those 'Arabized' whites noted by Marniche, such as the notorious Omani ruler Sayyid Said b. Sultan (d. 1856) who controlled the East African trade from Zanzibar in the 19th century (Figure 42).[821]

The East African Holocaust, therefore, was not the result of the Islamization of Africa, but of the *Aryanization* of Islam.

---

[819] Lovejoy, ***Transformations***, 25.

[820] Perry, "Perceptions of Race," 5; Drake, ***Black Folk***, 2:85, 152: "In early Islam, there were positive associations with blackness...The rabbinic and midrashic stories that interpret black skin as a curse was apparently not part of early Arab oral tradition. However...they became known after the seventh-century conquests, among scholars in Mesopotamia who were developing Islamic religious thought. The scholars...some [were] Arabs, [most were] Persians."

[821] On Sayyid and the Omani Arab control of the 19th century see Segal, ***Islam's Black Slaves***, 146ff.

Figure 42

Sayyid Said b. Sulton, the notorious Omani Arab who controlled the 'East African Holocaust,' i.e. the 19th century slave trade based in Zanzibar

Appendix I

The Black God and the Ancient Mysteries

I. *Introductory Summary*

The religious texts of the ancient East and India, i.e. the hieroglyphic writings of ancient Kemet (Egypt), the cuneiform writings of ancient Sumer (Chaldea/Mesopotamia), and the Sanskrit writings of ancient India, record the history of God as a divine Black man. According to these texts, God was originally a luminous, formless essence hidden within a primordial* substantive darkness called 'waters'. At some point, this divine luminosity concentrated itself within the darkness and produced the atom or first particle of distinct matter, the 'golden egg' of ancient myth*. From this first atom there emerged many atoms, which the God used to build up his own luminous body. This body was anthropomorphic and thus this God was the first man in existence, a self-created man. This was a brilliantly luminous man, represented by the so-called 'sun-gods' of ancient myth. Indeed, the sun in the sky was said to be only a sign of the luminous anthropomorphic body of the creator-god.

This God's initial attempts at creation proved unsuccessful, as the brilliant luminosity of the divine form scorched material creation. As a solution the God veiled his luminosity with a body made from that same primordial dark substance from which he initially emerged. This divine black body refracted the divine light as it passed through the hair pores covering the body. This black body is therefore referred to in later literature as God's 'shadow' as it shades creation from the scorching heat of the 'sun' or luminous body of God. As the light passed through the hair pores of this divine black body it produced a dark-blue iridescence or glow. The ancients symbolized this visual effect by the semiprecious stone sapphire or lapis lazuli, which was a dark blue stone with golden speckles throughout. The God's body at this stage was thus depicted dark blue and said to be made of sapphire/lapis lazuli. Veiled in this (blue-)black body, the God successfully produced the material cosmos. The creator-gods of ancient myth were thus often painted dark blue.

Animals were used by the ancients to represent or symbolize various characteristics or attributes of the gods. The so-called 'attribute animal' of this black-bodied creator-god was the black bovine,* usually a bull. The bull symbolized the strength and fecundity of the creator-god. It also associated the God with the primordial dark waters, which the bull was believed to personify. As the God's black body was made from this primordial darkness, the black hide of the bull represented the black skin of the creator-god. This black body of God symbolized by the black bull was at the center of the 'mystery of God' in the ancient Mystery Systems. In ancient Kemet (Egypt), for example, the greatest mystery concerned the union of the sun-god Rēʿ, i.e. the luminous body of God, with the black god Osiris, the personification of the divine black body.

II. *The Black God in Antiquity*

Godfrey Higgins, in his still prodigious work, ***Anacalypsis***, observed:

> We have found the Black complexion or something relating to it whenever we have approached the origin of nations. The Alma Mater, the Goddess Multimammia, the founders of the Oracles, the Memnon of first idols, were always Black. Venus, Jupiter, Apollo, Bacchus, Hercules, Asteroth, Adonis, Horus, Apis, Osiris, and Amen: in short all the...deities were black. They remained as they were first...in very ancient times.[822]

Though made over a century ago, current History-of-Religions scholarship only confirms Higgins' observation. The major deities of Egypt, India, Asia, the Near East, Greece and Central and South America were indeed black. Of special note we may mention, in addition to those listed above, Min of Egypt,[823] Viṣṇu and **Kriṣṇa** India,[824] Buddha of Asia,[825] 'Il/'El/Al of the Near East,[826] and Quetzalcoatl of the early Americas.[827] The blackness of these deities did not necessarily

---

[822] ***Anacalypsis, an Attempt to Draw Aside the Veil of the Saitic Isis, or, An Inquiry Into the Origins of Languages, Nations, and Religions*** (1836; Brooklyn: A&B Book Publishers, 1992) 286.

[823] On Min and black gods of Egypt in general see Terence DuQuesne, ***Black and Gold God: colour symbolism of the god Anubis with observations on the phenomenology of colour in Egyptian and comparative religion*** (London: Da'th Scholarly Services, Darengo Publications, 1996) *passim*, esp. 18-23; Edmund S. Meltzer, " 'Who Knows the Color of God?'" ***Journal of Ancient Civilizations*** 11 (1996): 123-129; Jules Taylor, "The Black Image in Egyptian Art," ***Journal of African Civilization*** 1 (April, 1979) 29-38.

[824] On Viṣṇu and Kṛṣṇa see below.

[825] See photos of black Buddhas and some relevant data in Runoko Rashidi and Ivan Van Sertima, ***African Presence in Early Asia***(New Brunswick: Transaction Publishers, 1995 [Tenth Anniversary Edition]), e.g. 51-53, 82, 116, 118, 322, 335.

[826] Werner Daum, ***Ursemitische Religion*** (Stuttgart: W. Kohlhammer, 1985) and below.

[827] The anthropomorphic creator-god of Central Mexico, *Ehecatl Quetzalcoatl*, was black (Figure 43). See H. B. Nicholson, "The Deity 9 Wind 'Ehecatl-Quetzalcoatl' in the Mixteca Pictorials," ***Journal of Latin American Lore*** 4 (1978): 61-92; Eloise Quiñones Keber, "Topiltzin Quetzalcoatl in Text and Images," MA Thesis, Columbia University, New York, 1979; Fray Bernardino De Sahagan, ***A History of Ancient Mexico***, trans. Fanny R. Bandelier (Glendale, California: The Arthur H. Clark Company, 1932) 1:26. It is necessary to distinguish the historical-legendary figure, *Topiltzin Questzalcoatl* from the mythological-cosmological figure, Ehecatl-Quetzalcoatl. The ethnic identity of the former has been a matter of speculation. While a number of

indicate that they were chthonic (associated with death and the underworld) or in any way malevolent. Indeed, in the various ancient traditions, it was the king of the gods, the creator deity himself, who was black.[828] The blackness of the creator deity, that is to say the creator deity's black *body*-how it originated, of what substance(s) it was composed, why it was black, etc.-was at the center of the 'mystery of God' in ancient Egypt, India, and Sumer/Akkad.

---

scholars cling to the post-Conquest myth of the legendary figure as a "bearded, white" foreigner (e.g. Graham Hancock, ***Fingerprints of the Gods*** [New York: Three Rivers Press, 1995] 102-05; Thor Heyerdahl, "The Bearded Gods Speak," in Geoffrey Ashe et al [edd.], ***The Quest for America*** [London: Pall Mall Press, 1971] 199-238; Constance Irwin, ***Fair Gods and Stone Faces*** [New York: St. Martin's Press, 1963] 33-47), the Totec ruler was likely either a native or maybe an African immigrant (B.C. Hedrick, "Quetzalcoatl: European or Indigene?" in Carroll L. Riley et al [edd.], ***Man Across the Sea: Problems of Pre-Columbian Contacts*** [Austin and London: University of Texas Press, 1971] 255-265; Ivan Van Sertima, "Among the Quetzalcoatls," in idem, ***They Came Before Columbus: The African Presence in Ancient America*** [New York: Random House, 1976] 71-89; Negel Davies, ***The Aztecs: A History*** [Norman: University of Oklahoma Press, 1980] 258-9). But regardless of the ethnic identity of the legendary figure, the mythological creator-god, Ehecatl-Quetzalcoatl, was black, as is shown, for example, in the cosmological narrative of Vindobonensis Obverse and the Codex Vaticanus. See Jill Leslie Furst, ***Codex Vindobonensis Mexicanus I: A Commentary*** (Albany: State University of New York, 1978) 100, 123-26; Eduard Seler, ***The Tonalamatl of the Aubin Collection: An Old Mexican Picture Amnuscript in the Paris National Library*** (Berlin, 1901) 45-7; idem, ***Codex vaticanus nr. 3773 (codex vaticanus B) eine altmexikansiche bilderschrift der Vatikanischen bibliothek*** (Berlin, 1902) 1:7 figure 1. Indeed, according to post-Conquest pictorial representations, the historic-legendary figure, as Totec priest, often dressed up as the god Ehecatl. In so doing, he painted his body black. See De Sahagan, ***A History***, Back; Keber, "Topiltzin," 65, 79, 86. On pre- and post-Conquest pictorials of Topiltzin Quetzalcoatl see Eloise Quiñones Keber, "The Aztec Image of Topiltzin Quetzalcoatl," in J. Kathryn Josserand and Karen Dakin (edd.), ***Smoke and Mist: Mesoamerican Studies in Memory of Thelma D. Sullivan*** (BAR International Series 402[i], 1988) 329-343. On the relation of the two Quetzalcoatls see Henry B. Nicholson, "Ehecatl-Quetzalcoatl vs. Topiltzin Quetzalcoatl of Tollan: a Problem in Mesoamerican Religion and History" in ***Actes du XLIIe Congrès international des amâricanistes. Congrès du centenaire: Paris, 2-9 septembre 1976*** (Paris: Socièlè des amèricanistes, 1976) 35-47.

[828] See below.

Figure 43

Ehecatl Quetzalcoatl, Black creator-God of Central America lifting the Primordial* Sky

III. *The Black God and his Black Bull*

In antiquity various aspects of the gods were represented zoomorphically. That is to say, different animals were used to symbolize distinct characteristics or attributes of a deity,[829] who was otherwise anthropomorphic. The paramount 'attribute animal' of the black creator-god was the black bovine*, usually a bull (Figure 19). The bull represented potency, fecundity, and primordial materiality, all essential characteristics of the creator-god.[830] The color of the bull was not arbitrary. As René L. Vos

829 On the 'attribute animal' of ancient Near Eastern religion see Erik Hornung, ***Conceptions of God in Ancient Egypt: the One and the Many*** (Ithaca: Cornell University Press, 1982)109-25; P. Amiet, ***Corpus des cylinders de Ras Shamra-Ougarit II: Sceaux-cylinres en hematite et pierres diverses*** (Ras Shamra-Ougarit IX; Paris: Éditions Recherche sur les Civilisations, 1992) 68; "Attribute Animal" in idem, ***Art of the Ancient Near East***, trans. J. Shepley and C. Choquet (New York: Abrams, 1980) 440 n. 787.

830 On the symbolism of the bull see Mircea Eliade, ***Patterns in Comparative Religion***, translated by Rosemary Sheed (1958; Lincoln and London: University of Nebraska Press, 1996) 82-93; Karel van der Toorn, Bob Becking and Pieter W. van der Horst (edd.), ***Dictionary of Deities and Demons in the Bible***, 2nd Edition (Leiden

pointed out, "Color reflected the nature of a god" and thus the skin color "constituted the vehicle of the divine nature of a sacred animal."[831] Over against the golden lion or falcon, which symbolized morning/midday sunlight, the black bovine symbolized night and materiality.[832] The black bovine was associated with the black primordial waters from which the creator-god emerged;[833] it thus came to symbolize the black

---

and Grand Rapids, MI.: Brill and Eerdmans, 1999) s.v. "Calf," by N. Wyatt, 180-182; ***ERE*** 2:887-889 s.v. Bull, by C.J. Caskell. See also René L. Vos, "Varius Coloribus Apis: Some Remarks of the Colours of Apis and Other Sacred Animals," in Willy Clarysse, Antoon Schoors and Harco Willems (edd.), ***Egyptian Religion: The Last Thousand Years, Part 1. Studies Dedicated to the Memory of Jan Quaegebeur*** (Leuven: Uitgeverij Peeters en Departement Oosterse Studies, 1998) 715, who notes that the bulls of Egypt "materialize upon the earth the creative forces of the hidden demiurge (creator-god)."

831 "Varius Coloribus Apis," 711.

832 Asko Parpola, "New correspondences between Harappan and Near Eastern glyptic art," ***South Asian Archaeology*** 1981, 178 notes: "Indeed, the golden-skinned hairy lion is an archetypal symbol for the golden-rayed sun, the lord of the day…Night…is equally well represented by the bull, whose horns connect it with the crescent of the moon." On the bull and the moon-god in ancient Near Eastern mythology see also Tallay Ornan, "The Bull and its Two Masters: Moon and Storm Deities in Relation to the Bull in Ancient Near Eastern Art," ***Israel Exploration Journal*** 51 (2001) 1-26; Dominique Collon, "The Near Eastern Moon God," in Diederik J.W. Meijer (ed.), ***Natural Phenomena: Their Meaning, Depiction and Description in the Ancient Near East*** (North-Holland, Amsterdam, 1992) 19-37. On the falcon as symbol of the sun-god see J. Assmann, ***Liturgische Lieder an den Sonnengott. Untersuchungen zur ägyptischen Hymnik I*** (MÄS 19; Berlin, 1969) 170-1.

833 Parpola, "New correspondences," 181 suggests that "the dark buffalo bathing in muddy water was conceived as the personification of the cosmic waters of chaos". In the *Ṛg Veda* the cosmic waters are cows (e.g. 4.3.11; 3.31.3; 4.1.11) and in *Pañcaviṃśa-Brāmana* 21.3.7 the spotted cow Śabalā is addressed: "Thou art the [primeval ocean]." On water and cows in Indic tradition see further Anne Feldhaus, ***Water and Womanhood. Religious Meanings of Rivers in Maharashtra*** (New York and Oxford: Oxford University Press, 1995) 46-47. The black bull (*k' km*) of Egypt, Apis, personified the waters of the Nile which was regarded as a type of Nun, the dark, primeval watery mass out of which creation sprang (See Émile Chassinat, "La Mise a Mort Rituelle D'Apis," ***Recueil de travaux relatifs a la philology et a l'archeologie egyptiennes et assyriennes*** 38 [1916] 33-60; E.A. Wallis Budge, ***The Egyptian Book of the Dead (The Papyrus of Ani). Egyptian Text Transliterated and Translated*** [New York: Dover Publications, Inc. 1967] cxxiii). See also the Babylonian Enki (Figure 9), called *am-gig-abzu*, 'black bull of the Apsû (primordial waters).' See W.F. Albright, "The Mouth of the Rivers," ***AJSL*** 35 (1991): 161-195, esp. 167. The Babylonian Tiamat (primordial salt-waters) seems also to have been presented as a bovine in the *Enūma Elish*: see B. Landsberger and J.V. Kinnier

material body that the creator-god will form for himself,[834] the black skin of the bovine signaling the black skin of the deity.[835] Thus, the hide of the sacrificial bull of ancient Sumer/Akkad, which was required to be 'black as asphalt (Figure 30),' was ritually identified with the skin of the Sumerian/Akkadian creator-deity Anu.[836]

This association between divine and bovine skin is explicitly articulated, for example, in the Indic[837]* scripture *Śatapatha-Brāhmaṇa*[838] with regard to the black *tārpya* garment worn by the king during the Indic royal consecration ceremony called *Rājasūya*. During this ceremony the king ritually impersonated

---

Wilson, "The Fifth Tablet of Enuma Elis," ***JNES*** 20 (1961): 175 [art.=154-179]. On the black bull and the black waters of creation see also Vos, "Varius Coloribus Apis," 715, 718.

[834] Thus the Buchis bull of Armant, whose name means something like "who makes the *ba* dwell within the body." See Dieter Kessler, "Bull Gods," in Donald B. Redford (ed.), ***The Ancient Gods Speak: A Guide to Egyptian Religion*** (Oxford: Oxford University Press, 2002) 30.

[835] See e.g. the black skin of the Egyptian deity Min (Figure 14), the 'creator god *par excellence*," and his black bovines (H.Gauthier, ***Les fêtes du dieu Min*** 2 vols. [Le Caire, 1931; IFAO. Recherches d'Archéologie] 2:55-57; ***DDD*** s.v. "Min," 577 by K. van der Toorn; Veronica Ions, ***Egyptian Mythology*** [Middlesex: The Hamlyn Publishing Group Ltd., 1968] 110; G.A. Wainwright, "Some Aspects of Amūn," ***Journal of Egyptian Archaeology*** 20 [1934]: 140 [art.=139-53]), the black-skinned Osiris and the black bull Apis (Vos, "Varius Coloribus Apis," 716; idem, "Apis," ***DDD*** 70) as well as the Indic Yamā with his black skin and black buffalo [P. van Bosch, "Yama-The God on the Black Buffalo," in ***Commemorative Figures*** [Leiden: E.J. Brill, 1982] 21-64). In contrast, but making the same point, see the white-skinned Śiva and his white bull Nandi.

[836] In one description of the Babylonian *kalū*-ritual the slaying and skinning of the black bull is mythologized as the god Bēl's slaying and flaying of the god Anu, whose characteristic attribute animal was the black bull. See Daum, ***Ursemitische Religion***, 204; E. Ebeling, ***Tod und Leben nach den Vorstellungen der Babylonier*** 2 vols. (Berlin-Leipzig, 1931) 1:29; C. Bezold, ***Babylonisch-assyrisches Glossar*** (Heidelberg: C. Winter, 1926) 210 s.v. sugugalu; Georgia de Santillana and Hertha von Dechend, ***Hamlet's Mill: An essay on myth and the frame of time*** (Boston: Gambit, Inc., 1969) 124. On Anu see further Herman Wohlstein, ***The Sky-God An-Anu*** (Jericho, New York: Paul A. Stroock, 1976).

[837] I will use 'Indic' throughout this work to refer to the traditions of ancient India, as opposed to 'Indian,' which is popularly, though erroneously, associated with the indigenous groups of the early Americas.

[838] Brāhmanas are Vedic texts dealing with priestly sacrifices and rituals.

the creator-god and divine king Prajāpati-Varuṇa.[839] The black *tārpya* garment worn by the king represented the body of the royal creator-god (Prajāpati-Varuṇa) whom the king impersonated here.[840] Regarding the *tārpya* garment and by implication its divine counterpart, ***Śatapatha-Brāhmaṇa*** 3, 1, 2, 13-17 notes:

> it (i.e. the *tārpya* garment) is indeed his (i.e. king's) own skin he thereby puts on himself. Now that skin which belongs to the cow was originally on man. The gods spake, 'Verily, the cow supports everything here (on earth); come, let us put on the cow that skin which is now on man; therewith she will be able to endure rain and cold and heat. Accordingly, having flayed man, they put that skin on the cow, and therewith she now endures rain and cold and heat. For man was indeed flayed; and hence wherever a stalk of grass or some other object cuts him, the blood trickles out. They then put that skin, the (*tārpya*) garment, on him; and for this reason none but man wears a garment, it having been put on him as his skin…Let him, then, not be naked in the presence of a cow. For the cow knows that

---

[839] See J. Gonda, "Vedic Gods and the Sacrifice," ***Numen*** 30 (1983): 1-34; Walter O. Kaelber, "'Tapas,' Birth, and Spiritual Rebirth in the Veda," ***History of Religions*** 15 (1976): 343-386; Johannes Cornelis Heesternman, ***The Ancient Indian Royal Consecration: The rājasūya described according to the Yajus texts and annotated*** (The Hague: Mouton & Co., 1957).

[840] See Heesternman, ***Ancient Indian Royal Consecration*** on the somatic significance of the ritual garments. Specifically, the black antelope skins represent the black skin of the divine king Varuṇ[a], who personifies the primordial waters. On the black skinned Varuṇ[a] see *Śatapatha- Brāhmana* [11.6.1]. On Varuṇ[a] and the black sacrificial garments see further Alfred Hillebrandt, ***Vedic Mythology***, trans. from the German by Sreeramula Rajeswara Sarma, 2 vols. (Delhi: Motilal Banarsidass Publishers, 1999; reprint) 2: 41, 44-45. On VaruÖ[a] in Indic mythology generally see ibid. 2:1-47; Alain Daniélou, ***The Myths and Gods of India*** (1964; Rochester, Vermont: Inner Traditions International, 1985) 118-121; F.B.J. Kuiper, *Varuṇ[a] and Vidūṣaka.* ***On the Origin of the Sanskrit Drama*** (Amsterdam/Oxford/New York: North-Holland Publishing Company, 1979); Sukumari Bhattacharji, ***The Indian Theogony: A Comparative Study of Indian Mythology From the Vedas to the PurāÖas*** (Cambridge: Cambridge University Press, 1970) Chapter One.

she wears his skin, and runs away for fear lest he should take the skin from her.[841]

In explaining the relation between the black ritual garment and the black cow skin, it is here recalled that the latter actually was once man's own skin, who lost it to the cow (man was 'flayed'). This black bovine skin apparently once covered man's fleshy skin as an exterior layer, according to this mythical account. In place of this lost exterior layer, man was given the black *tārpya* garment. Now whenever the cow sees a naked man it flees in fear of him trying to retrieve his original 'garment,' the black skin that now protects the cow from inclement weather. It must be kept in mind that the Vedas are the literary work of the invading Indo-Aryan tribes, and this description of the flaying of man's black skin reflects the actual experience of the indigenous 'black, snub-nosed' Dasyus tribes who were indeed flayed by the Aryan hordes. This historical flaying is mythologized in the ***Ṛg*** *Veda* (I. 130-8) where the Aryan deity Indra is described as tearing off the black skin of the Asura, the gods of the pre-Aryan black tribes.[842] In this ***Rājasūya*** or consecration ritual the human king is impersonating the divine king, God, whose skin is represented by the bovin skin. The black garment/bovine skin represents the black skin of the pre-Aryan black gods. Asko Parpola has demonstrated that both the *tārpya* garment and its divine

---

[841] Trans. J. Eggeling, ***The Śatapatha- Brāhmana according to the text of the Mādhyandina school***. I-V. ***Sacred Books of the East*** (Oxford, 1882-1900) II: 9f.

[842] On the historical conflict between the invading Aryans an
d the indigenous black tribes of India, and its mythic portrayal in the Vedas as the conflict between the Devas and the Asuras, see Ram Sharan Sharma, ***Sūdras in Ancient India. A Social history of the lower order down to circa A.D. 600*** (Delhi: Molilal Banarsidass, 1980) Chapt. II; Daniélou, ***Myths and Gods of India***, 139-146. On the racial background of the Asuras see also R. Ruggles Gates, "The Asurs and Birhors of Chota Nagpur," in T.N. Madan and Gopāla Śarana (edd.), ***Indian Anthropology. Essays in Memory of D.N. Majumdar*** (New York: Asia Publishing House, 1962) 163-184.

analogue, the 'sky garment' of the gods (i.e. the divine body), are associated with the skin of the mythic 'bull of heaven.'[843]

III.1. *The Blue-Black Creator-God*

In his *Praeparatio Evangelica* (III, 115a, 7) the fourth century church historian Eusebius of Caesarea quoted from Porphyry's (ca. 233-309) lost work, *Concerning Images*, a note on an Egyptian view of the Creator: "The Demiurge (creator-god), whom the Egyptians call Cneph, is of human form, but with a skin of dark blue, holding a girdle and a scepter, and crowned with a royal wing on his head."[844] While we have by now come to expect the divine human form, the dark blue skin requires some explanation. Indeed, the leading gods of the ancient Near East were not just black, but blue-black. This dark 'blueness' of the divine body had profound significance. It was not just any blue, but sapphire blue.[845] In biblical tradition and in ancient and medieval texts generally the term 'sapphire' denoted the semiprecious stone lapis lazuli.[846] Considered the "ultimate

---

[843] ***The Sky-Garment: A Study of the Harappan religion and its relation to the Mesopotamian and later Indian religion*** (SO 57; Helsinki, 1985); idem, "The Harappan 'Priest-King's' Robe and the Vedic Tārpya Garment: Their Interrelation and Symbolism (Astral and Procreative)," ***South Asian Archaeology*** 1983, vol. 1, 385-403. On the garments of the gods in ancient Near Eastern tradition see A. Leo Oppenheim, "The Golden Garments of the Gods," ***Journal of Near Eastern Society of Columbia University*** 8 (1949): 172-193; Herbert Sauren, "Die Kleidung Der Götter," ***Visible Religion*** 2 (1984): 95-117; David Freedman, "**Ṣubāt Bāšti**: A Robe of Splendor," ***JANES*** 4 (1972): 91-5. See also Alan Miller, "The Garments of the Gods in Japanese Ritual," ***Journal of Ritual Studies*** 5 (Summer 1991): 33-55.
[844] Trans. E.H. Grifford, 1903.

[845] The dark blue skin of the anthropomorphic deities of Egypt was *jrtyw* or **ḥsbḏ** (lapis lazuli), which is a blue-black: See Caroline Ransom Williams, ***The Decoration of the Tomb of Per-Nēb*** (New York: The Metropolitan Museum of Art, 1932) 52f; J.R. Harris, ***Lexicographical Studies in Ancient Egyptian Minerals*** (Berlin: Akademie-Verlag, 1961) 226.

Divine substance," sapphire/lapis lazuli possessed great mythological significance in the ancient Near East.[847] In its natural state lapis lazuli is dark blue with fine golden speckles[848] recalling the "sky bedecked with stars"[849]; thus the visible heaven is often said to be sapphiric.[850]

This sapphiric heaven, called the 'sky- garment' of the gods,[851] was associated with the divine body,[852] 'garment' being an

---

[846] Michel Pastoureau, ***Blue: The History of a Color*** (Princeton: Princeton University Press, 2001) 7, 21f; ***The Interpreter's dictionary of the Bible: an illustrated encyclopedia identifying and explaining all proper names and significant terms and subjects in the Holy Scriptures, including the Apocrypha, with attention to archaeological discoveries and researches into life and faith of ancient times*** 5 vols. (George Arthur Buttrick et al [edd.]; New York: Abingdon Press, 1962-76) s.v. "Sapphire," by W.E. Stapes; ***Dictionary of the Bible***, ed. James Hastings (New York: MacMillian Publishing Company, 1988) 497, s.v. "Jewels and Precious Stones," by J. Patrick and G.R. Berry.

[847] F. Daumas, "Lapis-lazuli et Régénération," in Sydney Aufrère, ***L'Univers minéral dans la pensée Égyptienne***, 2 vols. (Le Caire: Institut Français d'Archéologie Orientale du Caire, 1991) 2:463-488; John Irwin, "The L§ã Bhairo at Benares (V§r§ÖasÊ): Another Pre-Aśokan Monument?" ***ZDMG*** 133 (1983): 327-43 [art.=320-352].

[848] On Lapis Lazuli see Lissie von Rosen, ***Lapis Lazuli in Geological Contexts and in Ancient Written Sources*** (Partille: Paul Åströms förlag, 1988); idem, ***Lapis Lazuli in Archaeological Contexts*** (Jonsered: Paul Åströms förlag, 1990); Rutherford J. Gettens, "Lapis Lazuli and Ultramarine in Ancient Times," ***Alumni de la Fondation universitaire*** 19 (1950): 342-357.

[849] See Irwin, "Lāṭ Bhairo," 332.

[850] Exod. 24:10; Ez. 1:26 (LXX); William Brownlee notes "This dome (of heaven) was thought of as sapphire in color, and as crystalline and transparent." ***Ezekiel 1-19*** (Waco, TX: Word Books, 1986), 13. Nut, the ancient Egyptian sky goddess, "glistens like lapis lazuli." See Assmann, ***Liturgische Lieder***, 314ff. text III 4. The association of the heavens with precious stones is found in Babylonian cosmologies as well, which may have influenced biblical cosmology. According to W.G. Lambert, the Babylonians associated their three heavens (upper/middle/lower) with stones, the lower deriving its blue from the jasper stone ("The Cosmology of Sumer and Babylon," in Carmen Blacker and Michael Loewe (edd.), ***Ancient Cosmologies*** [London: George Allen & Unwin Ltd, 1975] 58). In rabbinic literature, the firmament is often made of crystal, whench the heavens derive their light (See Louis Ginzberg, ***The Legends of the Jews*** [7 vols; Baltimore: John Hopkins University Press, 1911, 1939], vol. 1, 13).

[851] See especially Parpola, ***Sky-Garment***; idem, "Harappan 'Priest-King's' Robe"; Oppenheim, "Golden Garments." This designation arises from the golden star-like ornaments or appliqué work sewn into the garment recalling the star-spangled night sky.

[852] Amun-Re is "beautiful youth of purest lapis lazuli (*ḥwn-nfr n-ḫsbḏ-m3ʿ*) whose "body is heaven" (*ḥt. K nwt*). See J. Assmann, ***Sonnenhymnen in thebanischen Gräbern*** (Mainz: a.R., 1983) 5, #6:5; 124, # 43:14; A.I. Sadek, ***Popular Religion in Egypt***

ancient and widespread metaphor for body.[853] Thus, the leading deities of the ancient Near East had sapphiric-blue bodies. This is particularly the case with deities associated with fecundity or creation.[854] In Egypt, "The traditional colour of (the) gods' limbs (was) the dark blue lapis lazuli."[855] The ancient Near Eastern cult statue, which was considered the earthly body of the deity,[856] was

---

During the New Kingdom (Hildsheim, 1987) 14. See also Grey Hubert Skipwith, " 'The Lord of Heaven.' (The Fire of God; the Mountain Summit; The Divine Chariot; and the Vision of Ezekiel.)," ***JQR*** 19 (1906-7): 693-4 and illustrations in Othmar Keel, ***The Symbolism of the Biblical World. Ancient Near Eastern Iconography and the Book of Psalms*** (London: SPCK, 1978) 33-4. In Manichaean tradition, the Mother of Life spread out the heaven with the skin of the Sons of Darkness according to the testimony of Theodore bar Khonai, *Liber Scholiorum* XI, trns. H. Pognon in ***Inscriptions Mandaïtes des coupes de Khouabir***, II (Paris: Welter, 1899) 188. In the *Greater Bundahišn*, 189, 8 the cosmic body is said to have "skin like the sky." See also the anthropomorphic body of Zurvan, called *Spihr*, which is associated with both the blue firmament and a blue garment: see R.C. Zaehner, ***Zurvan, A Zoroastrian Dilemma*** (Oxford, 1955; rep. 1972), 11f, 122. The stars covering the garment signified rays of celestial light emanating from the hair-pores of the divine skin (see below). Thus, in some depictions of this 'sky-garment,' the garment itself is missing and the stars are painted on the very skin of the anthropos. See e.g. the golden statue found in Susa and published by R. de Mecquenem, ***Offrandes de fondation du temple de Chouchinak***, (Paris, 1905) vol. II, Pl. XXIV 1*a*. See also Oppenheim, "Golden Garments," 182 Fig. 2.

[853] Geo Widengren, ***The Great Vohu Manah and the Apostle of God: Studies in Iranian and Manichaean Religion*** (Uppsala: A.-B. Lundequistska Bokhandeln, 1945) 50-55, 76-83; J.M. Rist, "A Common Metaphor," in idem, ***Plotinus: The Road to Reality*** (London: Cambridge University Press, 1967) 188-198; Dennis Ronald MacDonald, ***There is no Male and Female: The Fate of a Dominical Saying in Paul and Gnosticism*** (Philadelphia: Fortress Press, 1987), 23-25.

[854] John Baines, ***Fecundity Figures: Egyptian Personification and the Iconology of a Genre*** (Wiltschire: Aris & Phillips and Chicago: Bolchazy-Carducci, 1985) 139-142.

[855] Lise Manniche, "The Body Colours of Gods and Man in Inland Jewellery and Related Objects from the Tomb of Tutankhamun," ***Acta Orientalia*** 43 (1982): 5-12 (10). On the color of the god's skin as indicative of its status and role, with the sapphiric-bodied deity as 'king of the gods' see Robins, "Color Symbolism," in Redford ***Ancient Gods Speak***, 58-9; Monika Dolińsks, "Red and Blue Figures of Amun," ***Varia aegyptiaca*** 6 (1990): 5-6 [art.=3-7]. On the association of a deities skin color and character see also John Baines, "Color Terminology and Color Classification: Ancient Egyptian Color Terminology and Polychromy," ***American Anthropologists*** 87 (1985): 284 [art.=282-97]

[856] On the ancient Near Eastern cult of divine images see Neal H. Walls (ed.) ***Cult Image and Divine Representation in the Ancient Near East*** (American Schools of Oriental Research Books Series 10; Boston: American Schools of Oriental Research, 2005); Zainab Bahrani, ***The Graven Image: Representation in Babylonia and Assyria*** (Philadelphia: University of Pennsylvania Press, 2003); Michael B. Dick (ed.), ***Born in Heaven, Made on Earth: The Making of the Cult Image in the Ancient***

ideally made of a wooden core platted with red gold or silver, overlaid with sapphires,[857] all of which signified substances from the body of the deity: "his (i.e. Rē''s) bones are silver, his flesh is gold, his hair genuine lapis-lazuli."[858] But the hair too was a

Near East (Winona Lake, Indiana: Eisenbrauns, 1999); idem, "The Relationship between the Cult Image and the Deity in Mesopotamia," in Jiří Prosecký (ed.), ***Intellectual Life of the ancient Near East: Papers Presented at the 43rd Rencontre assyriologique international, Prague, July 1-5, 1996*** (Prague: Oriental Institute, 1998) 11-16; T. Jacobsen, "The Graven Image," in P.D. Miller Jr., P.D. Hanson and S.D. McBride (edd.), ***Ancient Israelite Religion: Essays in Honor of Frank Moore Cross*** (Philadelphia: Fortress Press, 1987) 15-32, esp. 16-20;

857 When King Nabu-apla-iddina of Babylon (ca. 887-855 BC) restored the image (*ṣalmu*) of the god Shamash, it was made of "red gold and clear lapis lazuli": L.W. King, ***Babylonian Boundary-Stones and Memorial-Tablets in the British Museum: With Atlas of Plates*** (London: British Museum, 1912) 120-127, #36 IV 20. Lugalzagesi, *ensi* (governor) of Ummah, during his sack of Lagash (ca. 2340 B.C.E.) is said to have plundered the temple of the goddess Amageštin and robed her "of her precious metal and lapis lazuli, and threw her in the well." H. Steible, ***Die altsumerischen Bau- und Weihinschriften*** (Freiburger Altorientalische Studien 5; Wiesbaden: F. Steiner, 1982): Ukgagina 16:6:11-7:6. The reference is likely to the goddesses cult statute. See Michael B. Dick, "The Mesopotamian Cult Statute: A Sacramental Encounter with Divinity," in Walls, ***Cult Image***, 49. See also the lament of Ninšubur on the occasion of Inanna's 'Descent to the Netherworld" (II. 43-46):

> O Father Enlil, let no one in the Netherworld kill your child!
> Let no one smelt your fine silver along with crude ore! (on the translation of this line see A.R. George, "Observations on a Passage of 'Inanna's Descent'," ***JCS*** 37 [1985]: 109-13)
> Let no one cleave your fine lapis lazuli along with the lapidary's stones!
> Let no one cut up your boxwood along with the carpenter's timber!
> Let no one in the Netherworld kill the young woman Inanna!

Inanna's statue is thus made of boxwood (*taškarinnu*), plated with silver and overlaid with lapis lazuli. Cf. the *eršemma* of Ningirgilu (*CT* 15 23). On the above passage as a reference to Inanna's cult statue see also Giorgio Buccellati, "The Descent of Inanna as a Ritual Journey to Kutha?" ***Syro-Mesopotamian Studies*** 3 (1982): 3-7. On Egyptian cult statues and lapis-lazuli see Daumas, "Lapis-lazuli et Régénération," 465-67. On the materials used for the construction of divine images see Victor Hurowitz, "What Goes In Is What Comes Out – Materials for Creating Cult Statues" in G. Beckman and T.J. Lewish (edd.), ***Text and Artifact – Proceedings of the Colloquium of the Center for Judaic Studies, University of Pennsylvania, April 27-29, 1998***, Brown Judaic Series, 2006 (in press).

858 Gay Robins, "Cult Statues in Ancient Egypt," in Walls, ***Cult Image***, 6; idem, "Color Symbolism," 60; Claude Traunecker, ***The Gods of Egypt***, translated from the French by David Lorton (Ithaca and London: Cornell University Press, 2001) 44; Dmitri Meeks, "Divine Bodies," in Dimitri Meeks and Christine Favard-Meeks, ***Daily Life of the***

metaphor for rays of light emanating from the hair-pores covering the body[859] and lapis lazuli was considered 'solidified celestial light'.[860] The deity's whole body was therefore depicted blue.[861] Mediating between the gold flesh and lapis lazuli 'hair' of the creator deity is the divine black skin signified by the bull hide. The black bull, Ad de Vries informs us, "mediated between fire (gold) and water (lapis lazuli), heaven and earth" (inserts original).[862] The light of the 'golden flesh' passing through the hair-pores of the divine black skin therefore produced a sapphiric 'surrounding splendor' (Figure 53)[863]

Egyptian Gods, translated by G.M. Goshgarian (Ithaca and London: Cornell University Press, 1996) 57; Hornung, ***Conceptions of God***, 134.

859 Ad de Vries, ***Dictionary of Symbols and Imagery*** (Amsterdam and London: North-Holland Publishing Company, 1974) 39 s.v. Beard; Marten Stol, "The Moon as Seen by the Babylonians," in Diederik J.W. Meijer (ed.), ***Natural Phenomena: Their Meaning, Depiction and Description in the Ancient Near East*** (North-Holland, Amsterdam, 1992) 255.

860 On lapis lazuli as "solidified celestial light" see Robins, "Color Symbolism," 60. On rays of light emanating from the divine hair pores see for example *Śatapatha-Brāhmaṇa* 10, 4, 4, 1-2: "When Prajāpati was creating living beings, Death, that evil, overpowered him. He practiced austerities for a thousand years, striving to leave evil behind him. 2. Whilst he was practicing austerities, lights went upwards from those hair-pits of his; and those lights are those stars; as many stars as there are, so many hair-pits there are." Translation by Eggeling. See also below. On ancient Near Eastern parallels see Parpola, ***Sky-Garment***, 74.

861 Thus the blue bodied deity Amun. See Traunecker, ***Gods of Egypt***, 44; Wainwright, "Some Aspects of Amūn"; Dolińsks, "Red and Blue Figures of Amun."

862 ***Dictionary of Symbols and Imagery***, 69 s.v. Bull. As the 'bull of heaven' the bovine has sapphiric associations as well. See e.g. the statuette from Uruk, Jemdet Nasr period (c. 3200-2900 BC) with trefoil inlays of lapis lazuli: H. Schmökel, ***Ur, Assur und Babylon: Drei Jahrtausende im Zweistromland*** (Stuttgart, 1955), plate 8, top. In the *Epic of Gilgamesh* (Old Babylonian Version, Tablet IV 170-3) the Bull of heaven has horns of lapis lazuli. Nanna-Sin, moon-god of Sumer and Babylon, is the 'frisky calf of heaven' and the 'lapis lazuli bull.' See Ornan, "The Bull and its Two Masters," 3; Stol, "The Moon," 255. On Nanna-Sin see further ***DDD***, s.v. Sîn 782-3 by M. Stol. See also the sapphiric bearded bull in Jeremy Black and Anthony Green, ***Gods, Demons and Symbols of Ancient Mesopotamia: An Illustrated Dictionary*** (London: British Museum Press, 1992) 44 s.v. bison.

863 See e.g. A. Massy, *Le Papyrus de Leiden I 347* (Ghent, 1885) 2 where an Egyptian deity is described as "robed in brilliance and wrapped in turquoise." See further Meeks, "Divine Bodies," 57.

III.2. *The Self-Created Blue-Black Creator*

Before creating the cosmos, according to ancient Near Eastern tradition, the black god created himself, or, rather, his body: "O Rēʿ who gave birth to righteousness, sovereign who created all this, who built his limbs, who modeled his body, who created himself, who gave birth to himself."[864] Ancient Indic and ancient Egyptian tradition give fairly detailed mythic accounts of the self-creation of the black god.[865] Most amazing is the remarkable similarity of these accounts. While one nation deriving its account from the other is improbable, it is likely that

---

[864] From Theb. Tomb 157: translation from J. Zandee, "The Birth-Giving Creator-God in Ancient Egypt," in Alan B. Lloyd (ed.), ***Studies in Pharaonic Religion and Society, in Honour of J. Gwyn Griffiths*** (London: The Egypt Exploration Society, 1992) 175 [art.=168-185]. See also the hieratic Coffin Text 714: "I (Atum) created my body in my glory; I am he who made myself; I formed myself according to my will and according to my heart." Translation from John D. Currid, in his ***Ancient Egypt and the Old Testament*** (Grand Rapids, Michigan: Baker Books, 1997), 58.

[865] On theo-cosmogony in Indic tradition, see, besides the primary Indic texts: David Leeming with Margaret Leeming, ***A Dictionary of Creation Myths*** New York and Oxford: Oxford University Press, 1994) s.v. Indian Creation, 139-144; Daniélou, ***Myths and Gods of India***; S.S. Dange (ed.), ***Myths of Creation. Papers read at the Seminar on 17th March, 1985*** (Bombay, 1987) Chapters 1-5; J. Gonda, " "In the Beginning," ***Annals of the Bhandarkar Oriental Research Institute*** 63 (1982): 453-62; F.B.J. Kuiper, ***Ancient Indian Cosmogony*** (ed. John Irwin; New Delhi: Vikas Publishing House, 1983); Wendy Doniger O'Flaherty, ***Hindu Myths: A Sourcebook Translated from the Sanskrit*** (London: Penguin Books, 1975); Bruce Lincoln, "The Indo-European Myth of Creation," ***HR*** 15 (1975): 121-145; Bhattacharji, ***Indian Theogony***; W. Norman Brown, "The Creation Myth of the Rig Veda," ***JAOS*** 62 (1942): 85-98. In Egyptian tradition, besides the standard accounts in treatments of Egyptian myth: Françoise Dunand and Christiane Zivie-Coche, ***Gods and Men in Egypt: 3000 BCE to 395 CE***, translated from the French by David Lorton (Ithaca and London: Cornell University Press, 2002) Chapter Two ("Cosmogonies, Creation, and Time"); Richard J. Clifford, ***Creation Accounts in the Ancient Near East and the bible*** (CBQMS 26; Washington, DC; Catholic Biblical Association of America, 1994) Chapter Four; J.P. Allen, ***Genesis in Egypt: The Philosophy of Ancient Egyptian Creation Accounts*** (YES 2; New Haven: Yale University, 1988). On Sumerian/Akkadian accounts of creation see Clifford, ***Creation Accounts***, Chapters Two and Three; Alexander Heidel, ***The Babylonian Genesis*** (2nd edition; Chicago and London: The University of Chicago Press, 1963); J. van Dijk, "Le motif cosmique dans la pensée sumérienne," ***Acta Orientalia*** 28 (1964): 1-59; Morris Jastrow, Jr., "The Sumerian View of Beginnings," ***JAOS*** 36 (1916): 122-135; idem, "Sumerian and Akkadian Views of Beginnings," ***JAOS*** 36 (1916): 274-299.

the similarities evince a widespread ancient Near Eastern mythic tradition concerning a self-created black creator-deity.[866]

According to this mythic tradition there was in the beginning only darkness, material darkness universally described as 'water.'[867] Hidden within this dark primordial water was the deity in a formless, luminous* state.[868] This primordial 'water' was characterized by what the Indic texts call *jāmi,* the unproductive state of non-differentiation of its constituent elements. All potential dualities (e.g. light/darkness, spirit/matter, male/female), which are a prerequisite to the generative process, lay undistinguished and negatively

---

[866] Speaking more broadly K.K.A. Venkatachari ("Babylonian, Assyrian and Other Accounts" in Dange, ***Myths of Creation***, 34) notes: "The myths regarding the creation of the universe and life, as found in the literature of the ancient civilizations bear remarkable similarity which is not easy to explain away, considering the lack of communication in the olden days and the fact that there was no print or other media as we have now."

[867] "At first there was only darkness (*tamas*) wrapped in darkness. All this was unillumined water." ***Ṛg Veda*** 10.129.1-6. An ancient Egyptian Coffin Text (Spell 80) mentions "the darkness *(kkyt)* of Nun." See Helmer Ringgren, "Light and Darkness in Ancient Egyptian Religion," in ***Liber amicorum. Studies in honour of Professor Dr. C.J. Bleeker. Published on the occasion of his retirement from the chair of the history of religions and the phenomenology of religion at the University of Amsterdam*** (SHR 17; Leiden: E.J. Brill, 1969) 143 [art.=140-150]. On the waters in Indic tradition see H.W. Bodewitz, "The Waters in Vedic Cosmic Classifications," ***Indologica Taurinensia*** 10 (1982): 45-54. In Egyptian tradition see Clifford, ***Creation Accounts***, 101-104; R.T. Rundle Clark, ***Myth and Symbol in Ancient Egypt*** (London: Thames and Hudson, 1959) 54-55. On the primordial waters in ancient myth see also Tamra Andrews, ***Legends of the Earth, Sea, and Sky: An Encyclopedia of Nature Myths*** (Santa Barbara, California: ABC-CLIO, 1998) s.v. Primordial Sea, 181-82; Eliade, ***Patterns***, Chapter Five; Philip Freund, ***Myths of Creation*** (New York: Washington Square Press, Inc, 1965) Chapter Four.

[868] For example the spiritual and featureless Brahman (neuter), which existed within the Indic primordial waters, was "brilliant, without body, sinewless": see E. Osborn Martin, ***The Gods of India: A Brief Description of their History, Character & Worship*** (London and Toronto: J.M. Dent and Sons, Ltd. And New York: E.P. Dutton and Co., 1914) Chapter 1; T.S Maxwell, ***The Gods of Asia: Image, Text, and Meaning*** (Delhi: Oxford University Press, 1997), 30; Kurian Mathothu, ***The Development of the Concept of Trimurti in Hinduism*** (Pali, India, 1974) 31-42. S.S. Dange, "Ṛgvedic Accounts," in Dange, ***Myths of Creation***, 10 notes: "In all the mythical accounts of Creation in the (Œg Veda), Water and Heat (i.e. a 'ray of light') seem to be the basic principles."

homogeneous; the ancient Egyptians called it the "state in which did not yet exist 'two things'." Creation begins with the distinguishing and separation of these elements.[869] How long this primeval,* homogeneous mass with its hidden divine luminosity existed is not indicated. At some point, however, God's luminosity concentrated itself within the primordial waters into a single point, producing the first distinguishable particle of luminous matter,[870] the mythical 'golden germ' or fiery a-tom,[871] the quark of modern-day quantum physics.[872] This soon

---

869 Hans-Peter Hasenfratz, "Patterns of Creation in Ancient Egypt," in Henning Graf Reventlow and Yair Hoffman (edd.), ***Creation in Jewish and Christian Tradition*** (JSOTSup 319; Sheffield: Sheffield Academic Press, 2002) 174 [art.=174-178]; John Irwin, " 'Asokan' Pillars: The Mystery of Foundation and Collapse," in Gilbert Pollet (ed.), ***India and the Ancient World: History, Trade and Culture Before A.D. 650*** (OLA 25; Leuven: Departement Oriëntalistiek, 1987) 87-93.

870 Dunand and Zivie-Coche, ***Gods and Men in Egypt***, 51 note: "Matter was already in Nun, waiting to be coagulated to a point where the dry contrasted with the unformed matter."

871 In Indic tradition the *Hiraṇya-Garbha* or 'Golden Germ"; see e.g. *Ṛg Veda* 10.121.7; *Atharva Veda* 10.7.28; *Matsya Pūraṇa* 2.25ff. On the golden germ see Daniélou, ***Myths and Gods of India***, 237-38; J. Gonda, "Background and variants of the HiraÖyagarbha Conception," in Perala Ratnam (ed.), ***Studies in Indo-Asian Art and Culture***, III (Delhi, 1974) 39-54; Mircea Eliade, "Spirit, Light, and Seed," ***HR*** 11 (1971): 1-30; Bhattacharji, ***Indian Theogony***, 330-1; F.B.J. Kuiper, "The Golden Germ," in idem, ***Ancient Indian Cosmogony***, 22-40; F.D.K. Bosch, ***The Golden Germ, An Introduction to Indian Symbolism*** (The Hague: Mouton, 1960). On the cosmogonic egg in Egyptian tradition see Clifford, ***Creation Accounts***, 106, 112; Clark, ***Myth and Symbol***, 56. On the Sumerian creator-god An/Anu planting the primordial seed see Clifford, ***Creation Accounts***, 26-29 and 39, where the author quotes an ancient Sumerian text entitled *Bird and Fish*, where mention is made of "the life-giving waters that begat the fecund seed."

872 The *Hiraṇya-Garbha*, according to Daniélou, ***Myths and Gods of India***, 234, is a "ball of fire from which the universe develops" and Von Franz, in her discussion of cosmogonic "Germs and Eggs" appropriately describes the mythical germ as "an enormous concentration of energy in...one center," ***Creation Myths***, 232. These descriptions identify the 'golden germ' with the quark (a-tom) of modern physics, the fundamental particle of matter, which is also a "ball" and "center of (fiery) energy." See Lawrence M. Krauss, ***Atom: An Odyssey from the Big Bang to Life on Earth...And Beyond*** (Boston: Little, Brown and Company, 2001); Leon Lederman with Dick Teresi, ***The God Particle: If the Universe is the Answer, What is the***

developed into an atom,[873] described mythically as the 'golden egg.'

III.2.1. *The Cosmogonic Egg and the Primordial Atom*

Ancient tradition described the primordial atom, in which everything (including God) was originally contained and out of which everything (including God) emerged, as an egg. [874] This 'Cosmogonic*' or 'Mundane' Egg symbolized the key to the mystery of Origins. Manley P. Hall, world-renowned scholar of the Occult, in his book ***MAN: The Grand Symbol of The Mysteries,*** observes:

Question (New York: Dell Publishing, 1993); Isaac Asimov, ***Atom: Journey Across the Subatomic Cosmos*** (New York: Truman Talley Books, 1992).

873 On the relation of the a-tom (quark) and the atom see sources cited above n. 502.

874 On the cosmogonic egg see Marie-Louise von Franz, ***Creation Myths*** revised edition (Boston and London: Shambhala, 1995), Chapter Eight ("Germs and Eggs"); de Vries, ***Dictionary***, 158-9 s.v. egg; ***ER*** 5:36-7 s.v. Egg by Venetia Newall; idem, ***An Egg at Easter: A Folklore Study*** (Bloomington: Indiana University Press, 1971) Chapter One; Eliade, ***Patterns***, 413-416; Anna-Britta Hellbom, "The Creation Egg," ***Ethnos*** 1 (1963): 63-105; Robert Wildhaber, "Zum Symbolgehalt und zur Ikonographie des Eies,' ***Deutsches Jahrbuch für Volkskunde*** 6 (1960): 7ff; H.J. Sheppard, "Egg Symbolism in Alchemy," ***Ambix*** 6 (August, 1958): 140-148; Freund, ***Myths of Creation***, Chapter Five; Martti Haavio, ***Väinämöinen: Eternal Sage*** (Helsinki, 1952) 45-63; Franz Lukas, "Das Ei als kosmogonische Vorstellung," ***Zeitschrift des Vereins für Volkskunde*** (Berlin, 1894) 227-243; James Gardner, ***The Faiths of the World: A Dictionary of All Religions and Religious Sects, their Doctrines Rites, Ceremonies and Customs***, 2 vols. (Edinburgh: A. Fullarton & Co., 1860) 1:797-8 s.v. Egg (Mundane). In Indic tradition see further F.B.J. Kuiper, "Cosmogony and Conception: A Query," ***HR*** 10 (1970): 100-104 [art.=91-138]; Gonda, "Background"; H. Lommel, "Der Welt-ei-Mythos im Rig-Veda," ***Mélanges Bally*** (Geneva, 1939) 214-20. On the cosmic egg as *prima materia* see also C.G. Jung, ***Psychology and Alchemy*** (2nd ed.; Princeton: Princeton University Press, 1968) 202. On the golden cosmogonic egg and the primordial atom see Freund, ***Myths of Creation***, Chapter 15; True Islam, ***The Book of God: An Encyclopedia of Proof that the Black Man is God*** (Atlanta: All in All Publishing, 1999) 148-151.

> The whole mystery of origin and destiny is concealed in the symbolism of that radiant gold egg...It was declared that such as understood this mystery had risen above all temporal limitations.[875]

Madame H.P. Blavatsky, Matriarch of Theosophy, says also:

> The 'Mundane Egg' is, perhaps, one of the most universally adopted symbols...Whence this universal symbol? The Egg was incorporated as a sacred sign in the cosmogony of every people on the Earth, and was revered both on account of its form and its inner mystery...It was known as that which represented most successfully the origin and secret of being. The gradual development of the imperceptible germ within the closed shell; the inward working, without apparent outward interference of force, which from a latent 'nothing' produced an active 'something,' needing naught save heat; and which, having gradually evolved into a concrete, living creature, broke its shell, appearing to outward senses of all a self-generated and self-created being-must have been a standing miracle from the beginning."[876]

The Egg symbolized *prima material*,[877] that 'primeval* substance in creation,'[878] or 'progenitive germ,'[879] from which the world evolved. As Philip Freund pointed out in 1965, this cosmogonic egg is the same as the 'primordial atom' of modern scientific theories on the origin of the universe.[880] In fact, the primordial atom, first proposed by Abbé Georges Lemaître, physicist at Louvain University, has since been called by scientists

---

[875] Manley P. Hall, ***MAN - The Grand Symbol of the Mysteries***, 1972, 69.
[876] Blavatsky, ***The Secret Doctrine*** 1:65,365.
[877] Jung, ***Psychology and Alchemy***, 202.
[878] Hillbom, "Creation Egg," 64.
[879] Freund, ***Myths of Creation***, 49.
[880] Ibid., 180.

"Lemaître's Egg" in recognition of its relation to the cosmogonic egg of the ancients. Isaac Asimov, for example, in his ***Atom: Journey Across the Subatomic Cosmos***, describes the beginning of the universe from a scientist's perspective in a way that radically approaches the beginning as described by these ancient religious texts:

> there was a time when the matter and energy of the Universe were literally squashed together into one exceeding dense mass. (The Belgian astronomer Abbé Georges Henri Lemaitre) called it the cosmic egg...If we consider the situation before the cosmic egg was formed, we might visualize a vast illimitable sea of nothingness...The nothingness contains energy...The Pre-Universe...had energy, and although all of its properties were otherwise those of a vacuum, it is called a false vacuum. Out of this false vacuum, a tiny point of matter appears where the energy, by blind forces of random changes, just happens to have concentrated itself sufficiently for the purpose. In fact, we might imagine the illimitable false vacuum to be a frothing, bubbling mass, producing bits of matter here and there as the ocean waves produce foam.[881]

Here we have a world-renowned scientist describing the pre-cosmic world in terms of a primordial ocean of matter and a cosmogonic egg, language deriving from the ancient mythic tradition.

---

[881] Asimov, ***Atom***, 304-310 On the congruence between modern quantum physics and ancient Eastern thought see the still insightful Fritjof Capra, ***The Tao of Physics*** (3rd ed.; Boston: Shambhala, 1991).

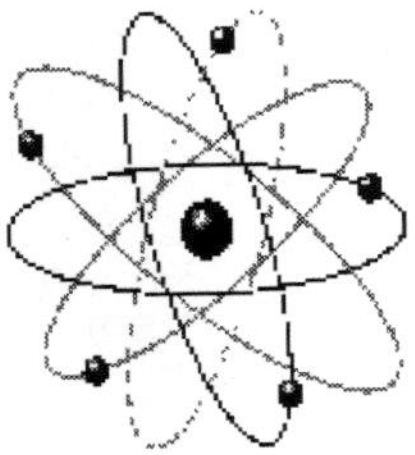

Figure 44
Newtonian Atom

Two different Eggs were recognized in ancient tradition. The first, the Universal Egg, was the black womb of Space in which existed that Primordial Energy – the Supreme All. The Sanskrit *Book of Dzyan* refers to it as the Eternal Egg.[882] Within this Universal Egg, the Supreme All self-fecundated and produced the Mundane or Golden Egg[883]; called "Golden" because the sparking of the Atom was the first visible manifestation of Light.

Proof that in fact the Golden Egg is a symbol for the A-tom from which the creator-God physically emerged is found everywhere. The *Egyptian Ritual* speaks of the "*egg conceived at the hour of the great one of the Dual Force*" (Sec. V., 2,3). The "Dual Force" is no doubt reference to the positive/negative polarity of the Primordial Energy which gave birth to the protons (+) and electrons (-) of the Atom. Occult philosophy depicts this Golden Egg with two poles, a positive on top and a negative on bottom.[884] The ancient Persians depicted two serpents, labeled Good and Evil, contending for the Mundane Egg (Figure 45). Hall notes that the ancients used the serpent to represent Electricity or Force.

---

882 Blavatsky, ***Secret Doctrine***, I: 28.
883 Hall, ***MAN - The Grand Symbol of the Mysteries***, 72.
884 Blavatsky, ***Secret Doctrine***, I: 556.

Electricity was commonly symbolized by the serpent because of its motion. Electricity passing between the poles of a spark gap is serpentine in its motion. Force projected through the atmosphere was called The Great Snake. Being symbolic of universal force, the serpent was emblematic of both good (positive) and evil (negative).[885]

Figure 45
Mundane Egg of the ancient Persians

The two serpents contending for the Egg are therefore symbolic of the contending protons (+) and electrons (-) within the Atom. The Orphic Mysteries depict the Egg with the Great Serpent coiled around it (Figure 46) like a mother snake coiled around its recently laid egg. This Great Serpent, Hall informs us, represents the "Fiery Creative Spirit," the God Force from which the Atom or Egg sparked.

[885] Hall, ***Secret Teachings of All Ages***, LXXXVIII.

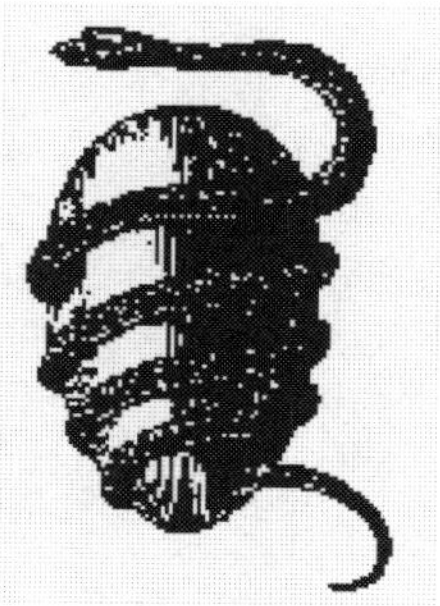

Figure 46
The Mundane Egg (Primordial Atom) born from the Cosmic Serpent (Divine Spirit/Latent Energy/God-Force

III.2.2. *The Primordial Atom and the Birth of God*

According to these ancient texts this 'egg' or atom (also depicted as a lotus plant)[886] began rotating and moving 'on the waters,' which movement originated time.[887] Within this atom the creator-deity now resided (Figure 47) and, eventually, from this atom he emerged as a luminous *anthropos* (man),[888] the so-

[886] See Bosch, ***Golden Germ***, 56-57.

[887] On the birth of time in Egyptian cosmogonic tradition see Dunand and Zivie-Coche, ***Gods and Men in Egypt***, 64-70.

[888] As von Franz remarks: "the motif of the human form of the first creative being, an anthropos figure…is another very widespread archetypal motif in creation myths." ***Creation Myths***, 34. See also Dunand and Zivie-Coche, ***Gods and Men in Egypt***, 48: "This (creator-)god was autogenous...He modeled his own body, and we must say that this was almost always anthropomorphically". See e.g. *Vādhūla-Sūtra* 6.4.109: "Brahman emitted [out of himself] Agni (the primordial spark of fire) and Prajāpati (a macrocosmic Agni) and he (Brahman) created the latter (viz. Prajāpati) in the form of a man." In ancient Near Eastern and Indic tradition, cosmogony (birth of the cosmos), theogony (birth and evolution of God/gods) and anthropogony (creation of man) are all revealed to be the same evolutionary process described from different perspectives. Thus, in Egyptian and Indic wisdom embroyogony, i.e. the development of the human embryo in the womb, recapitulates and therefore gives insight into the theo-cosmogonic process. See David Leeming and Margaret Leeming, ***A Dictionary of Creation Myths*** New York

called sun-god: Atum-Rē' of Egypt (Figure 48)[889] and Prajāpati-Brahmā of India (Figure 49).[890]

---

and Oxford: Oxford University Press, 1994) 31-33 s.v. Birth as Creation Metaphor; Jan Assmann, ***Egyptian Solar Religion in the New Kingdom. Re, Amun and the Crisis of Polytheism***, translated from the German by Anthony Alcock (London and New York: Kegan Paul International, 1995) 175; Ragnhild Bjerre Finnestad, ***Image of the World and Symbol of the Creator. On the Cosmological and Iconological Values of the Temple of Edfu*** (SOR 10; Wiesbaden: Otto Harrassowitz, 1985); F.B.J. Kuiper, "Cosmogony and Conception: A Query," ***HR*** 10 (1970): 91-183 [=***Ancient Indian Cosmogony***, 90-137]; Mircea Eliade, "Cosmogonic Myth and 'Sacred History'," ***Religious Studies*** 2 (1967): 171-83; Manly P. Hall, ***Man: Grand symbol of the Mysteries. Thoughts in occult anatomy*** Los Angeles: The Philosophical Research society, 1972). On the motif of the man-cosmos-God isomorphism see also Klaus Klostermaier, "The Body of God: Cosmos – Avatara – Image," in Robert B. Crotty (ed.), ***The Charles Strong Lectures 1972-1984*** (Leiden: E.J. Brill, 1987) 103-120; Alex Wayman, "The Human Body as Microcosm in India, Greek Cosmology, and Sixteenth-Century Europe," ***HR*** 22 (1982): 172-190; Brenda E.F. Beck, "The symbolic merger of Body, space and cosmos in Hindu Tamil Nadu," ***Contributions to Indian Sociology***, n.s. 10 (1976): 213-243; Leonard Barkan, ***Nature's Work: The Human Body as Image of the World*** (New Haven and London: Yale University Press, 1975); George P. Conger, "Cosmic Persons and Human Universes in Indian Philosophy," ***Journal and Proceedings of the Asiatic Society of Bengel*** n.s. 29 (1933): 255-270.

[889] "there was in the beginning neither heaven nor earth, and nothing existed except a boundless primeval mass of water which was shrouded in darkness and which contained within itself the germs or beginnings, male and female, of everything which was to be in the future world. The divine primeval spirit which formed an essential part of the primeval matter felt within itself the desire to begin the work of creation, and its word woke to life the world, the form and shape of which it had already depicted to itself. The first act of creation began with the formation of an egg out of the primeval water, from which broke forth Rā, the immediate cause of all life upon earth." Quoted from Budge, ***Egyptian Book of the Dead***, xcviii. See also Zandee, "The Birth-Giving Creator-God," 182: "Atum is 'complete' as an androgynous god. He unites within himself masculinity and femininity. He possesses all conditions to bring forth the all out of him. He was a Monad and made himself millions of creatures which he contained potentially in himself. He was the one who came into being of himself (*ḫpr ḏs.f*), who was the creator of his own existence, the *causa sui*." In a New Kingdom royal inscription Atum is described as he "who generates himself within the egg." See Assmann, ***Egyptian Solar Religion***, 112. Another image used by the Egyptians to depict the primordial atom out of which the creator-god emerged is the primordial mound (*benben*) that raised out of the primordial waters at the beginning of creation (see Clifford, ***Creation Accounts***, 105-6). This mound was the "first solid matter" brought from the bottom of the waters and it was identified with Atum himself (Traunecker, ***Gods of Egypt***, 77; Irwin, " 'Asokan' Pillars," 92. On the Primordial Mound see further idem, "The Sacred Anthill and the Cult of the Primordial Mound," ***HR*** 21 [1982]: 339-360; idem, "The Mystery of the (Future) Buddha's First Words," ***Annali Instituto Orientale di Napoli*** 41 [1981]: 623-664). It is no coincidence that this primordial atom is identified with and personifies Atum, the god born from that atom.

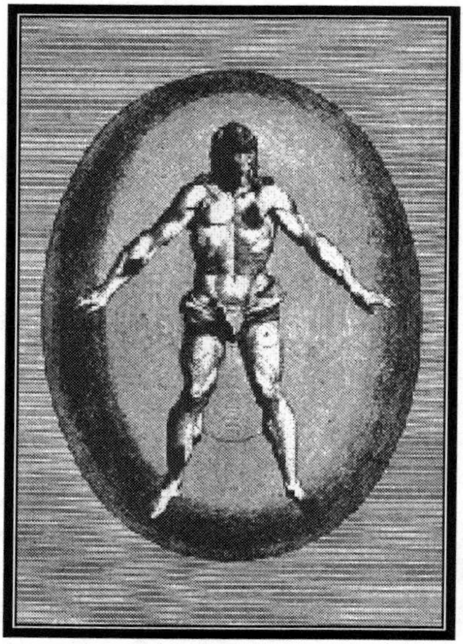

Figure 47

Indic Creator God Brahmā before emerging out of the Cosmogonic Egg/Primordial Atom (from Manly P. Hall, ***MAN: Grand Symbol of the Mysteries***). The Indic text, *The Laws of Manu*, relates:

> This universe was enveloped in darkness, unperceived, undistinguishable…Then the irresistible, self-existent Lord…seeking to produce various creatures…deposited in them (the primordial waters) a seed (quark). This (seed) became a golden egg (atom), resplendent as the sun, in which he himself was born as Brahmā, the progenitor of the word…Being formed by that first cause…that [Man (Purußa)] is called Brahmā…This egg, after the creator had inhabited (it) for a thousand years…burst open, and Brahmā, issuing forth by meditation, commenced the work of creation.

---

[890]See below and Martin, ***Gods of India***, 86, 87; Kurian Manthothu, ***The Development of the Concept of Trimūrti in Hinduism*** (Pali, Kerala, India, 1974) 54; Wendy Doniger and Brian K. Smith, ***The Laws of Manu*** (London: Penguin Books, 1991): 3-4.On Prajāpati-Brahmā and the cosmic man (Puruṣa) see ***ER*** 2:294 s.v. Brahman by Wendy Doniger; J.Gonda, ***Prajāpati's Relations with Brahman, Bṛhaspati and Brahmā*** (Amsterdam/Oxford/New York: North-Holland Publishing Company, 1989) Chapter IX; idem, "Beginning" 52-53; idem, "Background" 51-2; J.R. Joshi, "Prajāpati in Vedic Mythology and Ritual," ***Annals of the Bhandarkar Oriental Research Institute*** 53 (1972):101-125, esp. 114.

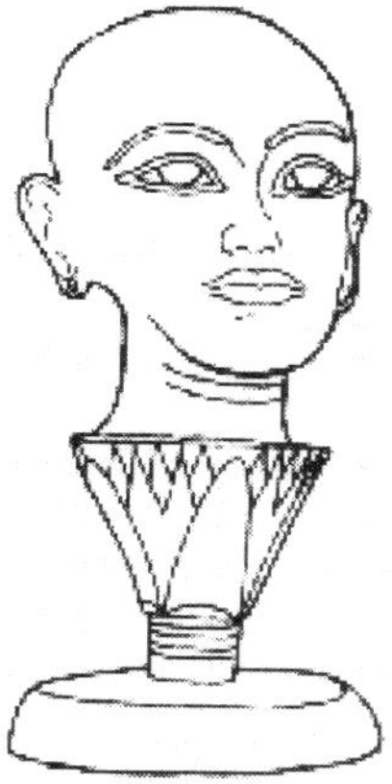

Figure 48

The anthropomorphic creator-god of Egypt, Rēʿ, emerging from the primordial atom, shown here as the mythical Lotus Plant.

Figure 49

The Indic creator-god Prajāpati-Brahmā (white anthropos) emerging from the lotus plant (primordial "seed" or atom). The lotus is emerging from the navel of Viṣṇu (primordial, universal soul) who is reclining on the primordial serpent Śesa (matter), himself resting on the primordial waters. These images represent the birth of the creator-god out of the primordial matter: "The anthropomorphic figure (Viṣṇu), the serpent coils that form his bed, and the water on which this serpent floats, are triune manifestations of the single divine, imperishable, cosmic substance, the energy underlying and inhabiting all forms of life."[891]

---

[891] Heinrich Robert Zimmer in Joseph Campbell (ed.), ***Myths and Symbols in Indian Art and Civilization*** (New York: Harper, 1962) 92.

The 'bursting forth' of the Creator God out of the egg/atom signifies that the atoms were used to build up the Creator God's body.

When the creator-god first emerged, the ancient sources tell us, he lacked the black-body. Indeed, he was light that separated from and emerged out of the darkness.[892] His body, we are told, was originally a body of light described variously as white gold, yellow gold or red gold (Figure 51).[893] The brilliance of this body surpassed that of the sun, which the creator-deity (sun-god) created only as a sign and a 'vicar.'[894] This brilliantly luminous body proved lethal to his future creation. His creatures were perishing at the sight of it and his cosmos was being scorched.[895] The creator-deity decided to cloak his luminosity in a bodily 'veil,' which he made from the primordial waters out of which he emerged. That primordial matter, black and aqueous, became the substance of his new body, which he wore over the luminous form like a garment, concealing its brilliance.[896]

---

892 See Ringgren, "Light and Darkness," 141-42

893On the golden, anthropomorphic body of Prajāpati-Brahmā see *Śatapatha-Brāhmaṇa* 10.1.4.9; 7.4.1.15; Shanti Lal Nagar, ***The Image of Brahmā in India and Abroad***, Vol. 1 (Delhi: Parimal Publications, 1992), 113, 134-43, 361-370; Km. Rajani Mishra, ***Brahmā-Worship. Tradition and Iconography*** (Delhi: Kanishka Publishing House, 1989) 50-57; Gonda, "Background"; The Egyptian sun-god is "the brilliant one (ḫ͗ỉ)," "white light (*whḫ ḥdḏwt."* See Ringgren, "Light and Darkness," 145. Rēʿ is "gold of the gods," "white gold" with a body "cast …from gold." See Assmann, ***Egyptian Solar Religion***, 27, 94, 95.

894 See Budge, ***Egyptian Book of the Dead***, xcvi.

895 See for example the tales in the *Mahābhārat* (O'flaherty, ***Hindu Myths***, 38-43) of Prajāpati-Brahmā's scorching the primordial creation with his 'fiery energy' and in the *Mārkaṇḍeya Prurāṇa* (Ibid., 66-70) of the sun-god Vivasvat whose form radiated excessive heat, scorching the three worlds. On Egyptian parallels see below. On the lethality of seeing the god's luminous body in Egyptian tradition see also Meeks, "Divine Bodies," 58.

896 The luminous, anthropomorphic Indic creator-deity Prajāpati-Brahmā is said to have, after the initial creation, wrapped himself in the primordial waters (Vāk/Virāj; see G.H. Godbole, "Later Vedic and Brahmanical Accounts," in Dange, ***Myths of Creation***, 13). He then became *haritah śyāvah*, dark brown (*śyāvah*, like night, *Ṛg Veda* 6.48.6.) with a ting of yellow (a yellow glow, *haritah*). See *Taittirīya Brāhmaṇa* 2.3.5.1; *Śatapatha-Brāhmaṇa* 6.2.2.2. On Vāk and the primordial waters see ibid., 6.1.1.9; *PaÕcaaveÒśa-*

Figure 50
Min, Egyptian black 'creator-god *par excellence*', who emerged from the primordial dark waters, from which his black body was formed

---

BrāhmaÖa 20.14.2; *Œg Veda* 10.125.3; *Jaiminīya-BrāhmaÖa* 2.252 (Vāk as primordial cow); Bosch, ***Golden Germ***, 52-53. On Vāk as primordial matter see Nagar, ***Image of Brāhma***, viii; Joshi, "Prajāpati," 113. On Prajāpati-Brahmā's copulation with Vāk as a metaphor for the reuniting of fire (breath) with water see Mishra, ***Brahmā-Worship.*** 11. On the fiery breath (Agni) and the waters see further Kuiper, "Golden Germ," 27-30; Bosch, ***Golden Germ***, 57-62.

In Egypt, Rēʿ transforms (*ḫpr*) his luminous body into a black body symbolized by the gods Atum and Osiris, both of whom had black bulls as their attribute animal; on Atum's black bull Mnevis see George Hart, ***The Routledge Dictionary of Egyptian Gods and Goddesses*** [2nd edition; London and New York: Routledge, 2005] 95 s.v. Mnevis; Ions, ***Egyptian Mythology***, 40). On Rēʿ darkening and transforming into Atum see See Ringgren, "Light and Darkness," 150; Karl W.Luckert, ***Egyptian Light and Hebrew Fire. Theological and Philosophical Roots of Christendom in Evolutionary Perspective*** (Albany: State University of New York Press, 1991) 73. Most often, Rē#'s black body is identified with the black god Osiris (Figure 16), who represents the black primordial waters of Nun; see Chassinat, "Mise a Mort Rituelle." On black Osiris as the netherworld body of Rē# see Hasenfratz, "Patterns of Creation," 176; Jan Assmann, ***The Search for God in Ancient Egypt***, translated from the German by David Lorton (Ithaca and New York: Cornell University Press, 2001) 41; idem, ***Death and Salvation in Ancient Egypt***, translated from the German by David Lorton (Ithaca and London: Cornell University Press, 2005) 188; Clark, ***Myth and Symbol***, 158; Martin Lev and Carol Ring, "Journey of the Night Sun," ***Parabola*** 8 (1983): 14-18; Albert Churchward, ***Signs & Symbols of Primordial Man: The Evolution of Religious Doctrines from the Eschatology of the Ancient Egyptians*** (Brooklyn: A&B Publishers Group, 1994, reprint) 63-66, 274-6, 322.

But some of this brilliance shown through the hair-pores of the new black body,[897] and this produced a dark-blue iridescence or glow. The result was the sapphiric body of the creator-deity.[898]

---

[897] See above and also *Mahābhārata* 5.129.11 which mentions "rays of light, like the sun's, [shining] from [Kṛṣṇa's] very pores." Translated James W. Lane, ***Visions of God: Narratives of Theophany in the Mahābhārata*** (Vienna 1989) 134. Now Kṛṣṇa, whose name means 'black' (A.L. Basham, ***The Wonder that was India*** [London: Sidgwick and Jackson, 1954] 305) is in many ways the paradigmatic blue-black god. As David R. Kinsley, ***The Sword and the Flute: Kali and Krishna, Dark Visions of the Terrible and the Sublime in Hindu Mythology*** (Berkeley: University of California Press, 1975) noted, Kṛṣṇa with his blue-black complexion is the "quintessence of divine beauty": "His appearance is redeeming in itself…Over and over again we read of his luminous dark complexion, large dark eyes, black curly hair. For devotees of Kṛṣṇa the image of their blue lord is the quintessence of divine beauty. The *Brahma-vaivarta-purāṇa*...describes Kṛṣṇa as emanating a blinding light…But Kṛṣṇa's devotees see within that dazzling light to an even more dazzling and redeeming image of their darling…(the) lovely image of Kṛṣṇa located in the center of this light. He is blue like a new cloud." The "dazzling light" is the light emanating through the hair-pores from the dangerously luminous form within the black body (his 'Universal Form', *viśvarūpadarśana*; see *Bhagavadgītā* 11; Lane, ***Visions of God***, 135-141). The description "luminous dark complexion" nicely captures the divine paradox.

[898] Thus Viṣṇu is "dark-hued, cloud-hued, sapphire-hued, gem-hued, ocean and sea-hued" (See S. Settar, "Vishnu-Krishna in Nammalvar's Tiruvaymoli [C.7-8th Cent. A.D.]," in G. Kamalakar and M. Veerender [edd.], ***Vishnu in Art, Thought, and Literature*** [Hyderbad: Birla Archaeological & Cultural Research Institute, 1993] 225) and Varuṇa, the "cloud-dark Lord of aquatic creatures," when he appeared to Arjuna was "the color of lapis lazuli, lighting up every direction" (*Mahābhārata* 3.42.5-6). The Viṣṇu of the Purānic Trimūrti or Triad is the creator-god (Prajāpati-)Brahmā with the luminous body cloaked within an aquatic body made from the primordial waters. Therefore, as Viṣṇu, (Prajāpati-)Brahmā is called "he who dwells in the [causal] waters, *Nārāyana*." By assuming this form (Prajāpati-)Brahmā showed mercy on creation. Thus, in his 'Viṣṇu' form he is called auspicious. On Viṣṇu see Daniélou, ***Myths and Gods of India***, Chapters Eleven through Fourteen; Arvind Sharma, "The Significance of Viṣṇu Reclining on the Serpent," ***Religion*** 16 (1986): 101-114; Nanditha Krishna, ***The Art and Iconography of Vishnu-Narayana*** (Bombay, 1980); Kalpana S. Desai, ***Iconography of VißÖu (In Northern India, Upto the Mediaeval Period)*** (New Delhi: Abhinav Publications, 1973);F.B.J Kuiper, "The Three Strides of Viṣṇu," in idem, ***Ancient Indian Cosmogony***, 41-55; Bhattachari, ***Indian Theogony***, Chapter Fourteen; Martin, ***Gods of India***, Chapter Three; J. Gonda, ***Aspects of Early VißÖuism*** (Utrecht; N.V.A. Oosthoek's Uitgevers Mij, 1954). See also Wendy Doniger O'flaherty, "The Submarine Mare in the Mythology of Śiva," ***JRAS*** 1971 9-27 and below.

While the luminous, fiery body was 'terrible' and destructive, the blue-black 'sapphiric' body was beautiful and auspicious, a mercy to the creatures.[899] "Blue as the sky, dark as the rain-cloud...Viṣṇu was the personification of beauty."[900] The act of cloaking the divinely luminous form in a black body was considered a divine sacrifice[901] - a sacrifice that resulted in the

---

In ancient Egyptian tradition see e.g. the famous story of the Withdrawal of Rēʿ **to** Heaven. After incinerating most humans with his fiery fury personified as his daughter, the ferocious lioness Sekhmet (who, incidentally, got out of hand), Rēʿ re-entered the primordial water (he mounted the back of Nut-Nun personified as the primordial cow). He thus concealed his luminous body within Nut-Nun. He is now "(he) who conceals his image in the body of Nut," "who conceals his image in his heaven." (P. Leiden I 344 v50.I. 4 and viii.7 in J. Zandee, ***Der Amunshymnus des Papyrus Lkeiden I 344***, 3 vols. [Leiden, 1992]. See also Assmann, ***Egyptian Solar Religion***, 70-72]. By concealing his luminous body within the body of Nut, Rē# becomes the sapphire-bodied Amun-Re, described as "beautiful youth of purest lapis lazuli (*ḥwn-nfr n-ḥsbḏ-m3ʿ*) whose "body is heaven" (*ḫt. K nwt*)." See above n. 31. In the Leiden Papyrus stored at the museum in Leiden (see Adolf Erman, "Der Leidener Amons-hymnus," ***Sitzungsberichte der Preussischen Akademie der Wissenschaften*** 11 [1923]: 66ff) Rēʿ's dangerously luminous body is described as his 'secret form' hidden within Amun (70-73). On the myth of Rēʿ's Withdrawal see Robert A. Armour, ***Gods and Myths of Ancient Egypt*** (2nd edition; Cairo and New York: American University in Cairo Press, 2001) 87-89; Clark, ***Myth and Symbol***, 181-186; Stephen Quirke, ***The Cult of Ra: Sun-Worship in Ancient Egypt*** (New York: Thames & Hudson, 2001) 35-6; Rudolf Anthes, "Mythology in ancient Egypt," in Samuel Noah Kramer (ed.), ***Mythologies of the Ancient World*** (Garden City, New York: Anchor Books, 1961) 17-22. On Amun's sapphiric body see above.

[899] Śiva too has two forms, his fiery form born from the golden egg called his 'terrible form' and his aquatic form described as "auspicious." See *Mahābhārata* 13.146.4; *Brahmāṇḍa Purāṇa*. See O'flaherty, "Submarine Mare."

[900] Devdutt Pattanaik, ***Vishnu, An Introduction*** (Mumbai, India: Vakils, Feffer and Simons, Ltd., 1999) 7.

[901] According to the cosmogonic account of Berosses, priest of Bēl-Marduk of Babylon, published in Greek ca. 250 BC, after cleaving the villainous primordial water (Grk. *Omorka*; Baby. *Tiamat*) and creating the cosmos, Bēl-Marduk's luminosity was unbearable for living creatures who were therefore perishing. Bēl-Marduk thus ordered a god to cut off his (i.e. Bēl-Marduk's) head (self-sacrifice); his blood was mixed with earth to form men and animals that could survive. See K.K.A. Venkatachari, "Babylonian, Assyrian and Other Accounts," in Dange, ***Myths of Creation***, 36-37. See also Brian K. Smith, "Sacrifice and Being: Prajapati's Cosmic Emission and Its Consequences," ***Religion*** 32 (1985): 71-87; Gonda, "Vedic Gods and the Sacrifice"; idem, "The Popular Prajapati," ***HR*** 22 (1982): 129-149; Joshi, "Prajāpati in Vedic Mythology and Ritual."

first human being (Allah The Original Man) and which permitted the creation of the (more densely) material world.[902]

This blue-black body of the deity was the most arcane secret of the ancient mysteries. In Egypt it was the mystery of the unity of Rēʿ and his black body Osiris (Figure 52).[903] As one text from a New Kingdom royal tomb associated with the mystery rites reveals: "It is a great mystery, it is Rēʿ and Osiris. He who reveals it will die a sudden death."[904] According to the *Book of Gates* this is the "Mystery of the Great God."[905] In Vedic India, "the central theme of what can be denoted by no other term than Aryan mysticism"[906] is the secret of Agni (fire) hidden in water (Varuṇa), *viz.* the mystery of the luminous Prajāpati-Brahmā (creator-god) hidden within the black and aqueous body.[907] The Akkadian 'bull-ritual' likewise associated the pelt of the black bull with the "mystery of Anu, Enlil, Ea(Enki) and of Ninmah," i.e. the black gods of Sumer/Akkad.[908]

---

902 This sacrificial 'incarnation,' if you will, is often represented metaphorically as the creator-god (re-)uniting with his wife/daughter, the celestial ocean (primordial matter) depicted as the primordial cow. When Rēʿ as Bull begets with the Divine Cow, i.e. Nut-Nun, the material world with its planets and humans are produced. Thus, "we are all cattle" (see G.S. Bedagkar, "Egyptian, Hebrew and Greek Accounts," in Dange, ***Myths of Creation***, 33). Prajāpati-Brahmā, (re-)uniting with Vāk (primordial water/primordial cow), produced the *idaṃ sarvam* or "phenomenal, material world," beginning with Manu, the first human, which is only Prajāpati-Brahmā himself in the phenomenal, material world: *Śatapatha-Brāhmaṇa* 6.6.1.19; 9.4.1.12; J. Gonda, "All, Universe and Totality in the Śatapatha-Brāhmaṇa," ***Journal of the Oriental Institute*** 32 (1982): 1-17; Joshi, "Prajāpati in Vedic Mythology and Ritual."

903 According to Jan Assmann "the most secret Arcanum known to the mysteries of the solar journey" is "the nocturnal union of Re and Osiris." Assmann, ***Egyptian Solar Religion***, 28; Idem, ***Death and Salvation in Ancient Egypt***, trans. from the German by David Lorton (Ithaca and London: Cornell University Press, 2005) 186. On Osiris as the black body of Rēʿ see above.

904 Assmann, ***Search for God***, 79.

905 Quoted in Assmann, ***Death and Salvation***, 189.

906 F.B.J. Kuiper, "The Bliss of Aša," ***Indo-Iranian Journal*** 8 (1964): 124 [art.=96-129;= ***Ancient Indian Cosmogony***, Chapter Four].

907 Kuiper, "Bliss of Aša"; idem, "Remarks on 'The Avestan Hymn to Mithra'," ***Indo-Iranian Journal*** 5 (1961): 36-60; idem, "The Heavenly Bucket," in idem, ***Ancient Indian Cosmogony***, Chapter 6.

908 Wohlstein, ***Sky-God An-Anu***, 118, 122.

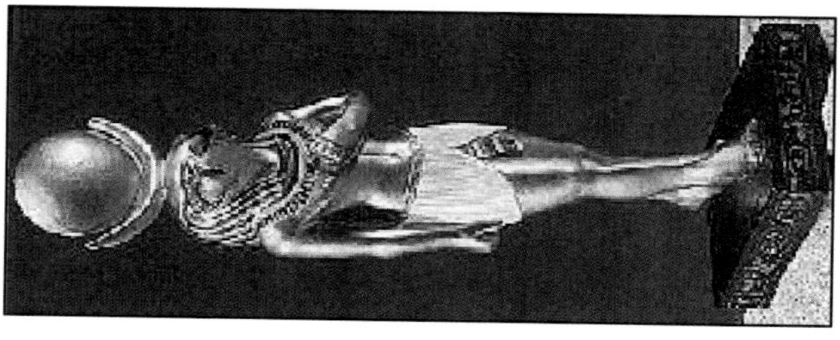

Figure 51

Rē' as Sun-God (luminous body)

+

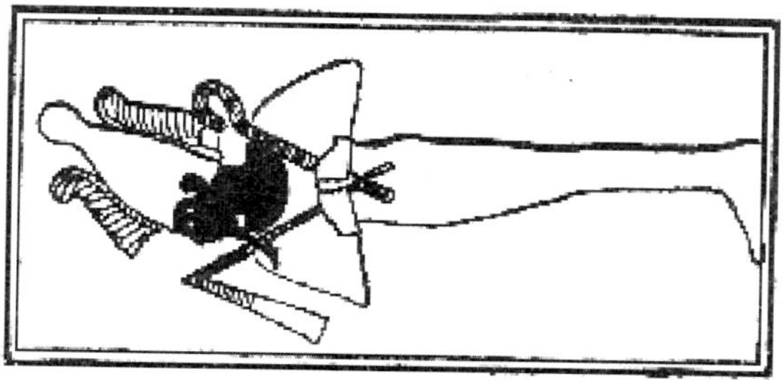

Osiris.
From the Papyrus of
Iuau, Plate XXII.

Figure 52

Osiris, black body of the Sun God Rē'

=

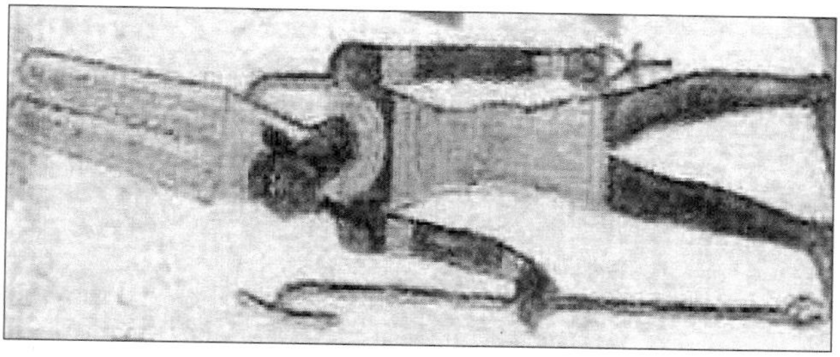

Figure 53

Amun- Rē'